Web Design Studio Secrets™

DEKE MCCLELLAND AND KATRIN EISMANN

WEB DESIGN
STUDIO SECRETS™

IDG BOOKS WORLDWIDE, INC.

AN INTERNATIONAL DATA GROUP COMPANY

Foster City, CA ▲ Chicago, IL ◆ Indianapolis, IN ▼ New York, NY

Web Design Studio Secrets™

Published by
IDG Books Worldwide, Inc.
An International Data Group Company
919 E. Hillsdale Blvd., Suite 400
Foster City, CA 94404
www.idgbooks.com (IDG Books Worldwide Web site)

Library of Congress Catalog Card Number: 98-72473

ISBN: 0-7645-3171-9

Printed in the United States of America

10 9 8 7 6 5 4

1K/RV/QZ/ZY/FC

Distributed in the United States by IDG Books Worldwide, Inc.

Distributed by Macmillan Canada for Canada; by Transworld Publishers Limited in the United Kingdom; by IDG Norge Books for Norway; by IDG Sweden Books for Sweden; by Woodslane Pty. Ltd. for Australia; by Woodslane (NZ) Ltd. for New Zealand; by Addison Wesley Longman Singapore Pte Ltd. for Singapore, Malaysia, Thailand, Indonesia, and Korea; by Norma Comunicaciones S.A. for Colombia; by Intersoft for South Africa; by International Thomson Publishing for Germany, Austria, and Switzerland; by Toppan Company Ltd. for Japan; by Distribuidora Cuspide for Argentina; by Livraria Cultura for Brazil; by Ediciencia S.A. for Ecuador; by Ediciones ZETA S.C.R. Ltda. for Peru; by WS Computer Publishing Corporation, Inc., for the Philippines; by Unalis Corporation for Taiwan; by Contemporanea de Ediciones for Venezuela; by Computer Book & Magazine Store for Puerto Rico; by Express Computer Distributors for the Caribbean and West Indies. Authorized Sales Agent: Anthony Rudkin Associates for the Middle East and North Africa.

For general information on IDG Books Worldwide's books in the U.S., please call our Consumer Customer Service department at 800-762-2974. For reseller information, including discounts and premium sales, please call our Reseller Customer Service department at 800-434-3422.

For information on where to purchase IDG Books Worldwide's books outside the U.S., please contact our International Sales department at 650-655-3200 or fax 650-655-3297.

For information on foreign language translations, please contact our Foreign & Subsidiary Rights department at 650-655-3021 or fax 650-655-3281.

For sales inquiries and special prices for bulk quantities, please contact our Sales department at 650-655-3200 or write to the address above.

For information on using IDG Books Worldwide's books in the classroom or for ordering examination copies, please contact our Educational Sales department at 800-434-2086 or fax 317-596-5499.

For press review copies, author interviews, or other publicity information, please contact our Public Relations department at 650-655-3000 or fax 650-655-3299.

For authorization to photocopy items for corporate, personal, or educational use, please contact Copyright Clearance Center, 222 Rosewood Drive, Danvers, MA 01923, or fax 978-750-4470.

ABOUT IDG BOOKS WORLDWIDE

Welcome to the world of IDG Books Worldwide.

IDG Books Worldwide, Inc., is a subsidiary of International Data Group, the world's largest publisher of computer-related information and the leading global provider of information services on information technology. IDG was founded more than 25 years ago and now employs more than 8,500 people worldwide. IDG publishes more than 275 computer publications in over 75 countries (see listing below). More than 90 million people read one or more IDG publications each month.

Launched in 1990, IDG Books Worldwide is today the #1 publisher of best-selling computer books in the United States. We are proud to have received eight awards from the Computer Press Association in recognition of editorial excellence and three from *Computer Currents'* First Annual Readers' Choice Awards. Our best-selling *...For Dummies*® series has more than 50 million copies in print with translations in 38 languages. IDG Books Worldwide, through a joint venture with IDG's Hi-Tech Beijing, became the first U.S. publisher to publish a computer book in the People's Republic of China. In record time, IDG Books Worldwide has become the first choice for millions of readers around the world who want to learn how to better manage their businesses.

Our mission is simple: Every one of our books is designed to bring extra value and skill-building instructions to the reader. Our books are written by experts who understand and care about our readers. The knowledge base of our editorial staff comes from years of experience in publishing, education, and journalism — experience we use to produce books for the '90s. In short, we care about books, so we attract the best people. We devote special attention to details such as audience, interior design, use of icons, and illustrations. And because we use an efficient process of authoring, editing, and desktop publishing our books electronically, we can spend more time ensuring superior content and spend less time on the technicalities of making books.

You can count on our commitment to deliver high-quality books at competitive prices on topics you want to read about. At IDG Books Worldwide, we continue in the IDG tradition of delivering quality for more than 25 years. You'll find no better book on a subject than one from IDG Books Worldwide.

John J. Kilcullen
John Kilcullen
CEO
IDG Books Worldwide, Inc.

Steven Berkowitz
Steven Berkowitz
President and Publisher
IDG Books Worldwide, Inc.

*Eighth Annual
Computer Press
Awards ≥1992*

*Ninth Annual
Computer Press
Awards ≥1993*

*Tenth Annual
Computer Press
Awards ≥1994*

XI
WINNER

*Eleventh Annual
Computer Press
Awards ≥1995*

IDG Books Worldwide, Inc., is a subsidiary of International Data Group, the world's largest publisher of computer-related information and the leading global provider of information services on information technology. International Data Group publishes over 275 computer publications in over 75 countries. More than 90 million people read one or more International Data Group publications each month. International Data Group's publications include: **ARGENTINA:** Buyer's Guide, Computerworld Argentina, PC World Argentina; **AUSTRALIA:** Australian Macworld, Australian PC World, Australian Reseller News, Computerworld, IT Casebook, Network World, Publish, Webmaster; **AUSTRIA:** Computerwelt Osterreich, Networks Austria, PC Tip Austria; **BANGLADESH:** PC World Bangladesh; **BELARUS:** PC World Belarus; **BELGIUM:** Data News; **BRAZIL:** Annuário de Informática, Computerworld, Connections, Macworld, PC Player, PC World, Publish, Reseller News, Supergamepower; **BULGARIA:** Computerworld Bulgaria, Network World Bulgaria, PC & MacWorld Bulgaria; **CANADA:** CIO Canada, Client/Server World, ComputerWorld Canada, InfoWorld Canada, NetworkWorld Canada, WebWorld; **CHILE:** Computerworld Chile, PC World Chile; **COLOMBIA:** Computerworld Colombia, PC World Colombia; **COSTA RICA:** PC World Centro America; **THE CZECH AND SLOVAK REPUBLICS:** Computerworld Czechoslovakia, Macworld Czech Republic, PC World Czechoslovakia; **DENMARK:** Communications World Danmark, Computerworld Danmark, Macworld Danmark, PC World Danmark, Techworld Denmark; **DOMINICAN REPUBLIC:** PC World Republica Dominicana; **ECUADOR:** PC World Ecuador; **EGYPT:** Computerworld Middle East, PC World Middle East; **EL SALVADOR:** PC World Centro America; **FINLAND:** MikroPC, Tietoverkko, Tietoviikko; **FRANCE:** Distributique, Hebdo, Info PC, Le Monde Informatique, Macworld, Reseaux & Telecoms, WebMaster France; **GERMANY:** Computer Partner, Computerwoche, Computerwoche Extra, Computerwoche FOCUS, Global Online, Macwelt, PC Welt; **GREECE:** Amiga Computing, GamePro Greece, Multimedia World; **GUATEMALA:** PC World Centro America; **HONDURAS:** PC World Centro America; **HONG KONG:** Computerworld Hong Kong, PC World Hong Kong, Publish in Asia; **HUNGARY:** ABCD CD-ROM, Computerworld Szamitastechnika, Internetto online Magazine, PC World Hungary, PC-X Magazin Hungary; **ICELAND:** Tolvuheimur PC World Island; **INDIA:** Information Communications World, Information Systems Computerworld, PC World India, Publish in Asia; **INDONESIA:** InfoKomputer PC World, Komputek Computerworld, Publish in Asia; **IRELAND:** ComputerScope, PC Live!; **ISRAEL:** Macworld Israel, People & Computers/Computerworld; **ITALY:** Computerworld Italia, Macworld Italia, Networking Italia, PC World Italia; **JAPAN:** DTP World, Macworld Japan, Nikkei Personal Computing, OS/2 World Japan, SunWorld Japan, Windows NT World, Windows World Japan; **KENYA:** PC World East African; **KOREA:** Hi-Tech Information, Macworld Korea, PC World Korea; **MACEDONIA:** PC World Macedonia; **MALAYSIA:** Computerworld Malaysia, PC World Malaysia, Publish in Asia; **MALTA:** PC World Malta; **MEXICO:** Computerworld Mexico, PC World Mexico; **MYANMAR:** PC World Myanmar; **NETHERLANDS:** Computer! Totaal, LAN Internetworking Magazine, LAN World Buyers Guide, Macworld Netherlands, Net, WebWereld; **NEW ZEALAND:** Absolute Beginners Guide and Plain & Simple Series, Computer Buyer, Computer Industry Directory, Computerworld New Zealand, MTB, Network World, PC World New Zealand; **NICARAGUA:** PC World Centro America; **NORWAY:** Computerworld Norge, CW Rapport, Datamagasinet, Financial Rapport, Kursguide Norge, Macworld Norge, Multimediaworld Norge, PC World Ekspress Norge, PC World Nettverk, PC World Norge, PC World ProduktGuide Norge; **PAKISTAN:** Computerworld Pakistan; **PANAMA:** PC World Panama; **PEOPLE'S REPUBLIC OF CHINA:** China Computer Users, China Computerworld, China InfoWorld, China Telecom World Weekly, Computer & Communication, Electronic Design China, Electronics Today, Electronics Weekly, Game Software, PC World China, Popular Computer Week, Software Weekly, Software World, Telecom World; **PERU:** Computerworld Peru, PC World Profesional Peru, PC World SoHo Peru; **PHILIPPINES:** Click!, Computerworld Philippines, PC World Philippines, Publish in Asia; **POLAND:** Computerworld Poland, Computerworld Special Report Poland, Cyber, Macworld Poland, Networld Poland, PC World Komputer; **PORTUGAL:** Cerebro/PC World, Computerworld/Correio Informático, Dealer World Portugal, Mac*In/PC*In Portugal, Multimedia World; **PUERTO RICO:** PC World Puerto Rico; **ROMANIA:** Computerworld Romania, PC World Romania, Telecom Romania; **RUSSIA:** Computerworld Russia, Mir PK, Publish, Seti; **SINGAPORE:** Computerworld Singapore, PC World Singapore, Publish in Asia; **SLOVENIA:** Monitor; **SOUTH AFRICA:** Computing SA, Network World SA, Software World SA; **SPAIN:** Communicaciones World España, Computerworld España, Dealer World España, Macworld España, PC World España, PC World Pro; **SRI LANKA:** Infolink PC World; **SWEDEN:** CAP&Design, Computer Sweden, Corporate Computing Sweden, Internetworld Sweden, it.branschen, Macworld Sweden, MaxiData Sweden, MikroDatorn, Natverk & Kommunikation, PC World Sweden, PCaktiv, Windows World Sweden; **SWITZERLAND:** Computerworld Schweiz, Macworld Schweiz, PCtip; **TAIWAN:** Computerworld Taiwan, Macworld Taiwan, NEW ViSiON/Publish, PC World Taiwan, Windows World Taiwan; **THAILAND:** Publish in Asia, Thai Computerworld; **TURKEY:** Computerworld Turkiye, Macworld Turkiye, Network World Turkiye, PC World Turkiye; **UKRAINE:** Computerworld Kiev, Multimedia World Ukraine, PC World Ukraine; **UNITED KINGDOM:** Acorn User UK, Amiga Action UK, Amiga Computing UK, Apple Talk UK, Computing, Macworld, Parents and Computers UK, PC Advisor, PC Home, PSX Pro, The WEB; **UNITED STATES:** Cable in the Classroom, CIO Magazine, Computerworld, DOS World, Federal Computer Week, GamePro Magazine, InfoWorld, I-Way, Macworld, Network World, PC Games, PC World, Publish, Video Event, THE WEB Magazine, and WebMaster; online webzines: JavaWorld, NetscapeWorld, and SunWorld Online; **URUGUAY:** InfoWorld Uruguay; **VENEZUELA:** Computerworld Venezuela, PC World Venezuela; and **VIETNAM:** PC World Vietnam.   5/7/98

To Elizabeth, whose food fills my tummy and whose eyes melt my heart. -D. M.

We wonder where we would be if we hadn't met. Thankfully those thoughts are only theoretical — to John with love, Katrin. And to my parents, who have lived for and given to my brother and me as only they could. - K. E.

FOREWORDS

Each time a new method of presenting content emerges, it seems we start all over again educating practitioners on the importance of good design. It happened during the transition from hot-metal type to cold type and again in the shift from traditional paste-up production methods to pages created in desktop-publishing applications. And now in the era of the Web page, we're still chanting the same mantra: Don't get so hung up in the bells and whistles of technology that you forget about the importance of good design and clear presentation. After all, most pages, whether on the Web or in print, exist to communicate information, not impress our friends and associates with how clever we are. That's where *Web Design Studio Secrets* can help.

By focusing on designers and Web publishers who are successfully practicing their craft, Deke McClelland has put together more than just a great how-to book. He's provided a rich framework to help us understand that design techniques and document structure, while grounded in certain basics, need to be fluid. What works for print does not necessarily translate to the Web. And what we're currently learning about communicating electronically will no doubt influence print pages in the future. It is a very exciting time for designers, editors, and publishers. All will benefit from the lessons in this book.

In addition to presenting new design challenges, the Web also throws into question our whole understanding of how documents are structured and viewed. The designer is no longer simply responsible for the visual look of a page, but is the architect of the navigation and retrieval systems of the document. By including chapters on navigation, tables, site management, and workflow, Deke has addressed the "hidden" design aspects of the Web that make it such a powerful presentation tool.

And let's not forget that the Web is a dynamic medium. Designers accustomed to two-dimensional, static thinking need to open their minds (and skill sets) to the worlds of 3D, VRML, film, video, animation, and sound. This book addresses those in the context of appropriate use and good design. Like it or not, technology has once again forced even the most talented designer to learn new techniques and new ways of thinking.

Like all the titles in the *Studio Secrets* series, this book is rich with colorful visual examples that add dimension to the text and graphically communicate an entirely separate layer of information. The CD-ROM included in the back of this book makes the information on these pages literally spring to life, and provides examples and resources that simply can't be constrained to print.

I can't think of anyone more qualified to bring this package of information together than Deke McClelland. He's the author of over 30 books on computer technology, a frequent contributor to every significant publication in the technology field, and a contributing editor to *Publish* magazine, which authorizes and approves this book series. We are proud to lend our name to both Deke and IDG Books Worldwide for what we hope is a productive, entertaining, and educational experience for you.

Gene Gable
President/Publisher
Publish magazine
GGABLE@PUBLISH.COM

The design and creation of Web pages has gone through several revolutions since it began as a way for scientists to distribute physics papers. First came the dull, text-heavy pages with basic gray backgrounds. Then came the slow, graphics-intensive sites with cryptic interfaces inspired by Myst. Now we are finally seeing the types of pages that let people easily do what they wanted to do from the beginning: find the information and software they need quickly and conveniently.

Let's face it: most of the Web sites in the world are there to deliver either a commercial or editorial message. While some sites focus on creating an "experience" and others on community or self-expression, the real business of the Web designer is (and should be) getting the right message across to the right audience. One of the hottest industry terms these days is "usability." This is a refreshing change. After years of obsession with Java, plug-ins, and other bleeding-edge technologies, we have settled into a time where the priority is on making pages that load quickly, can be searched, and can be found easily on Yahoo! and AltaVista.

This book is a great example of the trend away from the previous gee-whiz design focus, and the trend toward getting results. At our Web Design events we've worked hard to achieve the same kind of results that Deke McClelland and Katrin Eismann have with this book. In *Web Design Studio Secrets*, Deke and Katrin have assembled a collection of some of the industry's top Web design professionals to tell how they create great Web sites. A great site is one that meets the needs of the organization sponsoring it while creating an interesting and useful (and sometimes fun!) destination for the browser.

It's not about technology. It's about teamwork, communication, and understanding the needs of the client while facing the reality of a 28.8 world. This book shows how to do it right.

Steve Broback
President
Thunder Lizard Productions

Steve Roth
CEO
Thunder Lizard Productions

PREFACE

Web design is a bit like chess. Just because you know the basic rules doesn't mean you know the game. Sure, the bishop moves diagonally and the rook moves up and down, but how do you exploit these moves to confound your opponent and win the game? Granted, GIF and JPEG are the universal image formats on the Web, but how do you use these formats to produce attractive, fast-loading graphics?

The best way to get a feel for how chess is played is to watch the game in action. With a little observation, you get the hang of it. If you're inclined toward serious study, you can master the game. The same holds true for the world of online design. Browse through a few sites, check out the source code, and you begin to get a feel for how the Web works. If you're serious about making a living or establishing a firm presence on the Web, you can study the ways of those who have come before you and devise new and better techniques based on theirs.

This book is for serious students of online design. Chapter by chapter, we peer over the shoulders of 14 of the most capable professionals working on the Web. And they tell it all — from basic HTML and image manipulation to high-end production techniques and marketing your site to the masses. Their stories are instructional, packed with tips and tricks; enlightening, based on years of hard-won experience — and inspirational, rife with ideas and approaches you can start implementing into your site immediately.

But most important, the stories are real. Every artist covers a highly focused topic that he or she eats, drinks, and breathes. Each chapter features a successful artist crawling out of the trenches for a moment to explain in detail how to use HTML as a design tool, how to make your site easy to navigate, how to script buttons that highlight, how to create animated GIF and VRML files, and much more.

A FEW BORING DETAILS

Throughout this book, we assume you already know your way around the Web. There is no chapter that introduces you to the Internet or explains how to create your first line of HTML code. If the World Wide Web is completely new territory to you, we urge you to consult a primer and come back to this book in a couple of months when it will make more sense. We'd love to sell you a book, but we'd rather you get up to speed and learn in the most efficient manner possible.

This book is aimed specifically at designers, but even designers have to write and edit code when creating content for the Web. So in and amid the bright, colorful artwork, you'll come across occasional lines of HTML and JavaScript code. It just can't be helped.

That said, we're big believers that designers should have to focus on code as little as possible. To this end, we have tried to pull out only the code that is pertinent to the techniques the artist is demonstrating. This makes the medicine more digestible without oversimplifying the source code so it doesn't make sense.

If you want to dig deeper and examine the source code for yourself, we provide many of the original HTML files on the CD-ROM at the back of this book. Feel free to open the files in your favorite text or HTML editor and scan away.

FROM CRAFTSMAN TO ARTISAN

Web Design Studio Secrets is about the art of online design. It's like an intense three-week apprenticeship program at a leading design house, except you don't have to leave the privacy of your home or office, and your mentor won't ask you to fetch a cup of coffee and a bagel when business is slow. Assuming you're moderately familiar with how to create a Web page and you're looking to upgrade your talents, expertise, and general level of sophistication, you're good to go.

ACKNOWLEDGMENTS

This book is more than the mere product of two people sitting in dark rooms staring at screens and wishing they could go out to play. In addition to sitting, staring, and wishing, we spent countless hours on the phone talking to some shockingly talented and capable people. We were particularly lucky to work with 14 gifted, clever, generous, and good-humored artists whose patience never faltered as we asked one dumb question after another. Thanks for hanging in there, one and all.

Lest we forget, a book that addresses technology cannot be successful without the support of the companies and people that are shaping the industry. In addition to the many software vendors that have been a part of this project, we wish to thank Josef Pokorny from Kodak Professional, Joshua Weisberg from Intergraph Systems, and the astoundingly brilliant team from Thunder Lizard Productions. (If it was possible to be *too* good, there'd be two Steve's with a lot of explaining to do.) We count ourselves lucky to know them all.

Finally, thanks to Amy Thomas, the development editor and third author of this book. There is no way this book would have come together without her. Thanks to Ted Padova for lightning-fast turnaround. And thanks to the outstanding team at IDG Books Worldwide, including Andy Cummings, Marc Mikulich, Walt Bruce, and a bunch of editors, artists, and designers whose names escape us at the moment because, frankly, we're terrible with names.

Oh, and Deke wants to thank Katrin for coming in and saving his butt. Now you know what it's like to write a book. Pain, remorse, pain, frustration, pain, extreme remorse, pain, pain, utter exhaustion, strange otherworldly delirium, pain, pain, pain, and — quite suddenly — relief. I hope it was as fun for you as it was for me.

CONTENTS AT A GLANCE

CONTENTS

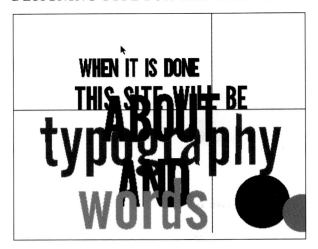

CHAPTER 5
HTML AS A DESIGN TOOL   91

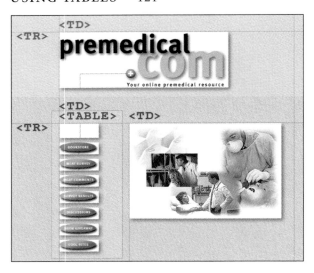

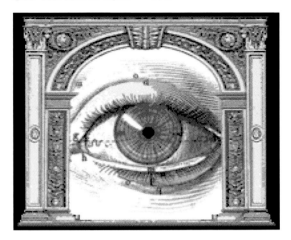

CHAPTER 10
FILMS AND VIDEO ON THE WEB   189

CHAPTER 11
IMMERSIVE ONLINE IMAGING   205

CHAPTER 14
ANNOUNCING YOUR WEB SITE   265

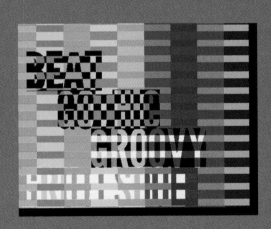

PART I
GENERAL
TECHNIQUES

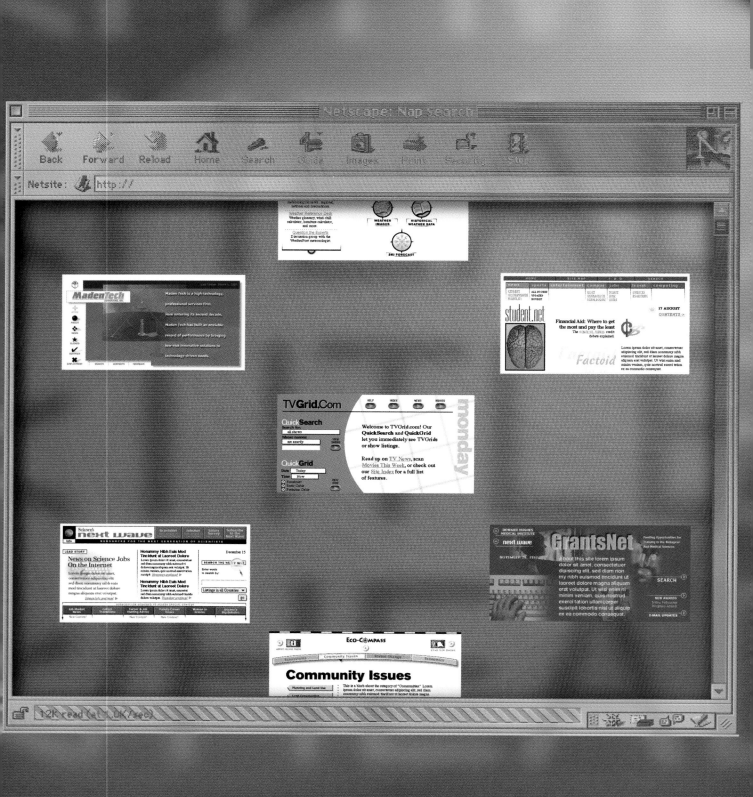

CHAPTER 1
DESIGNING FOR THE WEB

The Web presents a sizable challenge to even the most skilled graphic designers. In order to be successful in Web design, you must understand the added dimension of the medium. Many of the rules and techniques of traditional print composition still apply, but there are additional issues to consider and techniques to master. The challenge is to take traditional design skills and experiences and reshape and apply them with an understanding of how the Web works.

The most successful design is the one the viewer doesn't even notice.
TRACY KEATON DREW

WHERE TO BEGIN?

Tracy Keaton Drew studied graphic design before desktop computers were even used as tools of the trade. As Apple Computer, Aldus PageMaker, and Adobe PostScript were spawning desktop publishing in the mid-to-late 1980s, Tracy was working as the in-house designer in a large printing company. "I learned that to create the best design, you had to understand as much of the process as possible. I would talk to the strippers, the pressmen, the bindery. Everything that I learned in those areas was relevant to my design. When I began designing for the Web, I learned HTML. Understanding how HTML works improves my design, allowing me to better control the final appearance of the Web site. Getting into the code is much more interesting and easier than most designers think."

"Most importantly, Web designers need to understand the language of interaction. Your designs are no longer static and they are no longer two-dimensional.

You need to learn what the viewer reacts to, what attracts them to a site, and to structure the site so the viewer can find the information, service, experience, or product quickly and easily."

GETTING TO KNOW YOUR CLIENT

"Before I pick up a pencil or launch Photoshop, I always interview the client about the purpose and audience of the Web site. The more information that I can start with, the better my design proposal will be. As you can imagine, a client that is unsure about what they want can be a nightmare to work with. One part of a Web designer's role is to help the client define the objectives of the site. For instance, some clients want links to everything on the opening page: links to the mission statement, worldwide factory locations, client lists, complete product catalog, job openings, all the way through to a picture of the board of directors! Step back and help your client see what information is most important and relevant to the people they wish to attract to the site."

GETTING TO KNOW YOUR VIEWERS

Just as in traditional graphic design, designing for the Web requires defining your target audience and what appeals to them. You need to have a feel for your target viewers' experience using the Web, their likely patience, age, and gender, as well as whether they are at your Web site for entertainment, information, and so on. This will help you establish the tone and personality of your site. "For example, in the case of the FreeLoader site, the client wanted to appeal to a young audience, so I decided the site had to have a slightly irreverent look. The banners are playful through the use of a hand-written font with mixed upper and lowercase letters (1.1)."

Taking the time to technically "define" your viewers also includes determining their likely access speed, preferred computer platform, browser, and level of computer experience. "With the millions of people on the Web, you may wonder how you can define the ideal viewer. But the reality of the matter is, a Web site doesn't have the same reach that, say, a Super Bowl commercial does. The Web actually narrows your general audience." Once a Web site is up, the server can be configured to supply specific statistics including the speed at which people are accessing the site, whether they are accessing it from home or work, and how long they are staying in the site. This information allows you to do some fine-tuning and can serve as a reference for future site-design projects.

From a technical point of view, understanding the end-viewer in terms of computer platform, preferred browser, and access speed will influence your decisions about the size and complexity of the design, thereby influencing download time and the viewer's

ARTIST:
Tracy Keaton Drew

ORGANIZATION:
Keaton Drew Design
1728 Q Street, NW
Washington, DC 20009
202/518-0853
tkdrew@primenet.com

SYSTEM, MACINTOSH:
Power Mac 8500/120
Mac OS 8.0
5GB storage/112MB RAM

SYSTEM, PC:
IBM Aptiva M71
Windows 95
1GB storage/16MB RAM

CONNECTIVITY:
56.6 Kbps modem dial-up

PERIPHERALS:
NEC MultiSync x2 17-inch monitor, Wacom ArtZ tablet, Agfa Studio Star scanner, Connectix Color QuickCam

PRIMARY APPLICATIONS:
Adobe Photoshop 5.02 and Illustrator 7.0, Macromedia Director 6.0 and Extreme 3D, DeBabelizer 1.6, MetaCreations Painter 5.0, NetObjects Fusion, HTML Editor, and BoxTop ColorSafe, Netscape

1.1

Navigator versions 2–4, and Internet Explorer versions 2–4

WORK HISTORY:

<u>1984</u> — While studying traditional graphic design, saw a computer-enhanced Kodak ad and had the revelation to learn and work with computers — although there weren't any computers at the school.

<u>1986</u> — In-house graphic designer for printing company and learned that "to be a good designer I had to know what was going on behind the scenes."

<u>1987</u> — Acquired first Macintosh.

<u>1989</u> — Beta tested Adobe Photoshop.

<u>1990</u> — First job as an independent contractor at *The Washington Post*. News artist during the Gulf War, and DTP specialist to assist in electronic pagination of first weekly section.

<u>1992</u> — Six-month internship at the Kodak Center for Creative Imaging in Camden, Maine. "I came to the Center as a print-oriented graphic designer and left as a multimedia and interface designer."

<u>1993–95</u> — Design Director for "Digital Ink," *The Washington Post* online.

<u>1996</u> — Founded Keaton Drew Design. Clients include *The Washington Post*, the American Association for the Advancement of Science (*Science Magazine*), Student.Net, MediaOne, and Maden Tech. Teaches Web design courses at George Washington University.

FAVORITE PLEASURE:

Movie soundtracks — "I especially love soundtracks that were composed for a specific movie. It's the classical music of our time."

NOTE

FreeLoader was one of the first Web sites to use push technology, allowing viewers to configure their computers to automatically log on to the site and download the latest FreeLoader issue complete with huge graphics (1.2 and 1.3).

experience. "Always design with a specific audience in mind. Organize and support the information through clear design, avoiding distracting elements."

The GrantsNet.org Web site helps graduate and postdoctoral students studying the biological and medical sciences to find positions and grant money in their respective fields (1.4). The site needed to balance speed, simplicity, and clarity to quickly and easily give the viewer the essential information (1.5). The search engine was the most important aspect of this site (1.6). Most of the pages returned in searches are dynamically generated from databases of text and graphics. "In addition to designing the graphical interface, it was important that I could write the

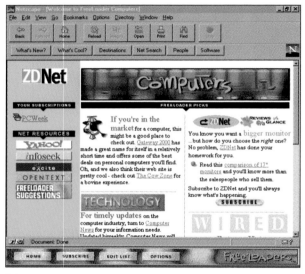

1.2

1.3

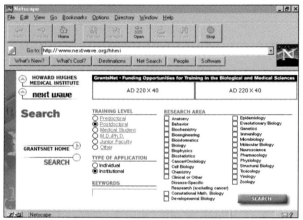

1.4

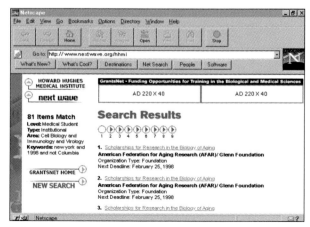

1.5

HTML and JavaScript since I was creating 'templates' that the Webmaster would be using to maintain the site and the database."

NEW GAME, NEW RULES

To avoid the "lost in interface" dilemma, Web designers need to distill information and categories carefully, underscoring the information with a consistent interface. Everything that goes into the user interface, from colors, controls, behaviors, navigation in and between screens, interactivity, and metaphors used, influence a viewer's experience. "Designing a Web site is similar to designing a mini-application, the viewer doesn't separate her experience from the design. If the design is poor and confuses the viewer, then the site has failed, no matter how relevant the information. The most successful design is the one the viewer doesn't even notice."

WHO IS IN CONTROL?

We all revel in the control that sophisticated software offers — from pixel-level image retouching to the ability to precisely fine-tune the word spacing of an important document. Designing for the Web requires an emotional 180-degree turn. You do not have the control that you're used to having over how the final result will look. You have no control over leading, letter spacing, and fonts when designing for 2.0 and 3.0 browsers (see Chapter 3 for more details). Further, you don't know for sure what computer platform, color depth, browser type, or version your viewers are using (unless you're developing an intranet), and all of these variables affect how content is displayed on the

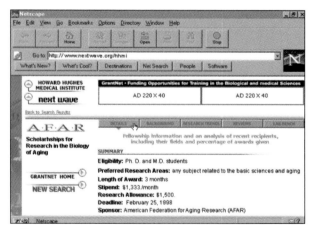

1.6

SELECTING FONTS

When it comes to selecting fonts, the rules are different for the Web than they are for print. "Blocks of serif 'body' text are easier to read in print, because the serif of one letter leads your eye gracefully to the next letter. Serifs help give type distinctive shapes, thereby increasing readability. But on the Web — or more accurately, on the screen — type is made up of pixels, and not continuous lines. If you were to count the number of pixels that are required to create a 10-point lowercase serif Times *h* and a 10-point lowercase sans serif Helvetica *h*, the difference is 17 versus 15 pixels. You can begin to see that serif fonts are more complex due to the nature of how they are displayed on the screen. In the illustration (1.7), Times, the serif font, is on the left and Helvetica, the sans serif font, is on the right. The smaller the typeface, the fewer pixels there are to display the letter. So there are fewer pixels, but you still have to add one or two pixels on either end of an ascender or descender because it's "serif" and because of the low resolution pixel display of computer monitors — it's getting messy. The bottom line? Sans serif fonts with a high x-height are the most legible onscreen."

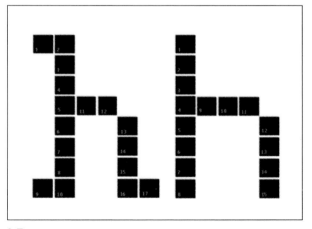

1.7

screen. "I always check a site throughout the design process on both Mac and PC. What happened with the Next Wave site is typical. The PC version (1.8) displays the pop-up boxes differently and has more white space above the navigation bar, while the Macintosh version shows the entire navigation bar (1.9)."

DESIGNING UP OR DOWN?

After identifying your audience, the next step requires a judgment call—design to the lowest common denominator (LCD) or assume that your viewers have more-advanced hardware and software. The decisions made at this stage will influence page weight and screen size. "Most of my clients request that I design for the average user—one that has an 8-bit color 15-inch monitor, uses either Netscape Navigator or Internet Explorer, preferably version 3.0 (I check all my designs on 2.0 and 4.0 browsers, too), uses a 28.8 modem, and leaves the default browser navigation options available (tool bar with text/icons and URL

indicator), which determines the size of available monitor real estate."

SPEED ISSUES

"I design the home page of a Web site to give the viewer a good first impression, just like the cover of a magazine should entice the people to read it. Guidelines that I try to follow when designing a top-level screen are to keep the weight of the page under 35K (add up the file size of the HTML document and all in-line files to arrive at your number), keep as much content as possible 'above the scroll line,' and don't overwhelm the viewer with too many choices. Under ideal conditions (a good phone line without noise), a 28.8 modem will take 15 seconds to download 30K of information. That includes all the HTML, graphics, advertisements, and whatever other bells and whistles you decide to use. On the Web, 15 seconds is a long time for viewers to wait to see if they are in the right place. I prefer to have my opening page be well under 30K, hoping that they will see the 'cover of the book' before clicking Ctrl/⌘+period to stop the page from loading."

An example of a site that needed to load quickly is *www.islandpress.com* (1.10). As a nonprofit environmental publisher, Island Press wanted their site to have a natural and serene look and feel. The icons, which look like woodcuts, and the simple yet graceful arch for the main navigation bar help create a hand-

1.8

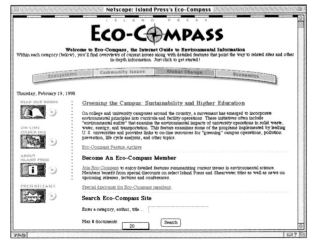

1.10

1.9

made low-tech atmosphere. As viewers go deeper into the site, details such as the small red triangle under the active topic (1.11) help them to easily orient themselves (1.12). As the information becomes more specific, the subsectional navigation clearly indicates the path that the user followed, how they got there, and how they can return to higher levels.

SITE NAVIGATION

The global and subsectional navigation throughout a site should give viewers confidence that they know where they are and how to get where they want to go. Navigation quickly becomes intuitive when you use

consistent treatment, placement, weight, and behavior for the site navigation. At the top level, the home page, the global navigation offers the viewer essential choices. For example, on the *www.student.com* site, the global navigation includes "About Us," "Contribute," "FAQ," "Search," "Site Map," and "Home." These are the choices the viewers should have available to them at every level of the site. When a viewer is browsing a specific area of the site, a second level of navigation

---

TIP

"A shortcut to adding up all the files to determine your page weight is to use an HTML validation service like *valsvc.webtechs.com/*. This site automatically checks your HTML to see if it is 'clean.' It will check pieces of code that you paste in or an entire page that is publicly available on the Web (1.13). It's a great service that helps me optimize my files and, subsequently, my design."

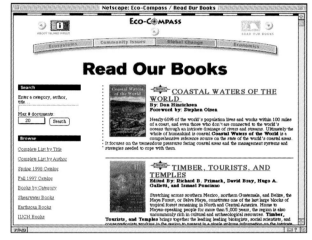

1.12

1.13

1.11

appears — one that reflects the specific content at hand. If a viewer clicks "Tuition & Financial Aid," he is offered nine choices including "Scholarships Open to All," "Buy Three Years — Get One Free," "Endowments Rise with Stock Market," and "More Students Default on Loans."

On Keaton Drew Design's Web site, the initial page reads quickly (1.15). The following portfolio pages (1.16) enable the viewer to see examples of Keaton Drew Design projects. Note the simple primary navigation that appears on the left side of the screen on all pages, and the subsectional navigation (the individual portfolio pieces) that enables the viewer to nonlinearly navigate throughout a category (1.17). It requires no further explanation and is intuitive to use.

COLOR ME SAFE

"**A**s a designer, you are used to working with the 16.7 million colors that a 24-bit system offers. You've even adapted to working within the limitations of color printing. Well, here you go again. Another reduction of your palette, but this time it is even more radical. You get 216 colors! The 216 color Web-safe palette is a compromise between browsers, computer platforms, and monitors. The established norm is an 8-bit monitor, but Macs and PCs do not use the same 256 color palette. They share only 216 colors and the remaining 40 colors vary between platforms. If you design with the Macintosh 256 color palette, your work will look great on a Macintosh. But the great majority of the people surfing the Web are using PCs, and the remaining 40 colors will dither on their machines. This can cause undesirable results." Designing with a Web-safe color palette will ensure that the majority of viewers will see colors that are consistent with your intention.

"I have to admit that I get tired of seeing the same gray-blue color on everyone's Web site. If I need a different tone of blue or if the 216 Web palette doesn't have the color I'm looking for, I'll use BoxTop's ColorSafe plug-in which creates a tiled non-dithering version of the color." (See the ColorSafe folder on the *Web Design Studio Secrets* CD-ROM.) Using the ColorSafe filter is the same as defining a pattern in Photoshop and then using the Fill command with that pattern to fill an area of the image. ColorSafe actually makes a 2 × 2 pixel tile of alternating tones to fool the eye into seeing one color (1.14). ColorSafe also converts RGB values to hexadecimal values and allows you to save your unique palette where you can name the colors anything you like. One word of caution though, this technique creates large GIF files.

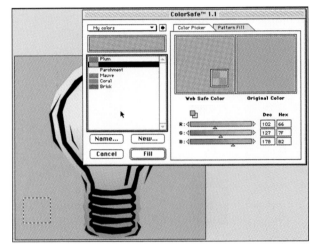

1.14

1.15

REAL ESTATE: KNOWING YOUR SCREEN SIZES

"As I begin to think about laying out a page, I start with a screen shot of an empty Web browser that is set using the default options. There is a common misconception that 640 × 480 pixels is a Web standard. That is a convention that remains from multimedia design and is not appropriate for Web design because it does not take into account how much monitor space the actual browser interface takes up. The viewing size of a default Netscape Navigator window on a Macintosh (1.18) is approximately 580 × 315 pixels and on a PC it's 635 × 314 (1.19).

It is surprising how many people do not resize their browsers or, even worse, surf the Web with the entire browser toolbar visible.

LIMITING SCROLLING

On the home page of a Web site, a viewer should not be required to scroll at all — all the important information should be within the monitor-safe rectangle. The viewer should understand where they are, what the site is about, what they are about to see when they delve deeper, and most importantly, how to use the site. "The initial page of a Web site is like the cover of a book — it gives you an impression of what is in the book and offers you a navigational scheme to explore the site, but it doesn't spell out every chapter like a table of contents would."

Just because viewers can scroll doesn't mean they want to scroll. One Web usability study (*www.useit.com/alertbox/9605.html*) has shown that a

1.16

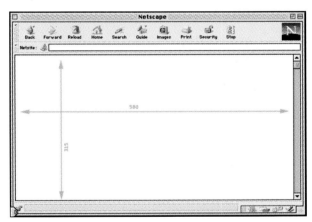

1.18

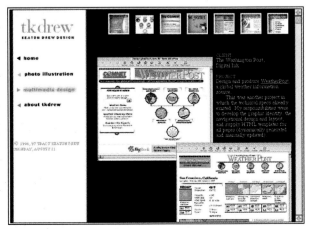

1.17

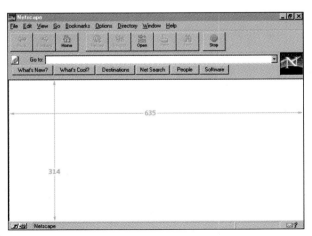

1.19

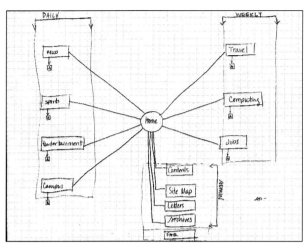

1.20

large majority of people will select an option that appears above the scroll line before they will scroll down to see what else is on the page.

The length of the page is just as important as the width. "Browsers and platforms influence the length of the page. PCs running Internet Explorer stretch pages, so I have to be careful to make sure that important information isn't lost at the bottom of the page." Of course viewers expect to scroll the deeper they get into the site. You expect that you may have to get through six screens worth of text before you finish reading an article, for example.

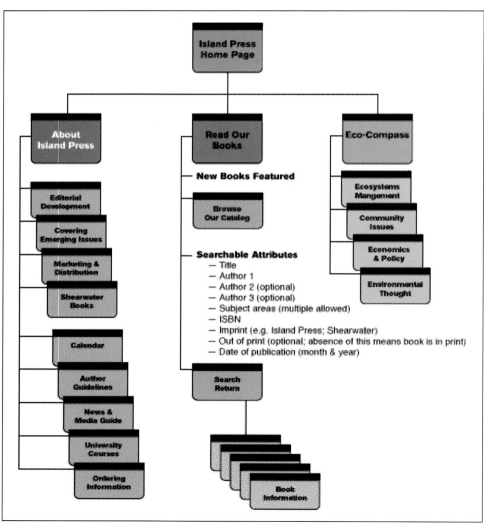

1.21

THE DESIGN PROCESS

"I always begin a site by planning out the site structure, either on paper (1.20) or with NetObjects Fusion. If I see certain areas are too content-heavy or one-sided, it is an indication that the structure isn't working. If one area has too much information and another one is sparse, I go back to the drawing board to find a better way to organize the information.

"Island Press wanted their Web site to be a useful electronic resource for booksellers, professors, and people conducting environmental research via the Internet. Originally, the site was called Island Press Books. It included a section called 'Eco-Compass,' which featured book reviews and resources for varying environmental topics. The first site map shows the original structure (1.21). I suggested elevating 'Eco-Compass' to become the top level, or home page, for the site to distinguish the site areas more clearly (1.22).

"Rather than having a home page that just links to subcategories, we reorganized the information so that the top level contained a timely and resourceful feature summarized and presented along with the other important options that a user might be looking for.

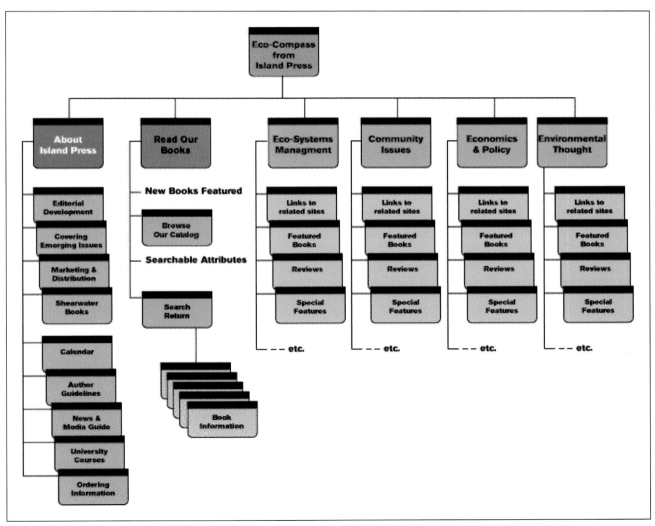

1.22

"After a site's scaffolding is in place, I begin to story-board each screen in the most fundamental way (1.23). I've found that if I begin to show a graphic design direction in these early sketches, the client almost always gets hung up on not liking a color, rather than looking at what choices are available on each screen (1.24).

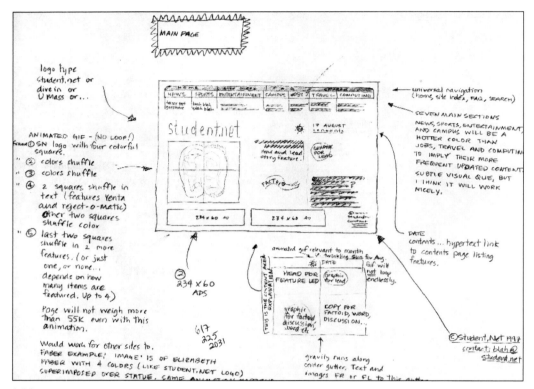

1.23

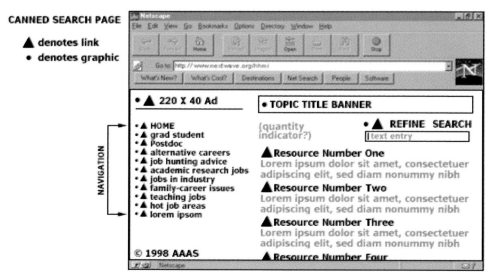

1.24

"After all the information structure is defined, and all content and navigation is applied to each screen in the structure, I begin to work on the visual appearance of the screen. My first step in establishing the graphical look and feel is to design the navigation elements."

DESIGNING BUTTONS

"I keep the style of navigational aids simple. I don't use cute names for buttons. I generally don't use pictures for buttons, and I strive to keep the text of the button to one — no more than two — words. Rather than saying 'In a Nutshell', the word 'Info' or phrase 'About Us' is more successful. It is very tempting to design cute little icons for each site, but this can backfire on you. Clarity and brevity are the key. If an icon needs an explanation, or can't be summed up and accompanied by one word, then bag it. This is especially important if the site will be accessed by an international audience. An analogy that I like to use is the up and down arrows on an elevator panel. The buttons need no description such as the wordy 'How to go up to a higher floor in this building.' The arrow or the word *up* are sufficient. It works. (For an interesting study on icons as buttons, see *www.sun.com:80/sun-on-net/uidesign/icons.html.*)

"After designing the navigation elements, I begin to work in even more detail, trying to work out the design treatment, layout, and placement of the navigation (global, sectional, and sub-sectional) (1.25 and 1.26)."

PHOTOSHOP AS A PAGE LAYOUT TOOL

"I use Photoshop to create my designs and get approval for concepts. I live by layers, guides, grids, and actions. I start with my screen shot of an empty browser. I use a PC screen shot if my client uses a PC, and a Mac screen shot if they are on a Mac. By hiding and revealing various layers, I can design any number of screens easily within the same file. To proof the design, I flatten and save the different screens, use the screens as comps (posted on the Web) for client approval, and print them out later to use as I write the HTML.

"Once I have all the screens in layers, I have to deconstruct them so I can drop them into the Web page. Precision cannot be underestimated when I'm cutting an image apart because I end up putting it back together with an HTML table. Most of my designs use tables for layout. And when possible, I use only one table since they can be complicated to code.

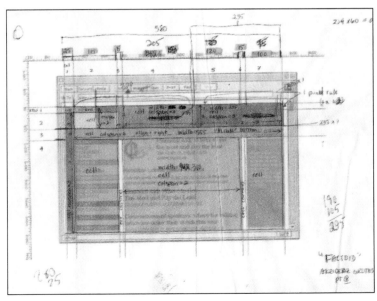

1.25

"Photoshop makes designing and writing these tables a breeze. I've come up with a production technique that speeds up the dissection of my comps into individual graphic files and helps me write accurate tables."

1. Start with an empty layer in Photoshop on top of a comped screen. (1.27)

2. Use the guides to draw accurate marquee selections that will represent each cell of each table (1.28).

3. "I illustrate the rows, columns, spanning rows and columns, and the individual cells."

4. Make each table cell a different color, and then, using the magic wand tool and the Info palette, select each cell by the exact width and height (1.29).

5. Check the math to make sure that all the cells add up to the width of the table.

6. Next, write the actual table in HTML using a text editor (1.30).

7. During this process, try to create as many cells as possible that won't require an actual graphic by using hexadecimal background colors instead of graphics. "I add these as I'm writing the HTML.

8. "Once I have the colored grid, by dropping the layer opacity down to 50 percent (1.31), I can see through to the active layer. With the magic wand set to zero tolerance and no antialiasing, I can select (1.32), copy, and paste the elements quickly into new documents (1.33). Working like this becomes automatic."

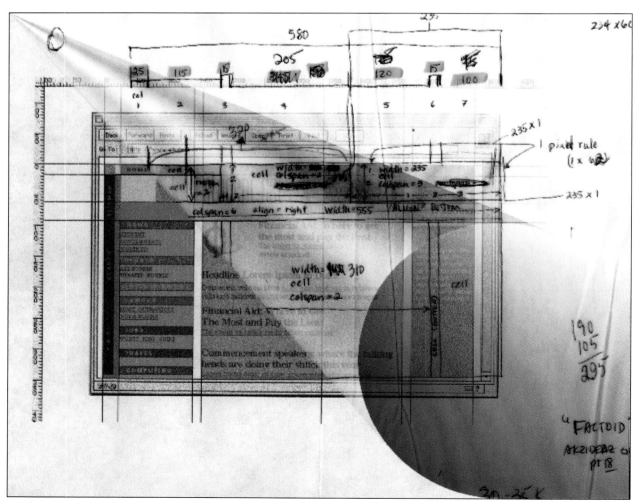

1.26

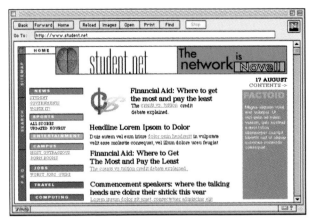

1.27

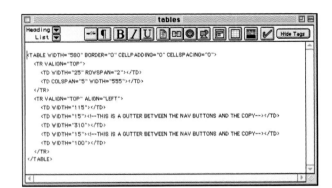

1.30

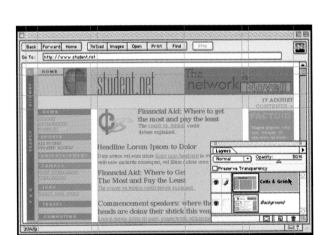

1.28

1.31

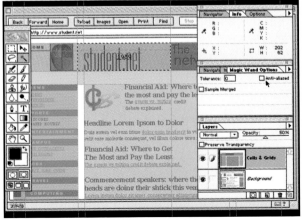

1.29

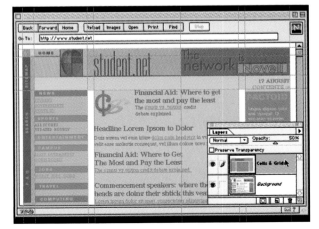

1.32

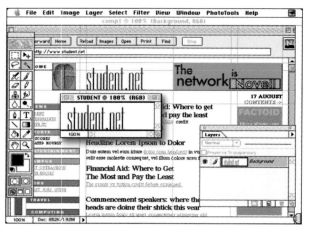

1.33

BUTTONS IN ACTION

Designing buttons is a snap when working with layers and actions. "When I use JavaScript rollovers for my buttons, each button has to be in three states: not clicked, mouse over, and mouse click. I start by copying one of the buttons from the layered Photoshop comp and making that my working document (1.34). Whenever I drop in new text, Photoshop creates a new layer, and by working with layer transparency I can see if the word is properly aligned. Creating the different states of the button can be made into an Action item (1.35 and 1.36)."

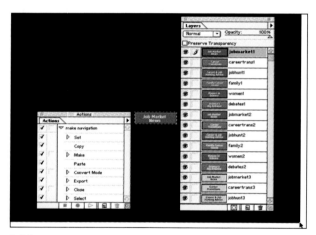

1.34

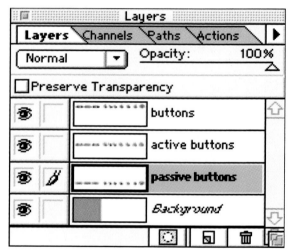

1.35

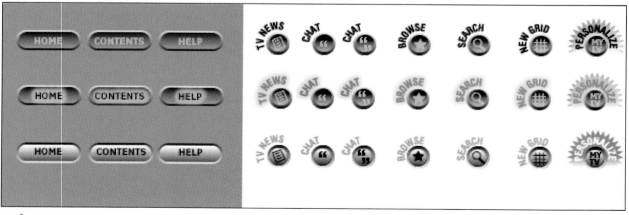

1.36

ENGAGING THE VIEWER

Refreshing your Web site regularly will entice viewers to return. Viewers like getting something back from a site: a sense of community, downloadable goodies, chat rooms, e-mail that actually gets answered, and most importantly, accurate and up-to-date information. "The *Washington Post* weather site challenged me to find a new approach to show world, national, and local weather (1.37) so that viewers could find up-to-the-minute weather information. As a reference site, the most important thing was for people to be able to access information quickly and easily. The client also wished to include graphical displays of weather data to support visual scanability (1.38). It was quite a balancing act."

ACTIONS IN ACTION

Working with the Photoshops Actions palette requires an understanding of what is and what is not actionable and a good grasp of the Photoshop command keys. In Photoshop 5.0, working with Actions has become much clearer and almost every tool and menu item is actionable. After building the buttons in the layered file, use Tracy's action to separate the files out into individual files. To use Tracy's action, start by loading the action Nav_butt.atn (on the *Web Design Studio Secrets* CD) into your Actions palette. Start the action at the top of the layer stack and work your way down.

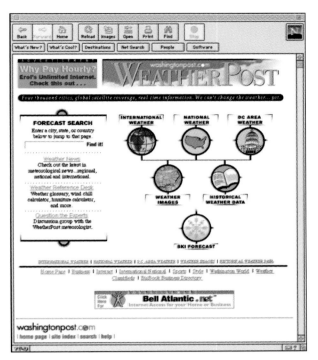

1.37

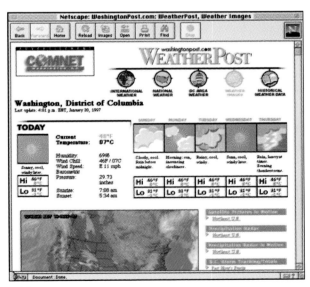

1.38

THE BOTTOM LINE

"In pricing out my Web design work, I follow the basic guidelines in *Pricing, Estimating & Budgeting* by Theo Stephan Williams, *Graphic Artists Guild Handbook : Pricing & Ethical Guidelines (9th Edition)* by Graphic Artists Guild, Rachel Burd (Editor), and *Web and New Media Pricing Guide* by Jp Frenza and Michelle Szabo. I calculate my costs: rent, equipment investment and depreciation, health insurance, my salary, and vacation to define my bottom line. Since I wear many different hats — designer, programmer, illustrator, project manager, site implementer, and tester — I've assigned each role a specific hourly rate. From the very first time that a client calls, I monitor every moment that goes into that job: phone calls, doing research, writing and presenting proposals, graphics production, and designing and implementing the site. This also helps me if I ever get into a tight deadline situation and I have to hire outside help. What the client doesn't see is how I have broken down the hourly rates. I did do that once and it turned into a slice and dice game. The client kept saying, 'Can't we trim this part or cut back on that part?' and it turned into a nightmare scenario.

"Doing Web design is so much more intensive on the back end than traditional design work. Keeping up to date is an ongoing process — sometimes I envy print designers. I mean, Quark doesn't change that much that quickly! The Web is constantly changing, and it requires a lot of time just to keep up with the changes in technology, so that you can deliver the best product possible. I spend a lot of time reading books and magazines, going to conferences, and surfing the Web, and that changes my hourly rate. But my clients don't flinch because I deliver the most up-to-date product possible."

FROM START TO FINISH

"Writing a proposal and design document is the most important step of any design project, especially since every project has different parameters. The design document includes the production schedule, budget, and job checklist of what has been completed. I use the design document to keep myself and the client on schedule. The client needs a schedule too since they are responsible for providing content in the form of images, text, logos, and so on.

"During the design process, I create a client viewing area on my Web site (1.39). I only give the URL to the client, and that way we can exchange ideas about the work in progress without having to have time-consuming face-to-face meetings. Clients love this way of working since they can see my progress (1.40) and add their input about their sites (1.41).

"Designing a Web site is rarely a cut-and-dry process. It's not like designing a glossy marketing brochure where once the job has gone to press the designer is done and can move on to the next project. Clients will want you to update or maintain the site. If not planned for, this can really eat into your profit margin. I often include future expenses, such as updating the site, as a line item on the project estimate. That way the client is aware that changes and maintenance will be a cost and we can discuss that before the budget is finalized. I always budget in at least four hours with the Webmaster to teach him about how and why I laid out the site as I did. Those four hours are always worth it for the site, the client, and my own sanity!

"The best thing about designing for the Web is that there aren't any hard or fast rules, and we are all learning as we go. The only way to learn it is to do it and enjoy the process."

1.39

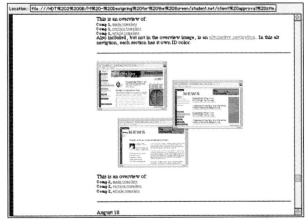

1.40

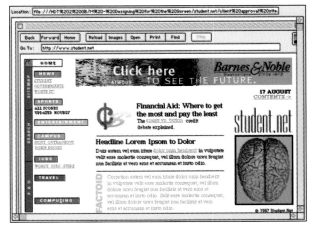

1.41

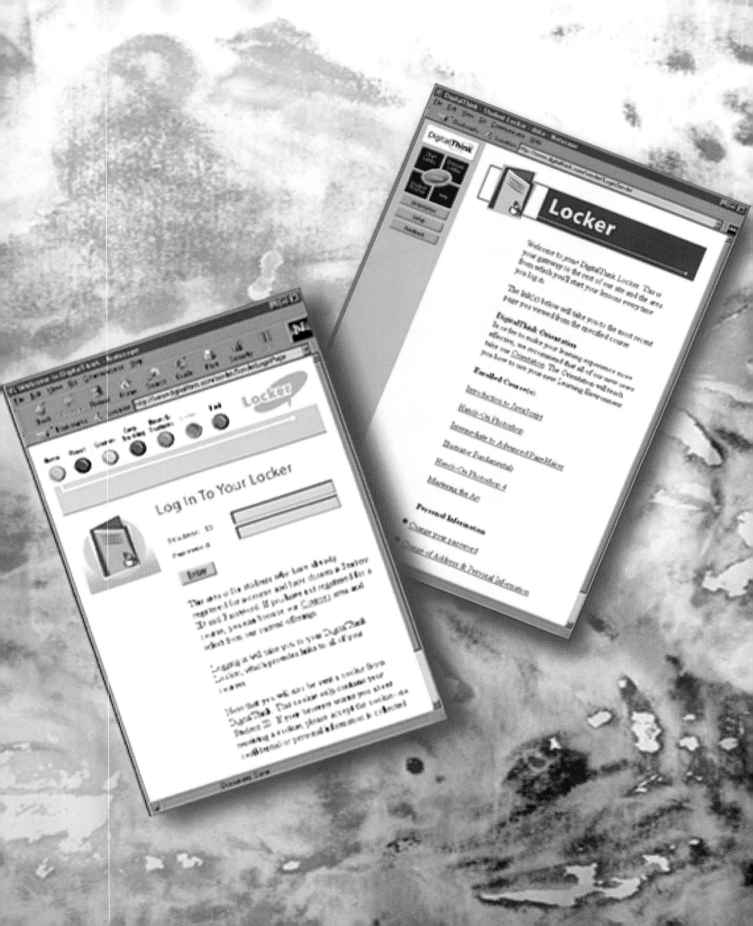

CHAPTER 2
MAKING YOUR SITE EASY TO NAVIGATE

In print media, navigation is an issue that both receives and warrants little attention. Most of the basic navigational protocols were developed long before any of us were born. If a sentence halts abruptly at the end of a page, the reader has only to turn to the next page to locate the remaining words. To help readers find the information they're looking for, the thoughtful designer provides a table of contents or, for a more complex document, an index. If a story jumps from one page to a nonsequential page later in a periodical, the reader can expect to see a short line offering guidance, such as "Continued on page 116." In the most extreme cases, a book might include footnotes along with a comprehensive bibliography to inform readers where they can go to further their knowledge.

Unfortunately, few of the navigational techniques you may have learned as a page designer are applicable to the Web. The rules of print navigation are based on the assumption that the pages are bound together in a sequential order. But electronic pages float freely; any order assigned to them is purely arbitrary. The default home page — *index.html* — isn't the first page in any traditional sense, whether the pages are arranged by size, date created, or alphabetical order. When you come right down to it, a site is nothing more than a random assemblage of unrelated documents. So as a designer, you begin from a point of absolute chaos.

The question then becomes, how do you ensure that your arbitrary ordering of information makes sense to your visitors? Do you work from a single navigation page and gradually spread out more and more links like the branches of a tree? Do you create multiple button groupings available from every single page so

In my opinion, pure information design is the basis of good navigation design.

CHRIS GOLLMER

2.1

any piece of information is just a single click away? Do you set up a network of navigational aides, including a site index, a help page, and a search option? Where do you begin, where do you stop, and how much can you tweak it when it comes time to add yet more pages to your site?

TWO THOUSAND PERCENT GROWTH IN TWO YEARS

To find out the answers to our questions, we turned to the online training firm DigitalThink (*www.digitalthink.com*, 2.1). Unlike most companies with a Web presence, DigitalThink exists solely on the Web. Granted, the company employs real people sitting at real desks in a real building somewhere in San Francisco, but the actual commercial business takes place online. DigitalThink *is* its Web site. We reasoned that if a site this large can keep its visitors moving, so can yours.

In the two years since its inception in January of 1996, the company has grown from three courses and a few hundred students to more than 50 courses and 26,000 students. The site itself contains thousands of pages, standardized multimedia elements as diverse as RealAudio interviews and Java applets, and separate "lockers" for every one of its students. This isn't just a Web site, it's an online service.

During this time of exponential growth, the primary navigational elements have remained fundamentally

ARTIST:
Chris Gollmer

ORGANIZATION:
DigitalThink
1000 Brannan Street
San Francisco, California 94107
415/437-2800
www.digitalthink.com
chrisg@digitalthink.com

SYSTEM:
Power Mac G3/266
Mac OS 8.1
4GB storage/128MB RAM

CONNECTIVITY, ISP:
OC-3, GlobalCenter Server environment:
UNIX

PERIPHERALS:
Mitsubishi Diamond Pro 21-inch monitor

PRIMARY APPLICATIONS:
Adobe Photoshop, Adobe Illustrator, Equilibrium DeBabelizer, HVS ColorGIF and JPEG

unchanged. Buttons have moved around on the page and new navigation elements have been added, but much of the original organization remains intact and continues to function every bit as well as it did in the company's start-up days.

The person responsible for DigitalThink's look and structure is Chris Gollmer, one of the company's first employees. "The DigitalThink site has grown significantly over the last couple of years. It's now much bigger than it was, so we're constantly adapting the old navigation systems to meet our new needs. In the beginning, we had one main home page with six main sections and an average of ten pages per section. It's gone way beyond that now, but it still works much the same way. We still have the six main sections, it's just that there may be hundreds and hundreds of pages behind them."

ALL IT TAKES IS TWO CLICKS

Gollmer's guiding principle is simple. "It has to work, it has to be functional. If it doesn't work for the end user, I don't care what our reasoning was, it doesn't work. What we have here is a piece of software, and what I'm doing is interface design. We use what works, we throw away what doesn't."

And according to the input Gollmer has received from DigitalThink's corporate and independent students, what works is major sections with a network of crosslinks. "Our students have to be able to access any major section of a site at any time. Some sites make you go down one path at a time. If you want to skip over to a different path, you have to back up. That might be fine for small sites, but we're hearing that you should never have to go back more than one step to get to the page where you want to be. Ideally, you should be able to get anywhere in our site in just two clicks. That's not always possible, but that's what we're working toward.

"In the beginning, I started very linear and just wrote everything down. I made diagrams and mocked up a basic organizational chart in Word. Just lists and names. No graphics, just text. The whole time, I was working closely with our Webmaster. We spent weeks just making sure the user could get around.

"Once you get the network of paths figured out and mock up the site in plain-gray HTML pages, then you can add all the bells and whistles. That's when you assign the look and feel, not before. In my opinion, pure information design is the basis of good navigation design. That's the way we approach the larger site now, too. It's all very bare-bones until we know it works."

CANDY-COATING THE INTERFACE

But the navigation tweaking doesn't end there. Even the bells and whistles are designed to help students get around. "When it came time to design the buttons, we came up with a sort of colorful candy treatment. We call the first-tier round buttons 'skittles' (2.2) and the

---

WORK HISTORY:

1978 — Mother enrolled Chris in his first oil-painting class when he was in first grade.

1990 — Enrolled in Design, Architecture, Art, and Planning school at University of Cincinnati.

1993 — Learned about competitive nature of business working for high-tech marketing-and-design firm.

1996 — Joined up as first member of the creative staff at Web-based training site DigitalThink.

FAVORITE ICE CREAM FLAVOR:

Ben & Jerry's Chubby Hubby ("It sounds bizarre, it looks bizarre — but when you taste it, it's just unreal.")

2.2

2.3

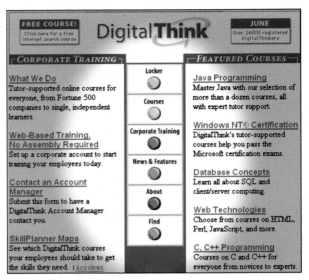

2.4

second-tier square buttons 'chiclets' (2.3). The buttons are soft and colorful. We got a lot of positive feedback because they aren't high-tech looking. People seem to think they make the site easier to use. They're also easy to spot because of the bright colors."

Gollmer also uses color to identify the main sections of the site. "The colors of the skittles tell you where you are. Red is always help or search, dark blue is company background, purple is for our large corporate accounts, light blue is the course catalog. Your locker, which is your gateway to all your courses, is always orange. Green is the news section and yellow takes you back to the home page.

"We have to stick with a few bright primary colors because of all the different platforms and monitor settings. Each color has to be really unique and easily identifiable. We did a lot of testing to find seven colors that we could separate very well regardless of what kind of screen you're looking at. We ended up with a rainbow palette. In the worse-case scenario, with a really dark, low-contrast monitor, the blue starts looking a lot like the purple and the orange looks like the red. But even then, users were able to distinguish the colors well enough to get around."

"I realize there's a group of people out there who may not be able to see the different colors. So we did our best to keep the value and hue of each color as unique

as possible, alternating between darks, lights, and mediums. But capitalizing on the use of color was key."

THE HOME PAGE SETS THE STANDARDS

Our tour of the DigitalThink site begins aptly enough at the home page. Smack dab in the center of the home page is a column of colored buttons, the main navigational skittles (2.4). "Centering the navigation bar was a tough sell at first. Everyone wanted to go with left-to-right buttons across the top or bottom. The problem is, we have two primary audiences that we have to address equally. There's the corporate training audience, then there are the home users who just want to take a Photoshop course. We're finding that the corporate trainers who come through with 100 or so employees at a time want a dedicated part of our site. So we used the navigation buttons to split the corporate stuff on the left from the individual course information on the right.

"It seemed a little risky when we did it, but it appears to be working fine. More than anything else, it's something different that you don't see very often. I think it makes the opening page more distinctive. And the navigator bar looks sort of like a podium, with our logo looking out over the top," a logo which Gollmer designed, we might add.

To find out what any one of the buttons does, you just move your cursor over it (2.5). Gollmer created the interactive buttons using the JavaScript `onMouseover` command. (For complete information on making interactive buttons, see Chapter 7.)

"JavaScript rollovers are typically used to create flashing hot spots. They're fun, but they have a tendency to be a little gimmicky. In this case, though, I tried to make the rollovers serve a specific purpose. When you mouse over a button, you get more information about a specific area. The button title changes from black on white to white knocked out of a blue stripe. And the skittle shows through somewhat transparent in the background. That way, you know it's still there and you can click on it if you want to. I think it helps point you in the right direction. It also saves you time by explaining where you're going before you go to the trouble of loading the page."

THE TWO-TIERED APPROACH

"In the early days of the site, we just had the round skittles at the top. As we started expanding, we developed subgroups within each group. We decided to add this gray bar below the skittles so we could increase the number of buttons and tie the new, second-tier chiclets in with the first-tier skittles. The gray bar accommodates up to six chiclets in all (2.6). But we still leave the gray bar in there even when there are no chiclets (2.7). I think consistency is really important. It's something that users feed on. If you change the navigational elements from one page to the next, you're going to confuse people.

"We make a big effort to integrate the colors from the skittle buttons into the pages. The balloon in the upper right corner of the page — which is modeled after the DigitalThink logo — changes colors to demonstrate the section you're in (2.8)." The gradient along the bottom of the spot illustration on the left side of the page also changes to reflect the key color. "That's a subtle treatment and I doubt most people notice it. But it does give you a sense of where you are in the site, and I think that's worth emphasizing and re-emphasizing in as many ways as you can. I always try to error on the side of too much consistency."

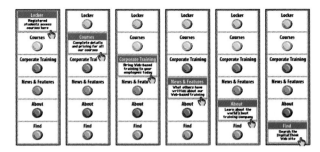

2.5

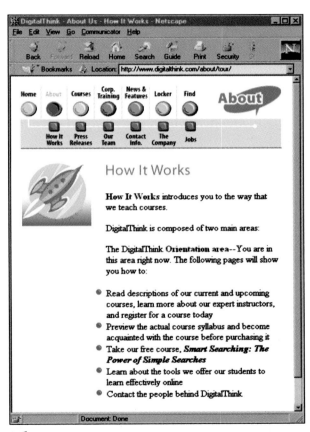

2.6

2.7

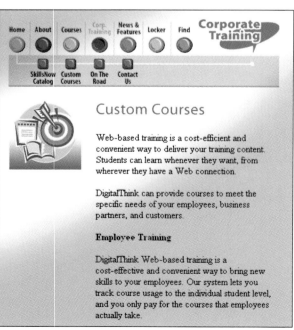

2.8

The beauty of the two-tiered approach is that it establishes an obvious hierarchy to the site structure. It also allows a user to switch to a completely different section of the site without backing out of the current section. "This goes back to my two-click principle. You should be able to move quickly to anywhere in the site you choose, without having to look at certain pages over and over again."

SPECIALTY NAVIGATION

The skittles and chiclets are the interstates and freeways of the DigitalThink site. They bind together the main areas and let you jump from one page to another in a matter of seconds. But if you're interested in touring DigitalThink's specific courses—which are, after all, the real purpose of the site—you have to get off the freeway and make your way into the suburbs. And when touring the garden district, you need a new map.

THE COURSE CATALOG

The one section of the site that's too large to fit the standard navigation model is the course catalog. "Setting up the standards for the course navigation was the toughest task because there's such a wide range of information relating to each course. We just couldn't squeeze it into the chiclet model. So we had to come up with something different that felt like an extension of the main navigation system and not a complete departure.

"To start with, I divided the page in thirds, with the major course topics on the left, the specific course information on the right, and an empty margin in between (2.9)." The thing to keep an eye on here is the blue bar that stretches across the top of the two columns. Gollmer uses the bar to show students where they are and where they've been. In some cases, the blue bar even offers a way back.

"If you click on one of the topics, like Design and Publishing, you see all the design and publishing courses we offer (2.10). Then if you look at the blue bar at the top, it still says Course Topics on the left, but on the right it says Design and Publishing. Now click on one of the course titles, such as Illustrator

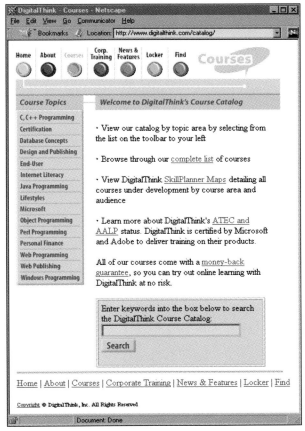

2.9

2.10

Fundamentals. The right half of the page contains a description of the course, just as you'd expect (2.11). But up top in the blue bar, it says Design and Publishing on the left, which is where you were, and Adobe Illustrator Classroom in a Book Series on the right, which is where you are. The Design and Publishing heading is actually a clickable button so you can back out. So you can go anywhere inside the Illustrator Fundamentals area — check out the training objectives, view the syllabus, read the instructor bio — and then back out to Design and Publishing in just one click.

"I call this the 'bread crumb trail' approach. If I can't show you all parts of the course catalog at once, I can at least make sure you can get back out to the last course topic in one step. And the main skittles are still there at the top of the page in case you want to switch to a different section of the site."

THE MARGIN BUTTONS

Things become additionally complicated when you start factoring in DigitalThink's diverse array of downloadable files and multimedia elements. "The site includes a series of horizontal 'margin buttons' that appear to the left of the main body copy. These buttons let you download files, search, and perform other operations. For the most part, they reside in a structured grid; the system allows these buttons to float vertically anywhere in the column. So I guess that strictly speaking, they aren't navigation buttons. But to the user, I think they feel like navigation elements. They help you get what you're looking for, they help you get around."

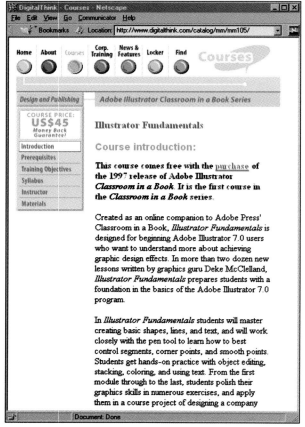

2.11

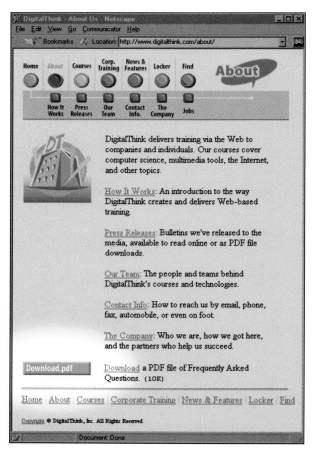

2.12

Like the skittles and chiclets, the margin buttons are color coded. "The colors have different meanings, but they're usually related. In the skittles, green means News & Features. It's stuff you don't absolutely need to know but you might want to check out. In the margin buttons, green means Download. Again, it's extra stuff—maybe you need it, maybe you don't. You might be downloading a JPEG image, you might be downloading an Excel spreadsheet, you might be downloading a PDF file (2.12).

"We use yellow for the official DigitalThink buttons. It's blue type against a yellow background to match the company logo. An example is the Register button, which lets you register for a course. The buttons that take you to the different author bios are yellow, too (2.13). Yellow is also the color of the Home skittle, which takes you to the home page. In most cases, the margin buttons and skittles are pretty much in sync."

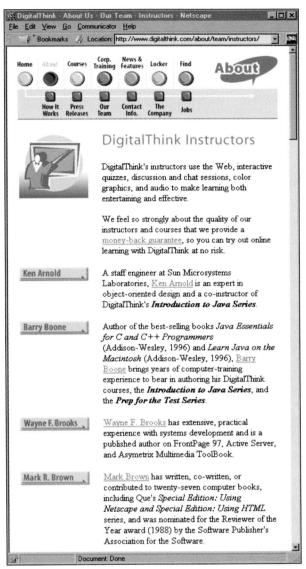

2.13

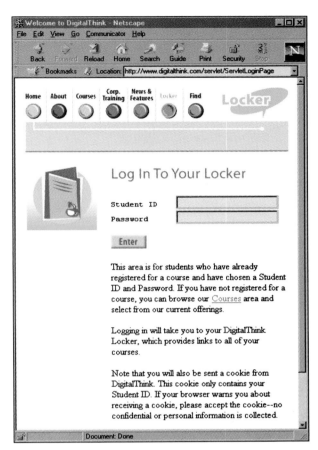

2.14

THE STUDENT LOCKER AND REMOTE CONTROL

Every student who signs up for a DigitalThink course gets a locker (2.14). This is where registered students sign in and gain access to their courses. "Originally, we called this area the home room. Now we call it the locker. It seems to be a good metaphor for our American students, but some of our international students don't quite get it. I think they're catching on, but we may still have some adjustments ahead of us.

2.15

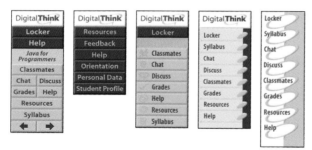

2.16

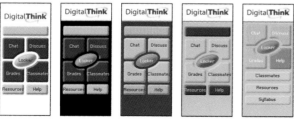

2.17

"Once you enter your locker, the skittles and chiclets go away and you see a yellow toolbar on the left side of the window (2.15). This element is only seen by registered students. From now on, as you study the lessons and take the quizzes, this toolbar is always with you. This way, you can concentrate on your course without being distracted by all the other areas of the DigitalThink site.

"I went through a lot of different looks for the toolbar (2.16). But then I finally settled on a remote control look (2.17). I actually went to a few big electronics stores to see what different remote controls looked like and decided what worked and what didn't." Gollmer finally arrived at two versions of the remote-control-style toolbar (2.18). The first appears in the locker area and the second follows you as you work inside the courses. "The differences between the two toolbars reflect the context that you're working in. In the locker, you need access to orientation and setup functions. In the courses, you need to be able to talk to tutors and classmates. But the basic concept stays the same.

"We decided to make the center Locker button look really different from the others because we wanted students to be able to get back to home base really easily.

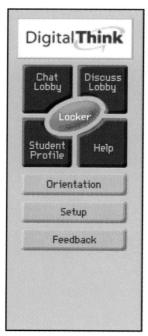

2.18

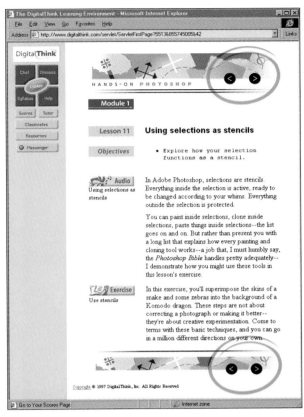

2.19

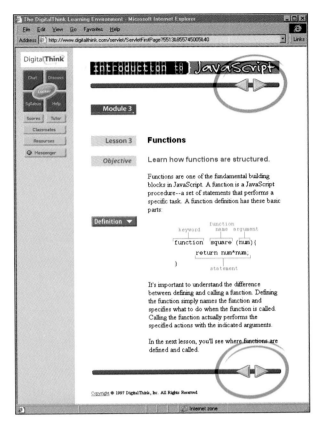

2.20

The shape and angle of the button match the balloon in the DigitalThink logo, just for a little extra continuity. The orange buttons are a little more recessed to make them blend in with the yellow background. This shows that the buttons have a lower priority."

MOVING THROUGH THE COURSE

"Once you enter a course, things become more linear. The courses are arranged into lessons, so Lesson 2 comes before Lesson 3. You have to work through it in a prescribed order, just like a traditional course.

"The buttons that let you go forward and backward are built into the banner art at the top of the page. We used to custom-design each banner with the navigation buttons folded into the art (2.19). But we found that some students had problems finding the buttons. The banners looked great, but they became too much fluff and not enough function."

"So we had to come up with a standardized system where the forward and back buttons are separated from the banner art that's specific to each course (2.20). We ended up going with the corporate DigitalThink blue and yellow. And since the arrows are so important for getting through the course, we made them really jump off the page so students don't miss them.

"Frankly, this is a lesson that we learned through trial and error. Personally, I liked the old way better with the buttons folded into the banner art. But it just wasn't working. A lot of people were trying to use the forward and back buttons built into their browsers. And of course that doesn't work because the browser's forward button doesn't let you go places you haven't been yet. So we had to come up with something that students would see again and again in every single course they take."

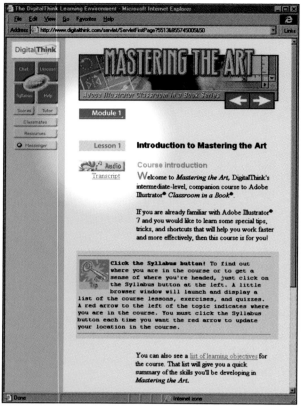

2.21

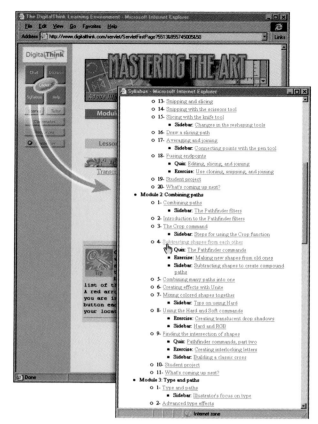

2.22

In addition to myriad buttons, Gollmer employs static navigation elements. You can't click on them, they merely show you where you are. "Every course is divided into ten or so modules which are subdivided into several lessons. You always need to know where you are in the course, so each page includes a dark blue tag to tell you what module you're in and a light blue tag for the lesson (2.21). The tags are a static form that grew out of the margin buttons. The only difference is that the tags are flat where the buttons are beveled," like the yellow Audio button in the figure.

What if you want to jump forward or backward to a different module in the course? "Clicking on the Syllabus button brings up a separate window that lists every module and lesson in the course (2.22). Just click on one of the links to go right to that page (2.23). That might not be something a user would think of automatically, but we explain how it works in the Help section."

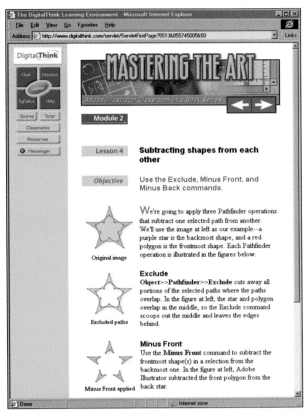

2.23

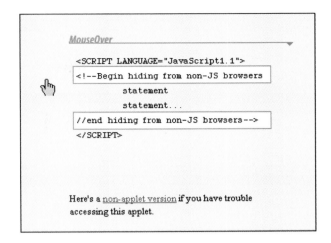

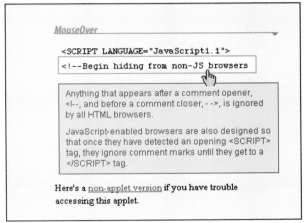

2.24

MOUSEOVER POP-UPS

DigitalThink's computer-related courses require lots of figures, many of which are interactive. Helping users to tell the static figures from the dynamic ones requires yet another navigational element. "We started using 1-pixel red outlines to highlight hot areas in an image. If you move your cursor over one of these outlined areas, you get a pop-up menu that explains how the highlighted operation works (2.24). We call these MouseOver graphics, after the JavaScript command. We actually code the MouseOver figures using JavaScript as well."

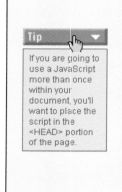

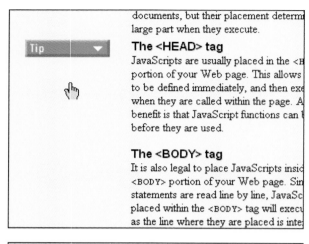

2.25

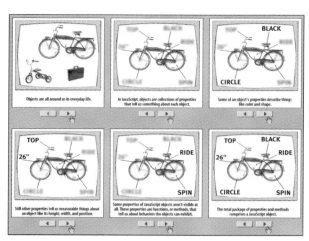

2.26

"The other style of JavaScript rollovers are the green Tip buttons (2.25). The little down triangle on the right side of the button shows that there's a drop-down element. Most people recognize the meaning of the down triangle because it's a common operating-system element. Hover the cursor over the Tip button to see the tip. Some people want to click on the button, and that works, too."

Why color the button green instead of red, like the MouseOver highlights? "The color goes back to our margin button coloring scheme. A tip is an extra bit of information, like a downloadable PDF file, so it's green. I think there's a chance people won't put that connection together. But I think it's safe to give it a try. If it really doesn't work and we get a lot of negative feedback, we'll have to go back and change it."

GUIDING STUDENTS THROUGH JAVA

Some courses offer interactive flip books (2.26), created using Java applets. "You can flip through these little picture books at your own pace. The coding is pretty complex. We developed the flip book idea internally and farmed out the actual coding to a Java contractor. But from a navigational standpoint, it's very simple. All we have is two arrow buttons. The buttons tell the students that they can scroll back and forth through the book. So each flip book acts like a miniature Web site inside the course page. You can go back and forth one image at a time.

"Another Java applet we use is the Messenger, which lets students and tutors talk to each other when they're online (2.27). It's just a basic chat tool. The little Messenger button in the remote control area flashes red if you have a message waiting. It's a simple two-frame animated GIF file that alternates between a red light and a red light with a burst behind it. I also designed the interface inside the Messenger window, which is nothing more than a series of buttons and a text-entry area."

THE ULTIMATE TEST

Gollmer warns his fellow designers that what seems obvious to them may not make a lick of sense to the end user. "When you're putting together Web graphics and other elements, you're working with the artwork day after day. You always see the buttons, you know what they do. It seems so obvious, it never occurs to you someone else might not get it."

The ultimate test comes when you put the site in front of the user. "If you want the best feedback you can get, ask an average person who's never seen your product and doesn't know anything about your navigation system to go through your site. You'll recognize very quickly what does work and doesn't. It can be a frustrating experience, but it's very illuminating.

"We also provide Feedback links that let students send us suggestions and comments about the site. Anything related to navigation or graphics comes directly to me or one of the other designers. We also have software to track the users and see where they're going. If they stop at a page and leave the site, we can know when that's happening. If it keeps happening at the same point over and over again, we know we have a problem."

As a designer, is it difficult to deal with what must be a never-ending supply of user feedback, much of it negative? "Sometimes. It's more fatiguing than anything. But you always have to bear in mind that users have the best intentions. If one user cares enough to tell you what's wrong, there are plenty more who feel the same way but don't care enough to respond. People are just being honest about the problems they're having. You can't take it personally.

"Besides, navigation design has a purpose. If the purpose isn't being met, then it needs to be fixed. You can't expect to take your beautiful design and put it on a pedestal. It has to do its job; otherwise, it's history."

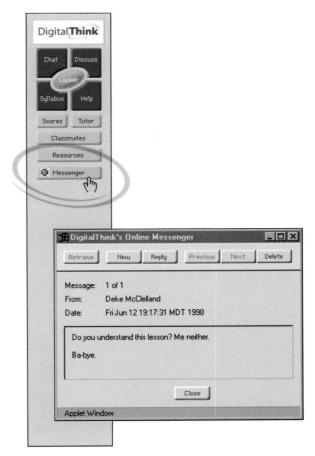

2.27

Netsite: http://www.catsprite.com/gallery2/sthrills.html

"super thrills"

mixed media on archival paper
approx. 6' x 5'

CHAPTER 3
CREATING WEB GRAPHICS

When an artist picks up a mouse and launches Adobe Photoshop or MetaCreations Painter, she brings a unique sensibility to the silicon and plastic workings based on an appreciation of art history, introspection, and passion that are essential to creating art.

For artists, computers and software are more than production tools. "Although it is true that machines have no soul, neither does a tube of polymer paint. It is the challenge of artists to breathe life into, give 'soul' to, a work of any medium. Working digitally allows me to explore, experiment, and combine art in ways that I couldn't before, and the limitations are easily outweighed by the possibilities. My Web site (3.1) has changed how I see and display my artwork. I have a gallery that is always open and where viewers are always welcome (3.2 and 3.3). I thrive on the e-mail and comments that people from all over the world have sent me. In a way, it is similar to the paint that would get under my finger nails and mark my clothing; it surprises and inspires me."

debi lee mandel — artist, illustrator, and creative director — lives and works in the mountains near Lake Tahoe in northern California. She balances her time between commercial and personal work, but the boundaries are often blurred. "My personal artwork obviously influences my commercial work. For me, creating a successful Web site is similar to hanging an art show. The exhibition space (the Web site) needs to compliment and support both the images and content of the site. Successful Web sites are effective and compelling if they work on technical, emotional, and visual levels."

I am constantly balancing my desire for the best image quality with the need for small, speedy graphics. It is a balance tempered through testing, visual inspection, and compromise, compromise, compromise.

debi lee mandel

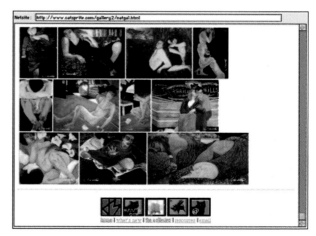

3.1

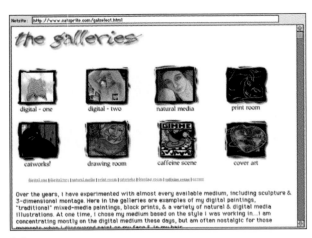

3.2

3.3

WEB GRAPHICS ESSENTIALS

Hanging a painting, linocut, drawing, or photograph on the walls of the Web or creating original art for the Web requires an understanding of resolution, file formats, color palettes, and techniques that allow images to load quickly and still look their best. "There is an incredible difference between creating artwork for the Web and repurposing existing artwork for Web display. Some of my natural media paintings are over seven feet wide and too unwieldy to handle easily, while some of the icons that I design for clients are so small that if I ever tried to reproduce them any larger than an inch wide they would just fall apart.

"Designing a Web site, be it personal or corporate, requires an understanding of the target audience and the technology. The objectives and requirements of a corporate site are very different than those of my personal Web site. For my own Web site, the target audience includes art directors, editors, and other artists, most of whom use Macintosh computers. They are coming to my site to see my portfolio (3.4 and 3.5) and are willing to wait a bit longer to see a higher-quality image. On the other hand, commercial Web sites such as *www.themoneystore.com* (3.6) have to load quickly and look best on the PC platform, so cutting down on every byte possible and using the Web-safe color palette is absolutely essential."

ARTIST:
debi lee mandel

ORGANIZATION:
catsprite studios
PO Box 2
Dutch Flat, California 95714
530-389-8312
www.catsprite.com
dlm@catsprite.com

SYSTEM, MAC:
Power Mac 7500/200
Mac OS 8.1
2GB storage/128MB RAM

Magnavox 17-inch monitor with VGA adapter
Power Mac 6100/60
Mac OS 8.1
2GB storage/72MB RAM
Apple 14-inch color monitor

CONNECTIVITY:
28.8 modem

PERIPHERALS:
Wacom ArtZ 6 × 9-inch tablet
UMAX S-12 scanner with transparency adapter
Hewlett-Packard 560c DeskWriter

Defining and envisioning a Web site's target audience influences the entire design process, from conceptualization and interface design to the selection of colors and file formats used. "For example, when I'm working on my own site I use the Macintosh 256 color palette since it includes the grays that are so important to my work. When creating original artwork for commercial sites (3.7), I know that most viewers will be browsing on a PC; therefore, I use the 216 Web-safe palette so that the artwork and graphics will look best on their machines. Using the Web-safe palette cuts down on dithering and unwanted color shifts.

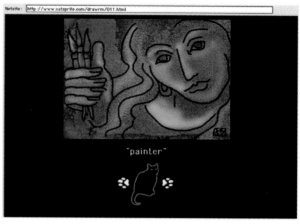

3.5

3.4

3.6

PRIMARY APPLICATIONS:

Adobe Photoshop 5.02 (with the original Gallery Effects filters) and Illustrator 7.0.1, MetaCreations Painter 5.0 and Expression, BBEdit, DeBabelizer, GifBuilder and Fetch.

WORK HISTORY:

After thirteen years as an artists' model in Europe and the U.S., "where I received the most diverse and thorough art education possible, I followed my heart to the mountains of Northern California."

1993 — Retrospective exhibition of "natural media" paintings. Due to the shear size of many of her paintings, heard to have said, "in my next life I want to be a miniaturist!"

1994 — Became enamored with the Macintosh computer to extend her creative palette. Became a miniaturist.

1995 – 97 — Designer and illustrator for one of the first multimedia companies. Clients include ABC-KGO-TV, Service-Master, Saturn Cars, Duraflame, and The Money Store.

1996 — Included in book *Painting With Computers,* by Mario Henri Chakkour Rockport Publishers, Inc.

1996 — First commissioned digital piece for 1997 Dianippon International Screen calendar.

1997 — Creative Director, at Freestyle Software. Clients include Sunkist, Sony, and Nestlé.

FAVORITE PLEASURE:

Floating down the river — weightless and without any deadlines.

"I prepare Web graphics with the 28.8 dial-up viewer in mind. In an ideal scenario a 28.8 connection will download 30K of information in half a minute. On commercial sites, my goal is to keep the total page weight between 15K and 30K. On my cat-sprite Web site, image quality has precedence over speed. I aim for each image in the gallery areas to be up to 30K, but sometimes more if absolutely necessary to properly view important details. These are tough decisions that every Web designer needs to make, site by site and image by image."

EVERY SINGLE BIT, BYTE, AND PIXEL COUNTS

Shaving files down to save bytes of information requires experimentation and an understanding of the different file formats. Not all graphics are created equally. A corporate logo requires a different treatment than a CEO's portrait. "The first thing I had to understand was the concept of resolution." *Resolution* — the amount of information required to display an image with the desired quality — impacts file size and download speed, which in turn impacts the viewer's experience. The mantra for creating Web graphics is "smaller, faster, better" and "I am constantly balancing my desire for the best image quality with the need for small, speedy graphics. It is a balance achieved through testing, visual inspection, and compromise, compromise, compromise."

The pixel resolution of monitors is the determining factor as to how many *pixels per inch* (ppi) to allocate to an image. Although monitor resolutions range from 70 ppi to 96 ppi, the majority of computer monitors come in at 72 ppi; therefore, the accepted display standard is 72 ppi. Since the monitor is the final output for any Web site, displaying an image at a higher pixel resolution will not add any image quality. Rather it slows the loading of the image and therefore degrades the viewer's experience.

FILE FORMATS

The great majority of images and graphics displayed on the Web today are in the *GIF* (Graphics Interchange Format) or *JPEG* (Joint Photographic Experts Group) format. "The names of the file formats reveal what they are best used for. Simply put, I use GIF for icons, illustrations, animations, and tiled backgrounds, and JPEG for photographs and art reproductions. The one exception to this is when I need to turn photos into icons that are 100 × 100 pixels or smaller."

3·7

GIF

Use the GIF format for images that are made up of solid colors such as logos (3.8), vector-based illustrations, and line art (3.9) or any image that uses transparency to "float" over a background. Here are a few important facts and useful advice about using the GIF format:

- It supports a maximum of 256 colors that must be indexed to either a Web or adaptive palette.
- It supports 1-bit transparency to drop out backgrounds, creating the illusion that the type or image is on top of the background (3.10 and 3.11).
- It's used to create GIF animations.
- It can be interlaced to download progressively.
- GIF is not appropriate for photographic images — with the exception of images that are smaller than 100 × 100 pixels.
- After indexing a file and saving it as a GIF, do not open and resize the image. If you require a different size graphic, reopen the original 24-bit file, resize, index, and save it again as a GIF.
- When an image contains fine type, do not dither when indexing the file. The dithering will break up the letters and make them difficult to read.

3.8

3.9

3.10

3.11

JPEG

Use the JPEG format for photos, paintings, and images with fine detail and important color gradations. Here's the lowdown on JPEG:

- It supports full 24-bit images.
- It uses *lossy* compression, so image information and quality are always compromised even when the human eye cannot detect the degradation.
- Avoid JPEG if fine type is included in an image. The compression artifacts will be most apparent where the type meets the solid color (3.12).
- After compressing an image with JPEG, do not open the image and retouch or re-edit and then recompress. The compression artifacts will be most apparent on the re-edited parts of the image. If you need to re-edit or resize an image, open the original 24-bit file, edit or retouch, and save it again as a JPEG.

Fine type will suffer
when you use
JPEG compression!

3.12

```
<A HREF="three.html">
<IMG SRC="honesty.gif" ALT="honesty"
BORDER=0 WIDTH=100 HEIGHT=100></A>
```

3.13

Future Choices

GIF and JPEG images are both supported by the standard browsers. In the future, we'll most likely be working with *PNG* (Portable Network Graphics), *WSQ* (wavelet scalar quantization), and *FlashPix* file formats. Presently, these all require plug-ins for the browser to display them. And no one likes being interrupted while Web surfing to go to a third-party Web site, download a plug-in, install it into the browser plug-in folder, quit, and relaunch only to be able to see a specific image. It better have been worth it!

FOR TEXT-ONLY VIEWERS

"Ideally, a viewer will come to my site and see the layout and graphics just as I designed them, but the Web is not an ideal place, and people do surf the Web with graphics turned off to speed up browsing. To give those viewers as much information as possible, I always use the image <ALT> attributes, which allows me to add a brief description about the graphic (3.13). At least 25 percent of all Web surfers choose to browse with Web graphics turned off (3.14), so if I

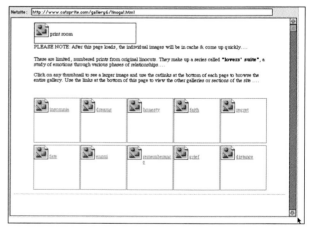

3.14

want them to have some information about the image, I add an `<ALT>` tag to the image code. The `<ALT>` tag is a brief text description of the image that displays in the box where the image would have been. If a text-only viewer decides he wants to load that graphic, he clicks on the image box and the image will load (3.15). In the catsprite gallery, visitors can then choose to view the image at full size (3.16). Of course, the impact of the page is lost, so any artist's preference is to have the page viewed as designed (3.17)."

THINKING GAMMA

"When I hang my paintings for a show, I pay careful attention to the lighting and placement of every piece. That way I know that the work will look its very best. When people surf the Web, I have little or no control over how they view my images. But this doesn't mean that I don't care. I know that most users viewing the commercial sites I create are on PCs and that PC monitors are approximately 20 percent darker than Apple monitors. So I know I will need to correct for this. The gamma of a standard Mac is 1.8 and the gamma of a PC is usually 2.2 or higher. The higher the gamma, the darker the images will display. I check all of the images at the common PC gamma and then use Photoshop Curves to match the image quality at the Mac settings. It all comes down to identifying your target audience and fine-tuning the images for them. If most of your viewers are coming to your site on a PC, make the images look good at the higher (in other words, darker) gamma. If you know that most people are looking at the images on Macs, make the images look their best at the 1.8 gamma."

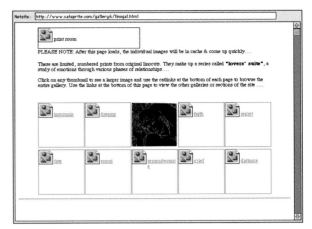

3.15

3.16

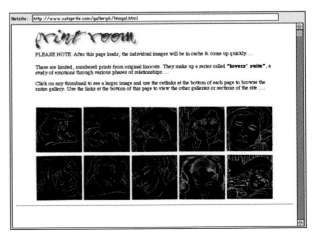

3.17

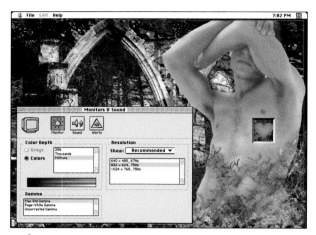

3.18

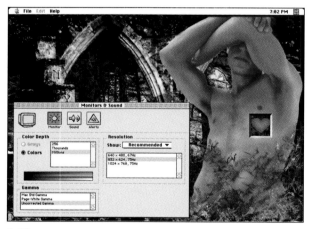

3.19

On a Macintosh, the simplest way to test how an image will look at the darker gamma is to access the Monitor & Sound control panel and select Uncorrected Gamma (3.18 and 3.19). On both the Mac and PC, you can preview images via Photoshop 5.0 by using the Color Preferences RGB settings (3.20 and 3.21).

PLAY IT SAFE WITH WEB-SAFE COLOR PALETTES

Color palettes play a very important role when repurposing existing graphics and when creating original content. The *Web-safe color palette* is made up of 216 colors that are shared by the Macintosh and PC platforms. The remaining 40 colors are not shared by the two platforms. If you create images with the full 8-bit 256 color palette on one platform, 216 of the colors will look fine and the remaining 40 colors will dither. *Dithering* occurs when the monitor display tries to display a color that is not in the shared 216 color palette. Imagine mixing red and yellow glitter to make orange glitter—from a distance it will look orange but as you get closer you'll see the separately colored speckles. Dithering becomes most apparent in large, flat surfaces, especially on 8-bit color monitors. It can also add "bulk" to the final file size.

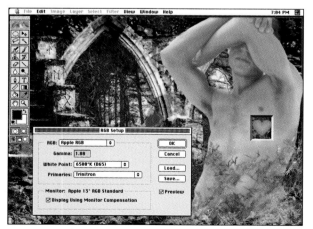

3.20

3.21

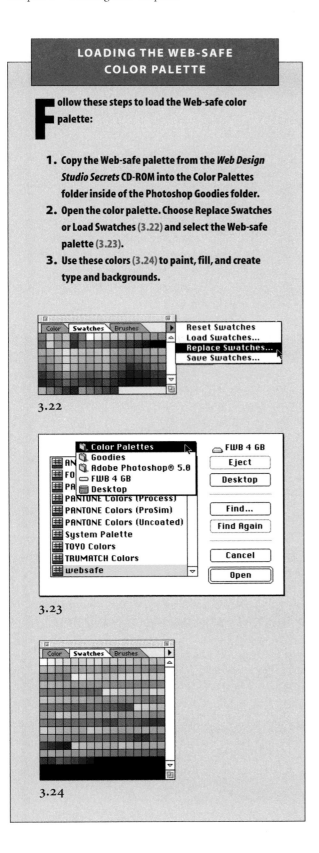

LOADING THE WEB-SAFE COLOR PALETTE

Follow these steps to load the Web-safe color palette:

1. Copy the Web-safe palette from the *Web Design Studio Secrets* CD-ROM into the Color Palettes folder inside of the Photoshop Goodies folder.
2. Open the color palette. Choose Replace Swatches or Load Swatches (3.22) and select the Web-safe palette (3.23).
3. Use these colors (3.24) to paint, fill, and create type and backgrounds.

3.22

3.23

3.24

DETERMINING FILE SIZE

"Photoshop isn't honest. You can't just read the file size off of the lower left-hand corner of the file while the file is open in Photoshop. That number represents the X times Y resolution of the image and it doesn't say a thing about how much disk space the file actually uses up. If you close the file and read the file size next to its file name you're being had again!"

"To determine the actual file size, you need to Get Info on the file and read the second number in parentheses—the one expressed in bytes (3.25). It is that number that is the honest assessment of file size." The first number represents how much space the file requires due to the 32K block Macintosh hard drive architecture. On a PC, seeing the actual file size is much simpler since the actual file size is displayed by right-clicking the file and reading the properties.

"After preparing all the GIF and JPEG files, the very last thing I do is to drag them onto the shareware program GIF Prep 1.0.1 by BoxTop Software to delete the files' resource forks, header information, and icons." GIF Prep cuts another 10 – 20 percent off the actual file size. You can download this great utility at *www.boxtopsoft.com*.

3.25

ICON OR NO ICON?

"I like the icons that Photoshop adds to files. They help me to identify files quickly, but they are deadweight for a Web designer, adding 5–6K to each file's size." In Photoshop's preferences, either select Never Save or Ask When Saving to decide on the fly if you want an icon or not (3.26). In Photoshop 5.0, you have a second opportunity to not include the icon by checking Exclude Non-Image Data when saving the file (3.27). If you really like the icons and do not want to change your preference settings, you can also create an Action item to resave the files without icons as a final step before embedding them into the HTML document.

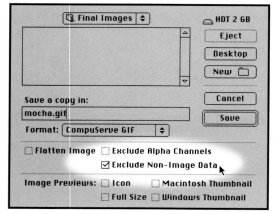

3.26

3.27

WORKING WITH EXISTING GRAPHICS

Most galleries on the Web are collections of paintings or photographs. The majority of images were created traditionally and need to be prepped correctly to display well on the Web. "Here's how I prep my images:

1. "Whether I start with a Kodak Photo CD image, a flatbed scan, or a vector illustration, I always start by cropping an image down to the essential information (3.28).

2. "After cropping the image, I view the image at 100% (accessed by double-clicking on the magnifying glass). That way I see the entire image and can decide if it is too large, to small, or just right (sounds like porridge!).

3. "Then I go to Image Size and resize the image to the pixel dimensions of 72 ppi, making sure that Resample Image is turned on (3.29).

4. "Whenever you resize an image, the quality will become a bit softer. You can use Unsharp Mask to bring back image crispness, but a sharpened image doesn't compress as well. Using Unsharp Mask to sharpen images requires a case-by-case judgment call.

5. "I use File ➤ Save a Copy since it allows me to flatten layers and doesn't override the image that I have carefully cropped and retouched. This copy goes into the Web Images folder. Now I just need to consider which file format to use to display the image on the Web. If the file is going to be a JPEG file, Save a Copy also lets me delete the file's alpha channels. If the file is going to be a GIF, I keep the alpha channel since it will help me define transparency later on in the process."

3.28

DO CATS PREFER GIF OR JPEG?

"I hold cats in high esteem and frequently use them literally and symbolically in my work, as exhibited on my Web site. When I was ready to convert 'intrigio in summer' and 'cat of kintyre,' I had to consider each image and decide which format would be best. The 'intrigio in summer' image is very graphical (3.30) with a limited color palette, making it ideal to export as a GIF file, while the 'cat of kintyre' image relies on subtle shading and softer values, especially in the stone wall (3.31), making it the perfect candidate to save in the JPEG format."

GIFS

GIF files can be created from existing graphics or from artwork that you are specifically designing for the Web. Converting existing graphics and artwork into GIFs requires experimentation to find out how few colors you can use while maintaining image quality.

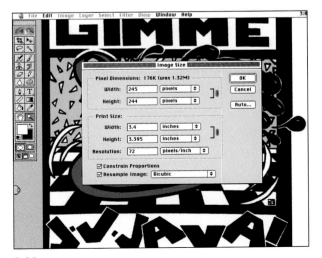

3.29

3.30

3.31

WORKING WITH WEB-SAFE COLORS AND EXISTING GRAPHICS

Converting an existing illustration to display well on the Web involves replacing the original colors with Web-safe colors, indexing the file, and exporting it in the GIF file format. Here are the steps:

1. Use Photoshop's magic wand tool set to zero tolerance with Anti-aliasing turned off to select large surfaces of color such as the green sunflower leaves in the 'intrigio in summer' image (3.32).

2. Choose Select ➢ Similar so that Photoshop selects all the similar values throughout the file (3.33 and 3.34).

3.32

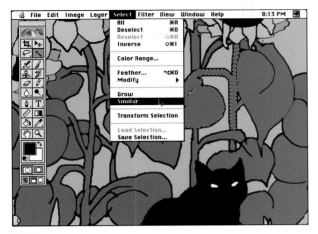

3.33

3. Select a color from the Web-safe color palette and option delete to force fill the selected area with the Web-safe green foreground color (3.35). Moving the toolbar next to the area to be filled helps to find the best color.

4. Repeat steps 2 and 3 until all surfaces have been filled from the Web-safe palette (3.36).

5. Zoom in to examine the file carefully. Use the pencil tool to retouch any errant pixels that may have been overlooked during the selection and fill process (3.37 and 3.38).

6. Save a Copy.

3.34

3.36

3.35

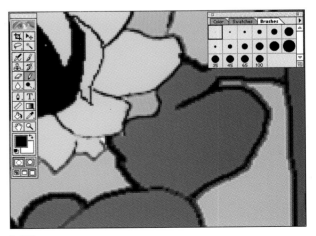

3.37

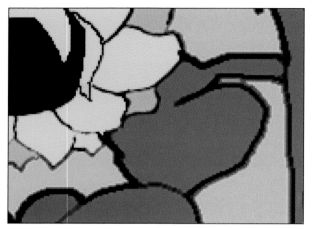

3.38

IMAGE COLOR LOOK-UP TABLES

Every image on the Web has its own color palette, also known as it's *CLUT* (Color Look-up Table). The browser accesses this color palette in order to display the image correctly. Most artists, designers, and photographers work with thousands, if not millions, of colors everyday, and the idea of converting images down to 216 colors seems barbaric. Interestingly enough, many images and graphics don't even need 216 colors to look great on the Web. Cutting the color palette down to the absolute essential colors results in a smaller CLUT that will yield smaller file sizes. Also, remember that no one is expecting exhibition quality image reproduction on the Web. Images need to look their best but still load quickly. debi uses the following Photoshop technique when indexing files.

1. Choose Image ➤ Mode ➤ Indexed Color (3.39). Select the Web palette and a Dither of None (3.40). Click OK.
2. Choose Image ➤ Mode ➤ RGB Color (3.41). Click OK. "I know that this sounds strange!"
3. Choose Image ➤ Mode ➤ Indexed Color. Select the Exact palette. Notice how few colors are actually required by the image (3.42). In this case, rather than using the full 216 Web palette, the image only requires 40 colors. The image uses more than the five dominant tones due to the antialiased brushes used when creating the original.
4. You can either save the image file as a GIF file or export it. Exporting allows you to define a color or alpha channel to serve as transparency (explained below). "I have also noticed files that are exported rather than saved as GIFs are approximately 10 percent smaller in final file size, and the Export command automatically removes the Photoshop icon from the file." Place this file into the Final Images folder.

Let's compare GIF and JPEG versions of the same image. In this case, "I tried JPEGing the 'intrigio in summer' image but the JPEG artifacts just ruined it (3.43). The GIF version is much cleaner (3.44)."

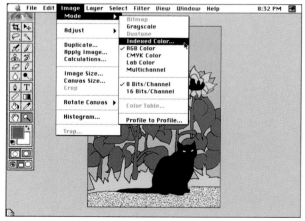

3.39

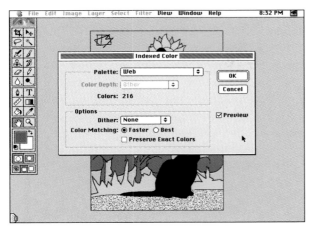

3.40

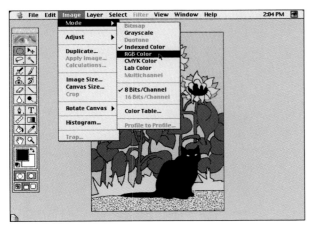

3.41

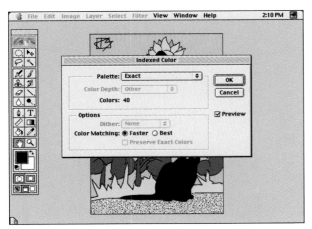

3.42

3.43

3.44

DO YOU DITHER?

Graphics may contain drop shadows (3.45) or color gradations, and photographs always include soft transitions and color blends. In all of these scenarios the process of indexing an image may cause obvious and ugly banding. Using the Dither option (3.46) can break up the banding you see, and although dithering will increase the file size slightly, sometimes the improvement of image quality offsets the trade-off of increased file size. Images made up of solid colors from the Web-safe color palette usually do not require dithering. Images with subtle tones will look better with a diffusion dither (3.47). "The most important thing about prepping graphics for the Web is to keep an eye on the image quality and file size. I'm constantly refining how I optimize images to save every byte possible while maintaining image quality."

3.45

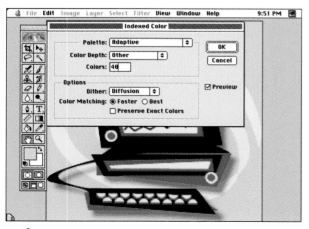

3.46

3.47

3.48

BATCH PROCESSING AND SUPER PALETTES

Converting a few images by hand is fine, but if you need to convert dozens of files, doing it by hand is tedious and inefficient and can add to repetitive motion injuries. The process of indexing multiple images is an ideal candidate for Photoshop's Actions. Another great time-saver when producing a large-scale Web site is to create a super palette, save the CLUT, and use it once. Then, when indexing images, select Previous palette and Photoshop will use the same palette over and over again. Here's how:

1. Create one Photoshop document with all relevant graphic files that contain all colors to be used in the Web site (3.48).
2. Index this file as described earlier (3.49).
3. Choose Image ≻ Mode ≻ Color Table (3.50) to view the Color Table (3.51).
4. Save the Color Table in your projects folder (3.52).
5. When indexing and exporting all files that require a similar color treatment, use Palette ≻ Previous to index the image with the super palette you created.

3.49

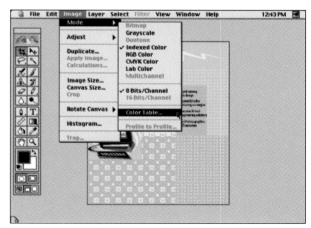

3.50

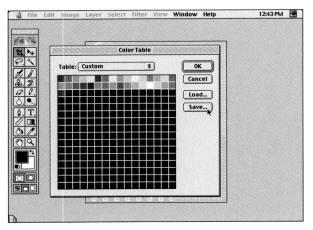

3.51

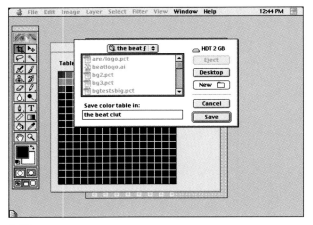

3.52

This technique will speed up file conversion and have an incremental positive effect on image downloading and display. Remember, every byte counts. You should also use super palettes when prepping files that will be used for GIF animations.

THE GOOD, THE BAD, AND THE TRANSPARENT

Wouldn't it be great to be able to stack images and text on top of one another at will! In 2.0 and 3.0 browsers, you can't have overlapping images, but by using the transparent option available in the GIF format, you can create the illusion of having an image, graphic, or text (3.53) float above a patterned background (3.54). You can define transparency via an alpha channel or by selecting one color in the image. The secret to making clean transparent GIFs without ugly white halos is to create the image in a Photoshop file in which the background layer is the same or similar (dominant) color as the final transparent GIF that you will be placing on top.

3.53

3.54

Color Technique

To define image transparency with Photoshop, follow these steps:

1. Create artwork in Photoshop and then fill the background layer with the Web-safe color that is (or is close to) the dominant background color of your Web site.

2. Flatten the image and index as described in the previous steps.

3. In the Gif 89 Export dialog box (3.55), use the eyedropper to click the background color or colors to be transparent (3.56).

4. Test the effect by dragging the GIF file onto an empty browser window (3.57).

5. By changing the General Preferences for the background of your Web browser or background file, you can check how the transparency will work by dragging the GIF file onto an empty browser window (3.58).

3.55

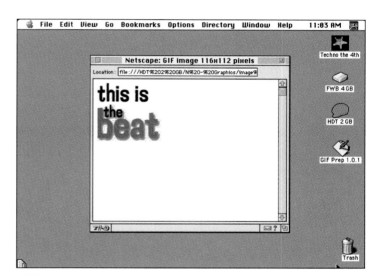

3.57

3.56

3.58

Alpha Channel Technique

Defining image transparency with an alpha channel yields better edge results, but the trade-off is that the file is a bit larger. Once again, which technique you should use depends upon the balance between image quality and file size. To define image transparency with an alpha channel in Photoshop, follow these steps:

1. Create the alpha channel (3.59). GIF transparency does not support any soft edges or transitions, so only use aliased tools such as the Pencil or Selection tools with Anti-aliasing turned off. (Note: You can create the mask in the RGB file since indexing an image does not affect the mask.) The white areas of the mask are what will be dropped out and the black will be protected (3.60).

2. In the Gif 89 Export dialog box, select Alpha 1 from the Transparency From pop-up menu (3.61).

3. Test the effect (3.62).

The quickest way to check transparency and edges is to drag and drop the GIF file onto an empty browser window. To improve this visual test, change the preferences settings to reflect the project's color or define the patterned background. (This is also a great way to read off the pixel dimensions from the file title without having to open the image in Photoshop.)

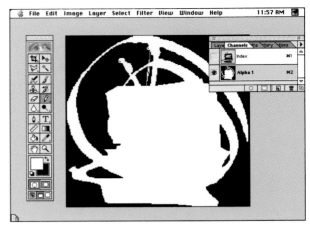

3.60

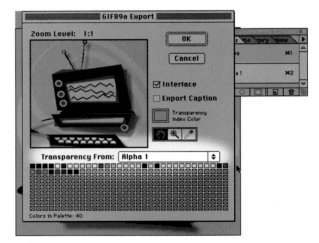

3.61

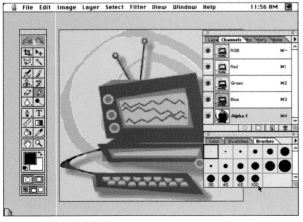

3.59

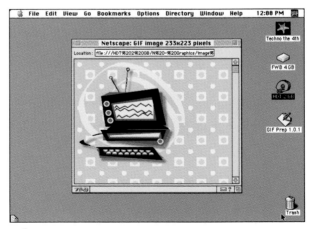

3.62

3.63

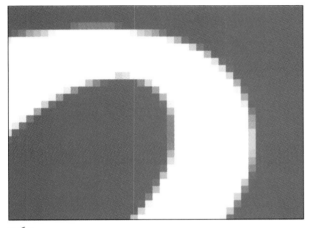

3.64

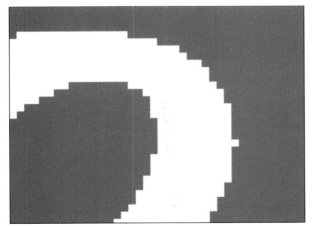

3.65

ANTIALIASING — FRIEND OR FOE?

Antialiasing is the series of tonal and color steps that soften edges and transitions. It is commonly used to avoid harsh, abrupt edges when working with text, selections, and painting tools (3.63). Visually, antialiasing is desirable since it creates a soft transition which helps to avoid the jaggy stair-step look. The problem with antialiasing is that it requires more colors to create these transitions, which increases final file size (3.64). debi lee uses antialiasing on type and avoids antialiasing when making selections (3.65).

INTERLACED GIFS AND PROGRESSIVE JPEGS

Interlaced GIFs and progressive JPEGs achieve similar effects: When an image first appears, it starts as a tiled/pixelated version and then the tiles become finer and finer until the entire file is in focus. "Interlace GIF files only when they do not contain any fine text (3.66)," debi advises. "It is very frustrating to try to read tiled text as it downloads. I do like progressive JPEGs, but not all browsers recognize them yet, and that is a compromise I cannot make right now."

3.66

WORKING WITH PHOTOGRAPHS AND PAINTINGS

To display paintings on her Web sites, debi does all the creative and retouching work on the high-resolution file and then resizes, converts or compresses, and saves the file.

Using Kodak Photo CD is a great way to input a lot of images quickly and inexpensively while still maintaining high image quality. The process starts with photographs from any film type (color negative, slides, and black and white) and format (35mm, medium, and large format). Photo CD Master includes five resolutions, the highest being 18MB, and Photo CD Pro includes six image resolutions, the highest being 72MB. As discussed below, debi acquires the files at the Base resolution when preparing files from Photo CD for the Web.

1. Photograph a painting, being careful to light the painting evenly and frame it squarely. Start with the best picture possible. Nothing ruins an art reproduction more than uneven lighting or when parts of the picture are out of focus.
2. Process and scan the 35mm film onto a Kodak Photo CD Master disk or a desktop scanner.
3. Acquire the image into Photoshop at the Base resolution of 512 × 768 pixels, which brings in the image at 1.13MB. "Although that is much larger than any image you will ever put on the Web, it is easier to finesse and retouch higher-resolution images and then size them down for Web display (3.67)."
4. Crop, fine-tune color and contrast, and retouch any dust or image imperfections (3.68).
5. Save the file to your Images folder.

3.67

3.68

3.69

3.70

JPEG

"JPEG compression works best with images that have many subtle tones such as photographs or paintings. You have to use JPEG carefully. If you overdo it, you'll be able to see the tiles (called 'artifacts') that JPEG uses to analyze an image.

"After I've cropped, retouched, and sized the image, I Save a Copy, selecting JPEG from the file formats (3.69). I like to start with a quality setting of 3. (The lower the quality setting number the more compression takes place and the lower the image quality will be.)" Click OK and save the file to a JPEG folder. To see the effects of JPEGing, close the image, reopen it, and compare it to the original file (3.70). "If the image still looks good, I'll close the compressed file and JPEG the original file again but with a lower quality setting. I call this finding my threshold of pain or

3.71

'putting my heart in a vise'. You hit a point where the JPEG artifacts degrade the image so much that you have to back off and use the higher-quality setting.

"Once you've found a setting, such as 3, that works for one type of image, this doesn't mean that 3 will be the magic number for all of your images. JPEG doesn't work well with images with a lot of fine detail, such as a photo of tree branches in winter, and you have to be especially careful when JPEGing portraits. JPEG artifacts (the little squares) can show up very quickly on flesh tones." The original uncompressed image (3.71) and a close-up of an over-JPEGged file reveals the square JPEG artifacts (3.72) very quickly. Also, notice the color shift that can occur when compressing too heavily with the JPEG format.

3.72

CREATING ORIGINAL GRAPHICS AND IMAGES

Working with the Web-safe color palette and cutting down on the use of antialiasing is the best place to start when creating original graphic content for the Web. "When designing icons and page headers, I start in Illustrator, working mainly in black and white (3.73).

"I use Hue/Saturation to colorize the graphic. Once again, I keep the Web-safe palette close to the image to eyeball the best color (3.74). The icons I designed for the Freestyle site are a good example of this technique (3.75).

 FREESTYLE

PORTFOLIO

COMPANY

CONTACT

PRODUCTS

HOME

3·73

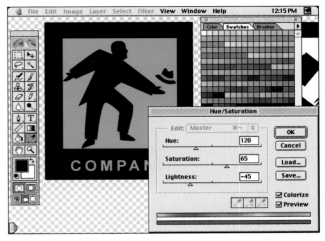

3.74

3.75

"I've experimented with ⌘/Ctrl + clicking the layer to load the transparency and then filling it with a Web-safe color, but I've noticed that the edges just aren't as clean as when I use the Hue/Saturation technique. It takes a bit of practice to get real close to a Web-safe color, but as you can see in the illustration (3.76), the edges of the text on the left have darker pixels, which Photoshop introduced. The text on the right uses a pure antialiasing, resulting in cleaner edges."

Using Fill with Preserve Transparency also results in very clean edges without the dark pixels that filling active selections can add.

"Another one of my favorite techniques is to use MetaCreations Expressions (a vector-based painting program) to 'hand-paint' masks, which I often use to rough up image edges that I'll then import into Photoshop as a mask channel mask."

1. Start with a black rectangle the exact size of the image for which you are making the mask (3.77).
2. Use a white brush to "erase" by painting on white strokes (3.78).
3. Save both as a native XPR (for editing later if necessary) and as a PCT file so you can open it in Photoshop.

3.78

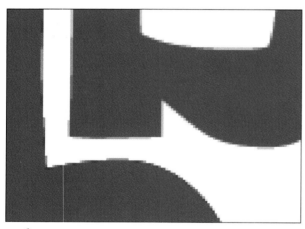

3.76

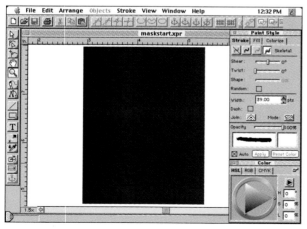

3.77

3.79

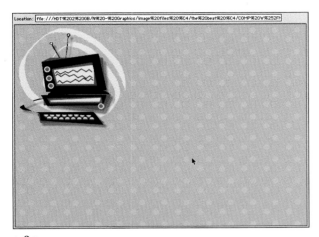

3.80

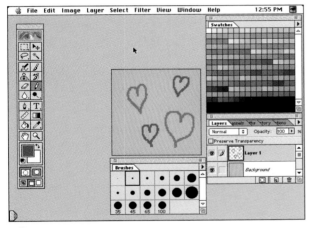

3.81

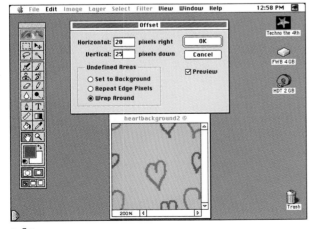

3.82

4. Open it in Photoshop and place into a new channel.

5. Load the selection, inverse, experiment with feathering, and delete to white (3.79). "Remember, all images on the Web are rectangles, and creating textured edges is a great visual trick to catch a viewer's attention."

TILED BACKGROUNDS

"A lot of clients want to have patterned backgrounds (3.80) on their Web sites, but this isn't always the best idea. When designing backgrounds, keep in mind that they *are* backgrounds and should enhance the look and feel of the Web site rather than dominate it. You see a lot of sites where the background makes the site hard to read. The rule here is not different than for print media. The background should be in the background and not dominate the site. I usually prefer to use a solid color as a background and white is still a very elegant solution for many Web sites."

To create a tiled background with Photoshop's Offset filter, follow these steps:

1. Start with a 48 × 48 pixel file at 72 ppi and fill it with a Web-safe background color.

2. On a new layer, create the pattern with the pencil or a hard-edged brush using Web-safe colors (3.81).

3. Save a Copy.

4. Open the new file and, using the offset filter, set to move approximately ⅓ of the image to the right and ⅓ down and choose Repeat Edge Pixels (3.82). Click OK.

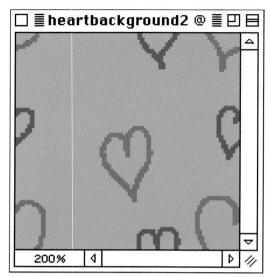

3.83

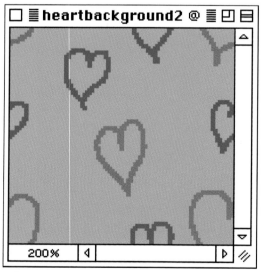

3.84

5. Press ⌘/Ctrl + F to cycle through the image to see if there are any empty areas that require additional attention (3.83 and 3.84) or if any element of the graphic is getting cut off on the edges.

6. Test the pattern by selecting the entire image, defining the pattern (3.85), and filling a larger empty file with the pattern (3.86). Or index the file, save it as a GIF, and define it as the background pattern in your browser.

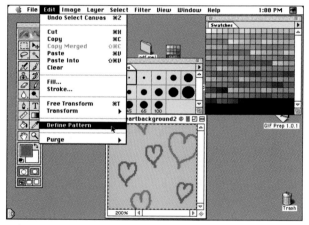

3.85

3.86

THE ARTIST AND ADVANCED WEB TECHNOLOGY

"The latest addition to my repertoire is designing for online, Java-based games and applications. The basic Web rules are the same, but the creation and optimization of graphics is a bit trickier. The controversy over the use of both Java and Shockwave technologies is still hot. The interactivity they provide is clearly an asset to any commercial Web site (as opposed to the mere 'eye candy' aspects that are more commonly found), but the extra download time sometimes results in the viewer loosing interest and surfing on. The challenge here is to further minimize file size while still creating beautiful graphics. The Java code, when done expertly, is minimal, and many of the simple graphics are created within the code itself. The secret, then, is knowing what the artist must create and what to leave to the programmers."

In this baseball example (3.87), the background, scoreboard, and moving parts were created to dither perfectly to the Web-safe palette. The moving parts (for example, the ball, bat, and shadows) are loaded only once. The code animates and resizes on the fly in addition to creating the necessary text for the baseball statistics and scores, making Java the most efficient interactive Web resource for designers.

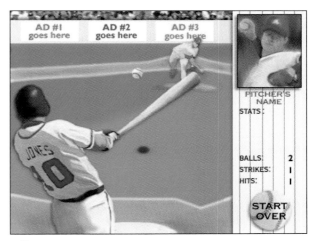

3.87

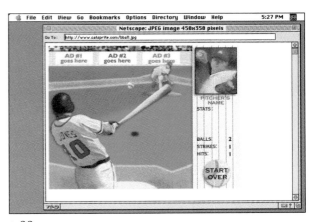

3.88

PUTTING YOUR BEST IMAGE FORWARD

"Every artist, designer, or photographer should have a Web site to display their work to the public and to serve as a portfolio to show potential clients. I also use my site to show and discuss work in progress with clients (3.88). Since I live in a fairly remote location, using my Web site as a client meeting room is a great asset, cutting down on long drives and large phone bills! One caveat of working on the Web is that there are always exceptions to the rules and I have to constantly keep up with the technical and aesthetic developments that are taking place."

CHAPTER 4
DESIGNING TYPE FOR THE WEB

The cultural associations created by type are powerful, yet often subconscious. They can be used to support or subvert the primary message of the written word. If a stop sign was set in swirling, wedding-invitation-type script, could you read it at 35 mph, much less still stop?

Typography and the written word are inseparable. We have been using letter forms to record events and share concepts for over 5,000 years. As typographic symbols evolved from the literal image of *a* steer to the abstract symbol of *every* steer, the power of the written word grew. As well as letterforms, typefaces became standardized. The history of type design is reflected in the fonts we still use every day, such as Garamond, Bodoni, Caslon, and Baskerville. In modern type design, Eric Gill, Adrian Frutiger, Matthew Carter, and Jan Tschichold are names of classic proportion that have added to our appreciation of the written word through the well designed letterform.

Typographers and designers do much more than lay out a page—they are responsible for the clarity of the written statement, influencing both the quality of the reader's experience and the comprehension of the written word. In both print and on the Web, a poorly designed page hinders readers if they cannot actually read the page. Today the time that a designer has to get a message across is scant. Readers only skim a page or scan the screen for a relevant piece of information. On the Web, your reader's eye is often distracted with animation, patterned backgrounds, and the inevitable blinking command of "click here!"

The real trick is to take what you know about print design and typography and combine it with an understanding of what you gain and lose on the Web.

MICHAEL WORTHINGTON

YOU WIN SOME, YOU LOSE SOME

"Designers understand that there is a lot that words can do that an image, video, or audio just can't. Try expressing an abstract concept such as *society* with an image that everyone can recognize — you can't. For a designer, the real trick is to take what you know about print design and typography and combine it with an understanding of what you gain and lose on the Web." Michael Worthington, typographer, designer, and teacher, has worked in many mediums — photography, interactive CD-ROM publishing, print, broadcast title design, and Web design. Throughout his career Michael has always been fascinated with how type can enhance or detract from the meaning of words. "Everyone talks about working with images on the Web, but I think it is much more exciting to work with words and type. As in any well-designed piece, the typography and the words themselves are essential to the look of the Web page."

Typography on the Web includes body text that is meant to be read, requiring legibility and visual hints that help orient the reader. But it also includes typography that adds a stylistic element to the site. When the monitor is the final output, "You lose the crisp letterforms and edges that you have in print and the sense of scale that a printed piece can convey. There is an incredible difference between holding a 4-inch-by-4-inch book in your hands or viewing a 6-foot-by-4-foot poster and looking through the frame created by the computer monitor. Sure you can look at a 6-foot-wide image or graphic on the monitor, but you're either only looking at a piece of it or a reduced version of it.

"Of course, the advantage of designing for the Web is that you can self-publish. One person can be the designer, writer, and publisher and it doesn't really cost you anything. I'm also intrigued by the fact that as I work on the computer, I am actually working on the finished piece — the distinction between a sketch and a final piece is disintegrating. The ability to make changes easily and the fact that the work is done and never done at the same time is definitely a two-edged sword. Working with the computer lets me experiment with ideas quickly, and I use the computer as a sketchbook, creating variations on an idea very quickly. If the final piece is going to be seen on the screen, most of the work should be done on the screen."

ESSENTIALS OF TYPOGRAPHY

Traditional print designers understand the impact of typefaces, taking their weight, legibility, size, and significance into account. Designers are also used to controlling the exact look and placement — including using grids and specifying the fonts, leading, tracking and kerning of type — to influence the final result of their work. The Web wreaks havoc on a designer's sense of perfection and control. But all is not lost, and you don't have to retreat to 12-point Courier with a `<blink>` tag. The Web also offers

ARTIST:
Michael Worthington

ORGANIZATION:
Worthington Design
3207 Glendale Blvd.
Los Angeles, CA 90039
home.earthlink.net/~maxfish
maxfish@earthlink.net

SYSTEM, MAC:
For browsing and creating Web graphics:
PowerPC 7500/100
System 7.6
1GB/114MB RAM
For motion graphics and high-resolution

Photoshop work:
PowerPC 9600/200
System 7.6
4GB/230MB RAM

CONNECTIVITY:
28.8 Kbps modem dial-up

PERIPHERALS:
Apple 17-inch monitors
UMAX Vista scanner

PRIMARY APPLICATIONS:
Adobe Photoshop, After Effects, and Illustrator; Macromedia Director, Infini-D, QuarkXPress, Sound Edit Pro, Web Weaver and GifBuilder (both shareware)

dimensions that the flat printed page just cannot—interactivity, depth, motion, and time.

Making the best design decisions requires an understanding of the audience, the medium, and the context and function of the piece. No one can prescribe hard and fast design rules and expect them to work for everyone. Typography is not about the right or wrong typeface; rather, the right typeface is the most appropriate typeface. Clothing offers an analogy: we all have different clothes ranging from casual to sporty to formal to business attire to clothing we'll never wear again. Depending on the situation at hand, you'll wear something different when you go mountain biking or go to a formal wedding. For purely illustrative purposes, clothing and fonts are used in a similar fashion—to express something about ourselves and the context in which we exist. Using an inappropriate typeface is like wearing beach clothes to a job interview—wrong first impression and you can forget the job!

MONITOR AS FINAL OUTPUT

The difference between reading a paragraph in a book or on a computer monitor is striking. Technical quality in desktop publishing is based on *Adobe PostScript*, a page description language designed specifically to define how a printed page looks. The vector graphics possible with PostScript allow for extremely smooth curves on type and high resolution

graphics (4.1 and 4.2). On the other hand, computer monitors are approximately 72 pixels per inch (ppi) in resolution, and each pixel is mapped to a specific Cartesian coordinate on an X Y grid. A pure bitmapped system would display everything with edges that look like stair steps (4.3 and 4.4).

The 72 ppi world of monitors and the Web is much too low to accurately and smoothly display vectors. The compromise between bitmap, low-resolution efficiency and vector-based precision and smoothness is *antialiasing*—the subtle shades of grays fool our eyes into seeing smooth curves where none can truly exist (4.5 – 4.7).

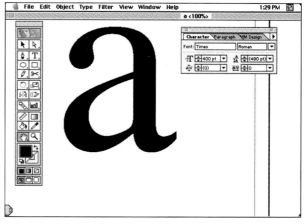

4.1

WORK HISTORY:

1984 — Studied photography in London, England. Began shooting for record sleeves and discovered interest in combining images and text.

1988 – 90 — Attended St. Martins School of Art in London, England, where students were left to their own devices. Worked with Macintosh SE-30s, FreeHand, and HyperCard.

1991 — Founded Studio DM with Colin Taylor. Created CD-ROM titles that included typographic movies.

1993 – 95 — Graduate work at California Institute of the Arts in Los Angeles, CA. Made 25th Anniversary CD-ROM for CalArts. Designed "HYPERTYPE," an interactive thesis examining the role of typography in the environment of the computer screen.

1996 – 97 — Worked with Inscape, Reverb, and Frankfurt Balkind Design. Art directed CD-ROM for the United Nations "Hot Spots". Designed Web sites for LA Eyeworks, X-Large Clothing, and Los Angeles Culture Net.

Present — Teaches graphic design, motion typography and interface design at California Institute of the Arts.

FAVORITE GUILTY PLEASURE:
Spiritual and physical procrastination.

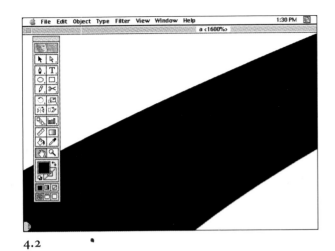

4.2

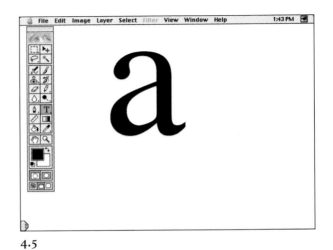

4.5

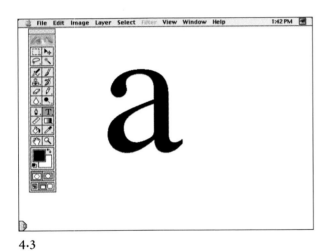

4.3

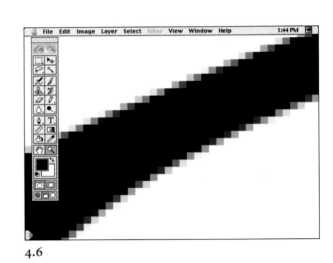

4.6

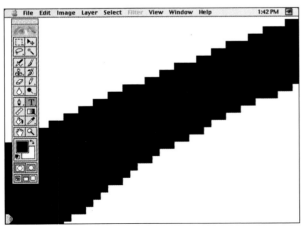

4.4

4.7

Antialiasing has its advantages and disadvantages. The advantage is that the shades of gray smooth out lines and curves, avoiding the stair-step look. The disadvantage is that all those shades of gray add to file size as the index color palette increases with every shade of gray. When laying out text in HTML, antialiasing is not an issue, but when creating text headlines in Photoshop, antialiasing plays a significant role. Here are some general rules to follow:

■ Always antialias text except when the text is small. Small is, of course, relative. As a good rule of thumb, between 10-point and 12-point is small for Web display. The only reason to use such small text from Photoshop is when you are designing buttons or image maps. Twelve-point body text should be created in HTML and not in Photoshop (4.8).

■ When bringing in text or a logo from FreeHand or Illustrator, antialias the rasterized EPS files (4.9).

■ To avoid unsightly halos around a logo or type when flattening and defining transparency, always flatten the image onto a background layer similar in color to the color of the Web page over which the piece will be placed. In this example (4.10 and 4. 11), the words are to be placed over a blue Web background. By flattening onto a blue layer and defining that blue as transparent, unsightly edges will be minimized (4.12). In the next example (4.13), the words are flattened onto a white background, and white is defined as transparency, which results in ugly halos.

■ JPEG will ruin fine type (4.14).

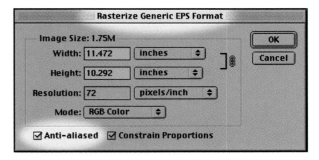

4.8

4.9

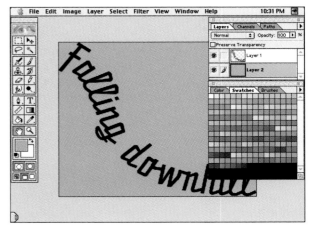

4.10

4.11

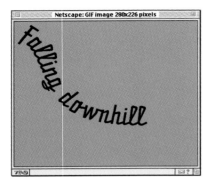

4.12

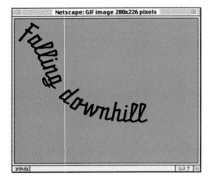

4.13

Serial commas work better than journalistic commas
use: "dog, cat, and mouse" versus "dog, cat and mouse"

4.14

Microsoft, Adobe, and a large number of type foundries have developed fonts that are specifically designed to read well on the monitor. Good resources for learning about type design are included on the CD-ROM at the back of this book in the Typography section. Make sure to visit *www.microsoft.com/typography/* and *www.w3.org/Fonts/* to stay up to date.

READ OR PRINT?

When you come across a Web page with a lot of text, what is the first thing you do? Do you scroll down to see how long the text is before making the decision to read the page? Or do you just print out the page to

read it later? Using a lot of text on a Web page works only as long as the design of the page and the selection of the fonts used help the reader understand the information — of course, this is assuming the reader is interested in the content! Breaking up large blocks of text into readable chunks (for example, paragraphs with clear headers and/or indents), working with contrast and shape to guide the viewer's eye, and using typography to support the words are all essential design techniques.

HTML

When designing for 2.0 and 3.0 browsers, HTML text and image text are the two fundamental methods to display text on the Web. The advantage of HTML text is it downloads extremely quickly. The primary disadvantage is that HTML text lacks the typographical controls to influence (to the pica) the sizing, font, tracking, kerning, and letter spacing, which you need to shape the look and feel of your text. In 3.0 browsers you may define which font the browser should use to display text, but that font must be installed in the viewer's fonts folder in the system folder.

Working with HTML text is recommended when laying out large bodies of text, especially body text which forms the bulk of a document. Headline text can also be HTML text, but most graphic designers use image text for this purpose. The basic elements you can control in HTML text are size, color, bold, italic, drop caps, small caps, and alignment. The HTML that forms the page controls all of these attributes. The final element you can specify is the font tag, which lets you tell the browser to use a specific typeface to display body text. See Chapter 5 for a thorough explanation of working with HTML, font tags, and tables.

SIZE

Controlling the size of headers and body text in HTML is straightforward. Headers go from 1 to 6, where 1 is the largest display type and 6 is the smallest (4.15). Body text uses the opposite convention: 1 is the smallest and 6 is the largest (4.16). This is to keep you on your toes in the middle of the night.

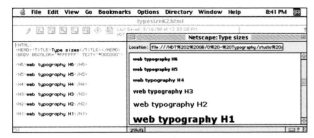

4.15

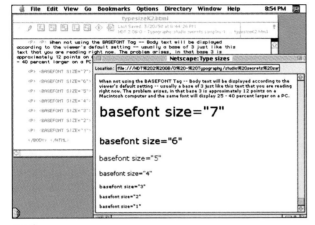

4.16

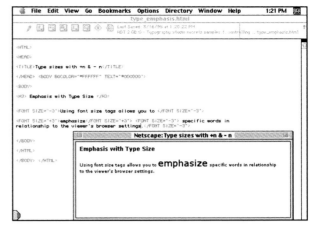

4.17

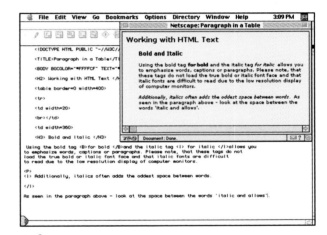

4.18

<FONT SIZE="+n or -n"> where n is −2 to + 4 allows you to increase or decrease body text in relationship to the viewer's font preference settings (4.17).

BOLD OR ITALIC TEXT

Using the <B> tag for bold and <I> for italic allows you to emphasize words, captions, or paragraphs. Note that these tags do not load the true bold or italic font face, and italic fonts can be difficult to read due to the low resolution display of computer monitors (4.18).

COLOR

Using Web-safe colors and taking the background into consideration are the two primary issues when selecting a color for body and headline text. The color of headers are defined within the original body tag. In this example (4.19), the background is a mild green, and the headlines appear as a burnt orange:

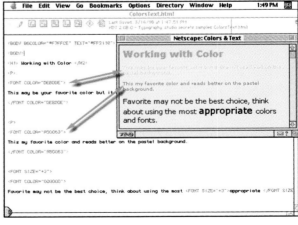

4.19

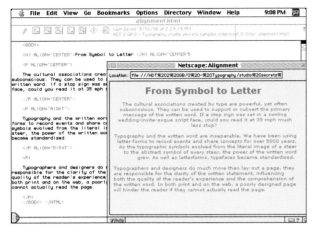

4.20

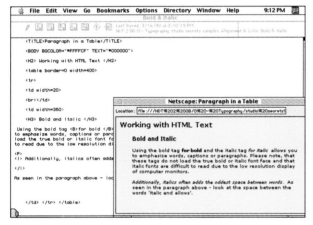

4.21

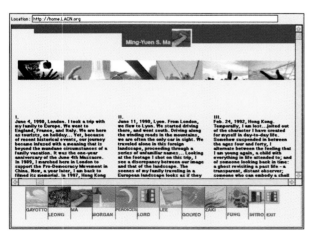

4.22

`<BODY BGCOLOR="#F7FFCE" TEXT="#FF3118">`. Body text can be defined letter by letter, word by word, or, better yet, by paragraph and subject at hand. Add the `<FONT COLOR="hex value of color">` to emphasize subject matter and guide the reader's eye through the text.

ALIGNMENT AND WIDTH

Alignment can be left, right, or center — sounds like a political talk show! `<P ALIGN="direction">` allows you to align a paragraph. The default alignment is left and force justify does not exist as an alignment tag (4.20).

More important than the alignment of a paragraph is the width of a paragraph. Think of a newspaper and how quickly you can scan the column for relevant information. Controlling paragraph width helps the reader to read quickly. We don't read a word letter by letter or a sentence word by word; rather, we visually grab chunks of text based on the shape of the words. Margins help the reader find the left side of the page more easily, which cuts down on rereading the beginning of the same sentence over and over again. Using a table with two columns and one row, where the left margin and body text column are defined in relationship to the width of a standard monitor, allows you to define the margin and body text to look sophisticated without a lot of work. A character width of ten to twelve words is a comfortable reading range (4.21). On the Los Angeles Culture Net site, (4.22) (www.lacn.org) Michael used tables to lay out essays and poetry. Each artist's page has a different treatment (4.23). See Chapter 5 for the HTML required to build a table.

FONT TAGS

Finally, designers can specify the font that the browser uses to display text — almost. As discussed in Chapter 5, embedding font tags allows you to specify the font used to display body text. The font, however, must be present in the viewer's system folder to be effective. The most conservative approach is to design with and specify fonts that are standard to the Macintosh and PC platforms. On the Macintosh, Helvetica, Courier, and New York (`<FONT FACE=helvetica,courier,newyork>`), and on the PC, Arial, Courier, and Times New Roman (`<FONT FACE=arial,courier,times-newroman>`) are safe bets. The font tag has been supported by Internet Explorer since version 1.0 and Netscape Navigator caught up with font tag implementation in the 3.0 version. To see what your font selection looks like, change your browser font preferences and go to *www.cen.uiac.edu/~ejk/fontsizes.* (4.24 and 4.25). The first test shows how clear Verdana is and the second shows Zapf Chancery.

Use sans serif fonts for body text. The *serifs* (the short cross-stroke at the base and top of serif fonts) use a limited number of pixels and can distract from the legibility of the text. Avoid fancy, baroque, script-type font for the same reason. The low resolution monitor makes the text hard to read (4.26).

DYNAMIC AND EMBEDDED FONTS

As of this writing, several options for automatic font display are in development, including *TrueDoc* and *OpenType*, both of which require 4.0 browsers to be effective. TrueDoc, developed by Bitstream, is implemented in Netscape Navigator 4.03 and is called "Dynamic Fonts." From a designer's point of view, TrueDoc empowers you to use any font, design with it, and not worry if viewers have the specific font loaded on their machines. TrueDoc records the font shape and then stores the shape in the efficient

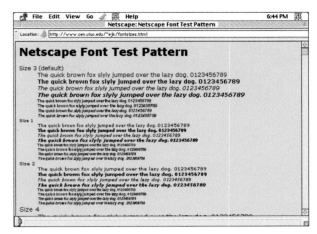

4.24

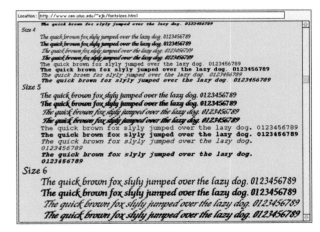

4.25

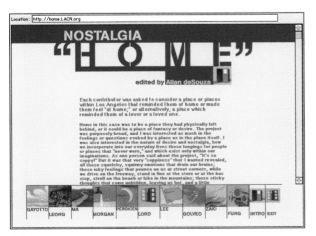

4.23

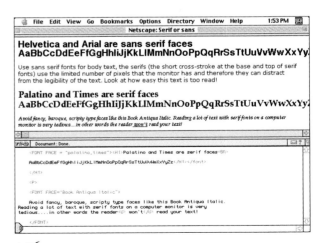

4.26

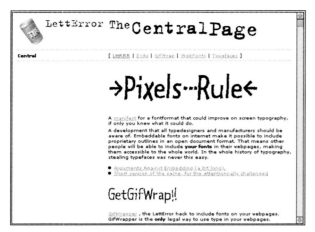

4.27

Portable Font Resource (PFR) file format. When a viewer comes to a Web site, the PFR is downloaded in the background and then played back. Only the required fonts are displayed on the page.

OpenType Embedding, developed by Microsoft and Adobe Systems, uses a different implementation. OpenType creates subsets and then compresses TrueType fonts while retaining the required hinting (antialiasing) information. When the viewer comes to a site implementing OpenType, an EOT file is created and the fonts are temporarily installed in the system, supposedly for use only in the browser. The creation of the EOT file requires a free Windows-only utility from Microsoft, called WEFT. Visit the Microsoft site at *www.microsoft.com/typography/web/embedding/weft/ default.htm* to download required tools and read extensive explanations addressing embedding fonts with WEFT.

Once again, designers and viewers alike are waiting to see which implementation will be accepted and, more importantly, available and consistent for both browsers. Presently, TrueDoc, which has been available for a few years, offers a number of benefits: it is used internationally (imagine designing a Web page in English and a viewer in Japan can read the page in Kanji!), supports JavaScript, and is a compact file format that renders text beautifully. OpenType, on the other hand, is still in development, and concerns have been voiced over the security of the EOT file.

COPYRIGHT ISSUES

Fonts are intellectual property and they fall under similar copyright protection that images, text, and music do. Unless you created the fonts from scratch yourself, you really shouldn't be distributing them. Visit the LettError site, a cutting-edge typography and design studio whose pointed opinions offer food for thought, at *www.letterror.com/LTR_central.html* (4.27).

IMAGES

The second implementation of typography for the Web is to use images as type. Working with all the typographical and design features that Illustrator or FreeHand offer, you can finesse, wrap, and play with the type and then bring the files into Photoshop for final image processing and format changes to a GIF or JPEG file. The advantages of this creative and typographic freedom to design words with any typeface and endless possibilities are obvious. The disadvantage is that the GIF or JPEG files add up in file size, slowing the download of the page. See Chapter 3 for techniques to optimize images.

As Michael explains, "A lot of the time, designers don't have images to work with, so they are experimenting with words and typography to make a stylistic statement. Creating your own typefaces, experimenting with letter forms, or even just scanning in objects that look like letters all allow you to create images with type. Deconstructing type and giving it multiple levels of reading allow the reader to interpret the type-image in numerous ways. 'Mean type, meaningless type, worthless, or worthington:' in this case it's a visual pun (4.28a and 4.28b). I like to fracture and break up the letterforms to give a reader different ways of appreciating the words. Working with type as images also questions the convention of how you read left to right, top to bottom (4.29a and 4.29b). Most importantly, it all depends on the context of the piece. If I was designing the definitive manual on brain surgery, I'd avoid using techniques that let the reader interpret the information in different ways!"

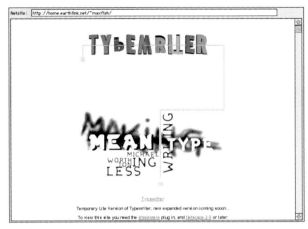

4.28A

4.28B

4.29A

NEW DIMENSIONS IN TYPOGRAPHY

"Designing with typography for the screen isn't just about reading the text; rather, it can include texture, juxtaposition, motion, interactivity, sound, depth, and time. By disrupting legibility, designers can add stylistic elements and dimensions inviting the viewer to explore and interpret the new medium. These added dimensions will change the way people write, as well.

"Typography is based on a set of rules, and even when you break those rules it's useful to know what you're breaking. The rules of spacing, sizing, arrangement, when to use lower case, and so on, vary depending on the piece. If you're being rebellious, it's

4.29B

better to know what you're doing to be rebellious. The appropriate selection and use of a font conveys a lot of meaning about the Web site. For example, for the L.A. Eyeworks site I designed a bolder, graphic, edgy typeface that conveys something about the company and their customers. It is also a reference to eye

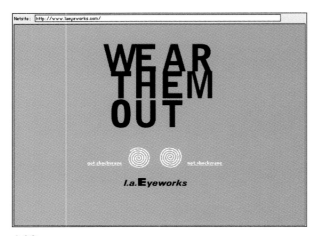

4.30

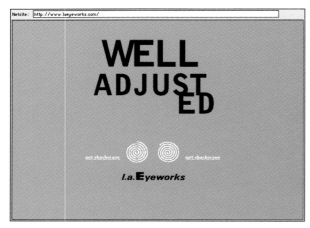

4.31

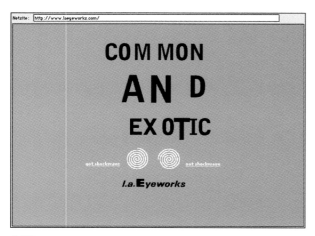

4.32

charts where the letters are spaced out, forcing the reader to look at individual letters and not just read whole words. If I had used a scripty Baroque italic typeface, the first impression of the site would be completely different (4.30, 4.31, and 4.32).

"L.A. Eyeworks doesn't have just one slogan to identify themselves with, so I designed the opening page with a simple GIF animation that includes a number of their slogans. I laid out the separate frames in Photoshop layers, and by including a 50 percent transparent layer between the slogans, I created a transition to avoid jolting the viewer with hard cuts from one slogan to the next. Working in layers also allows me to see the relationship the letterforms have to one another (4.33, 4.34, and 4.35)."

Another simple, yet effective, method to have words blend and interact is to place each word onto a separate Photoshop layer, duplicate each word, and then blur the duplicate. Save the separate layers as PICT or GIF files and animate them in GIF Builder (4.36–4.40).

FLASH AND SHOCKWAVE

"Before I designed for the Web, I did a lot of CD-ROM design work with Macromedia Director. I still use Director to create animations and to program interactivity, after which I save a Shockwave file that can be embedded into a Web site just like an image. Flash is good when you want to create animation without interactivity. Being vector-based, Flash allows you to scale and move objects, and it mathematically calculates the new size, shape, and position of each object while keeping the file sizes very reasonable. The benefit of Director is that it has its own programming language, Lingo, which lets me make a lot of things happen without a lot of file size overhead. For example, I could make a word move around the screen, change color, disappear, or explode—all depending on what the viewer does with the mouse. If the original word was only 2K, then I could do all that and the file would still only be 2K.

"In the X-Large site, I wanted to deconstruct and reconstruct the logo on the opening screen. In that case, I used Macromedia Director to block out the motion, taking the letterform and working with the negative

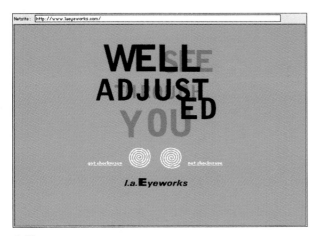

4.33

4.34

4.35

4.36

4.37

4.38

4.39

4.40

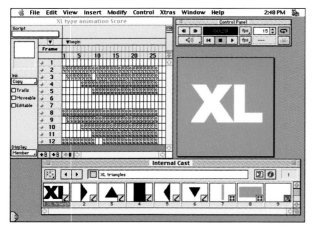

4.41

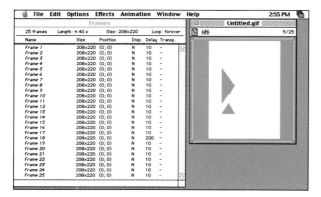

4.42

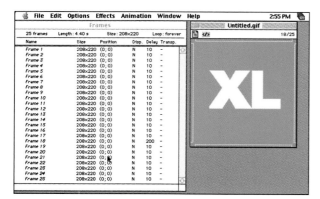

4.43

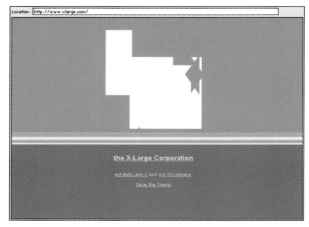

4.44

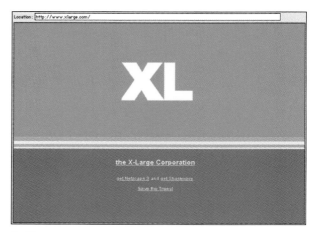

4.45

space and letter shape to create the animation (4.41). When I had the animation the way I wanted it, I exported the cast members as PICT files and brought them into GifBuilder to build the file in a file format that everyone can read over the Web (4.42–4.45). I contrasted the abruptness of the opening pages with a softer piece that I did in Shockwave. For the X-Large Girls clothing, the 'index' is a very soft image made up of a grid. When the viewer goes over an image with the mouse, the individual image comes into focus and is the hot spot for that particular piece of clothing (4.46–4.48).

4.46

4·47

4.48

4·49

"With Shockwave, anything that I can do on a CD-ROM, I can put on the Web if I can make the file small enough. I designed the typeface Bulimic for *Mute* digital newspaper in London. It gorges and vomits indiscriminately and I have no control over it." (4.49 – 4.54) To keep the files small, I work in 1-bit black and white. If I need to add color, I do it in Director using a cross-platform color palette and Lingo and it actually stays 1-bit, keeping the file size down. Admittedly, the edges are pretty ugly and aliased, but for what I get in return in terms of motion, interactivity, and sound, I can accept that compromise (4.55 – 4.59).

4.50

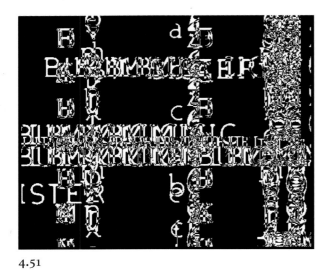

4.51

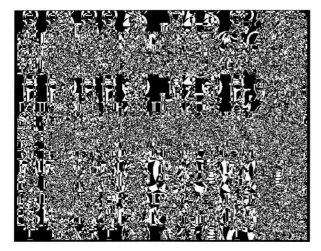

4.52

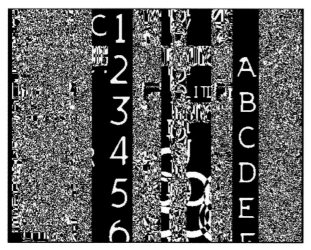

4.53

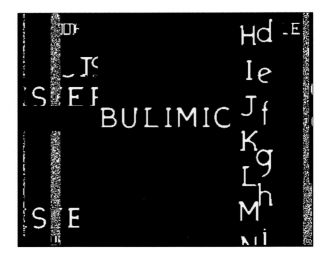

4.54

4.55

4.56

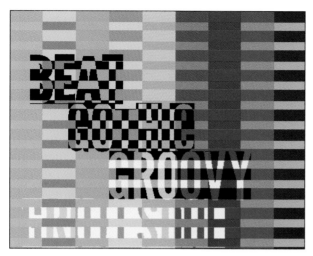

4.57

4.59

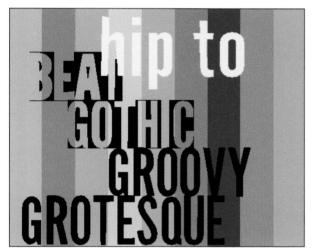

4.58

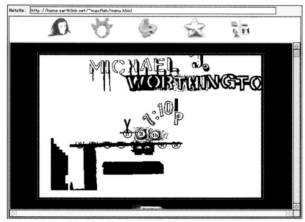

4.60

4.61

"For the Art Center poster, I created two pieces: one for the Web using Shockwave (4.60 and 4.61), and one for print (4.62). I started by creating twenty separate pieces of artwork in Illustrator, Photoshop, and even by scanning in found objects to create words and type. In Director, I programmed it to place the cast members on the screen randomly. Sometimes it will scale the pieces up or down or position pieces off the edge of the screen. In fact, I don't always know what it will be doing. The final effect is that it is randomly composing the type and the poster. I like that the machine has control over it. The piece is also a

4.62

play on analog and digital type — made by hand, scanned in, and then reworked in Photoshop, and cut into pieces and put back together in Director.

"In a piece I did for my own Web site, I wanted the viewer to control how the text would read. Depending on where a viewer puts the mouse, the text will move up or down, left, or right. Sometimes the text says, 'When this Site is done it will be about Typography,' and sometimes it says, 'This Site will be Design & Writing' or 'This Site will be Sign Writing' (4.63 – 4.65).

"I can also add sound to the pieces, and as long as the browser has the Shockwave plug-in installed, the site can be constantly changing. Think about a company's logo. There is no reason that it has to be one static piece. A logo could change over time, reflecting the diversity of a company, saying 100 things about a company rather than just one."

SUBSEQUENT DIMENSIONS

Creating true 3D on the screen is really complicated and, in terms of type, it certainly has been overused. For the typewriter logo, "I created the individual letters in Infini-D, lined them up on the wire that they are rotating around in Photoshop, and then animated them in GifBuilder (4.66 – 4.68).

"More interesting for me is the use of interactivity, which is something that I can't have in a book. Interaction between the reader and the designer fascinates me. If a reader can influence what a piece looks like, it takes away the idea of designer as hard-core control freak that in a sense speaks down to the audience. It's also fun to create something with flexibility, that people can read differently and interact with."

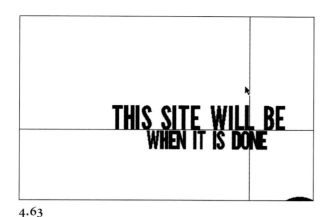

4.63

4.64

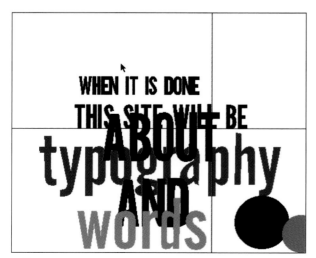

4.65

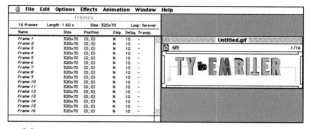

4.66

4.67

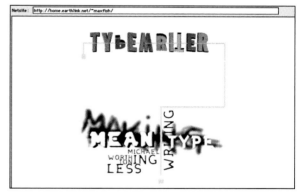

4.68

Type is a signifier. Whether it's for the Web, the printed page, broadcast design, or billboards, it's all about context, what the content of the project is, who the audience is, and who you are as a designer. "The Web is not replacing print; rather, we are in a period of transition that is simultaneously creating and defining the medium—just as the advent of photography irrevocably changed the medium of painting, freeing it to become abstract art. The Web frees type from existing in a flat, two-dimensional space. Typography can now include motion, depth, interactivity, and the fourth dimension of time, and it's fascinating to participate as the medium changes and redefines itself."

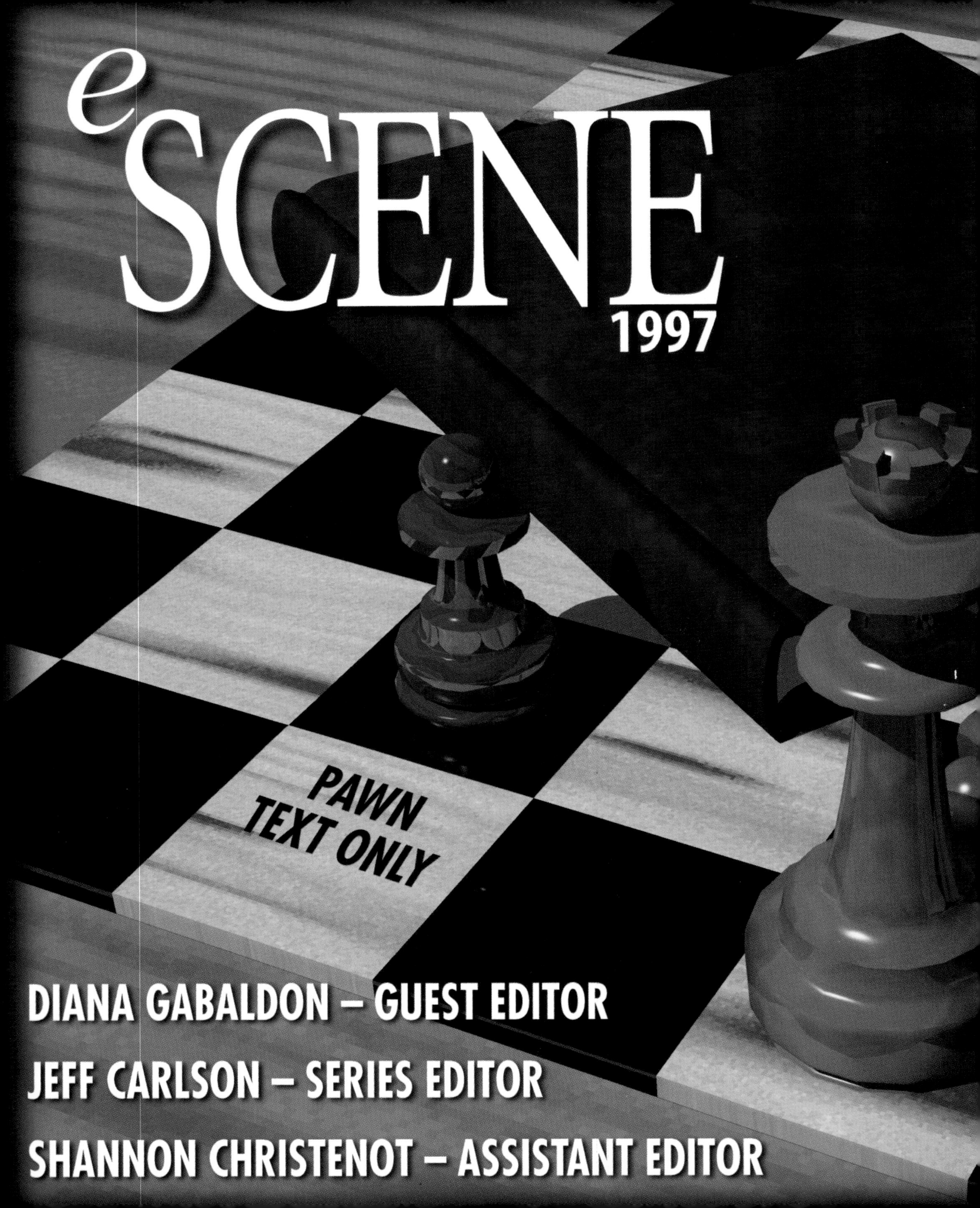

eSCENE
1997

PAWN
TEXT ONLY

DIANA GABALDON – GUEST EDITOR

JEFF CARLSON – SERIES EDITOR

SHANNON CHRISTENOT – ASSISTANT EDITOR

CHAPTER 5
HTML AS A DESIGN TOOL

Every day we work with sophisticated software to edit images, lay out pages, or track finances. Yet, how many people can explain how software really works? The millions of lines of code behind an image-editing program or a database would be gibberish to most of us. On the other hand, *HTML* (Hypertext Markup Language) is a simple text protocol used to structure Web pages—think of it as a translator between the designer's intentions and the viewer's browser.

To design a Web page, you gather images and text, make sketches, and begin to rough out layout and navigation. The design decisions you make about color, fonts, and image placement need to be expressed in a way Web browsers such as Netscape Navigator and Microsoft Internet Explorer can understand in order to properly display a Web page. HTML is the go-between, connecting your design and what the viewer sees. It tells the browser what color to use as a background, how large a headline should be, and where to go next when your viewer clicks a link. Simply put, design + HTML + browser = Web site.

Now that's not to say that every artist and designer must take up hard-core programming as a new career. Rather, understanding how HTML works allows you to take control of your page design with finesse and style. Understanding the possibilities and limitations of HTML allows professional Web designers and Web hobbyists alike to create compelling Web sites that can be viewed by anyone with a browser and an Internet connection.

HTML can be stretched, pulled, and prodded into unexpected shapes for use in Web design, but sometimes you just have to work around its shortcomings as a visual design tool.

JEFF CARLSON

Learning HTML requires a few hours to understand the basic rules and requirements. It's similar to navigating through a large subway system. At first you are hesitant, reading the map at every station, overwhelmed by the colored lines moving underground and backtracking missed connections. Yet within a few days, you are cruising through the subway with the ease of a native, not even glancing at the signs as you catch up with the daily newspaper of the person sitting next to you.

As Jeff Carlson, principle of Never Enough Coffee creations and managing editor of eSCENE and TidBITS explains, "The best thing about learning HTML is the instant feedback that working with it gives you. When I first started working with PageMaker, we would design pages that looked fine onscreen, but when we tried to output them at a service bureau, there would be a numbing number of PostScript errors to correct. With HTML I save the file, preview it in Netscape Navigator or Internet Explorer, and I can see right away if the HTML is working. Believe me, HTML is child's play compared to deciphering PostScript errors!"

DO I REALLY HAVE TO?

The first time you look at HTML code, your first instinct may be to quickly close the file. This is understandable, and that feeling of panic is being addressed by a great number of software manufacturers announcing WYSIWYG (What You See Is What You Get) tools on a daily basis, promising drag-and-drop simplicity with sophisticated features to make you a whiz bang Web designer overnight. "WYSIWYG tools are good to a point, but I don't know of a single professional designer who doesn't go in and tweak their HTML. Sure, not everyone warms to the idea of hand-coding HTML, but it is really the only way to be a control freak — I mean, designer. Admit it, designers and artists love being in control of the final product."

When the Web was first coming into its own, "there were no professional Web designers or Web layout tools. If you wanted to create for the Web, you had to learn HTML. It was that simple. Now that larger groups are developing sites, there's been a return to the model of compartmentalized job descriptions: designers design, coders code, writers write, and producers . . . manage. Too often, the people responsible for making the page work through their HTML skills get very frustrated when the star designer discovers that his design either won't work on today's browsers across today's Internet connections or that the design will undergo radical shifts before it hits the Web."

When you understand what HTML does and does not do well, you are able to design pages that load quickly and satisfy the designer inside of you. "At the very least, it's important to know enough about HTML to know what it's capable of, including it's limitations. HTML can be stretched, pulled, and prodded into unexpected shapes for use in Web

ARTIST:
Jeff Carlson

ORGANIZATION:
Never Enough Coffee creations
1619 Eighth Ave. North
Seattle, WA 98109
206/285-9121
www.necoffee.com
jeff@necoffee.com

SYSTEM, MAC:
Power Mac 7600/120
Mac OS 8.1
4.5GB storage/64MB RAM
NEC MultiSync XV 17-inch monitor

PowerBook 5300cs
Mac OS 8.1

CONNECTIVITY:
Work: 2-channel, 128 Kbps ISDN
Home: 33.6 Kbps modem
"The distinction between home and work is very blurred."

PERIPHERALS:
Wacom ArtZ 6 × 9 inch tablet

PRIMARY APPLICATIONS:
BBEdit 4.5, Adobe Photoshop 4.01, Macromedia FreeHand, Strata Studio Pro Blitz 1.75, Netscape Navigator, and Internet Explorer versions 2.0–4.0.

design, but sometimes you just have to work around its shortcomings as a visual design tool. It's definitely better to know the limitations beforehand — or at least know a good work-around for the effect you're trying to achieve — than face hours of frustration."

Fine, it's important to know about HTML, but that doesn't get us past the fact that it's still *code*. What if you're a designer who's more familiar with a Wacom pen than a `<WIDTH>` tag? Luckily, HTML differs from traditional code in one important way. "HTML is a shared language, so it's necessary for designers to learn it in order to join the Web conversation. People often compare HTML to Adobe's PostScript, pointing out that almost no one hand-codes PostScript anymore now that applications like PageMaker and QuarkXPress do it automatically. But PostScript remains a proprietary, highly-technical programming language. HTML, on the other hand, is open, flexible, and always changing. The best thing about learning HTML is that it doesn't require any expensive or proprietary software. Anyone with a copy of SimpleText or even Notepad can start to create Web pages."

WORKFLOW ORGANIZATION

A little bit of planning before we depart on our cross-country tour of HTML will help minimize the number of unexpected pit stops. Let's start with the vehicle we'll drive throughout this chapter and beyond. As mentioned, you can write HTML with the simplest text editors, such as SimpleText and Stickies on the Mac or Notepad on the PC. Notice we do not include Microsoft Word in that list. Word is a document editor, so everything that makes Word powerful — the ability to use multiple fonts, create outlines, and make your resume look great — will get in the way when writing HTML, because Word marks these attributes in its own format. The vehicle we use for this chapter is free, ubiquitous, and powerful — BBEdit Lite (*www.barebones.com*). BBEdit is the industry-standard HTML-editing application (on the Macintosh platform) and offers an HTML checker and preview function into any browser installed on your hard drive. On the PC, we recommend Allair's Home Site 3 (*www.allaire.com/ products/ homesite/30/index.cfm*).

FILE AND FOLDER HIERARCHY

You have mapped out the design of the Web site, gathered all the project assets, prepared all the images to be as small as possible, and the coffee is brewing. Pause a moment and take a look at your hard drive. Is your project neatly organized, or do you have a smattering of floppies, Zip disks, and folders scattered about, each containing bits and pieces of the Web site to be? If the answer to the latter is a sheepish yes, take a few minutes to organize the project's folder and file structure. Create one main folder named *Your Project Title*, and inside that create a subfolder named *images*. The

WORK HISTORY:

Mid '70s–'80s — Drew dozens of superheroes and then couldn't stop drawing Star Wars ships after driving two hours from Twin Falls, Idaho to see the movie in Wells, Nevada.

1985 — First experience with Aldus PageMaker 1.0.

1991–92 — Internship with the Publications Office at Whitworth College in Spokane, Washington.

1992 — Graduated college with a bachelor's degree in English.

1995 — Founded eSCENE, a Web site dedicated to publishing the Internet's best short stories. Learned HTML.

1996 — Managing editor of TidBITS.

1997 — Founded Never Enough Coffee creations. Web site clients include Microsoft, Doug Thomas's Movie Maven, Thunder Lizard Productions, ZAP, TidBITS, and NetBITS. Contributing editor and author for adobe.mag; contributor to *Macworld* magazine, *Adobe Magazine*, and *HOW*.

FAVORITE WEIRD FOOD:

Banana and Egg Sandwiches — Scrambled eggs and sliced bananas on buttered toast. Elvis would have definitely loved this one!

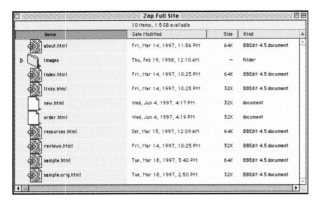

5.1

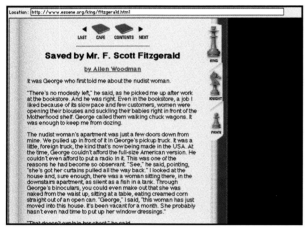

5.2

5.3

ZAP — How Your Computer Can Hurt You Web site has a simple folder hierarchy: one folder with all the HTML documents and one folder with the images including the opening GIF animation (5.1). (It's best that your Web image folder only contain *final* files.)

"With eSCENE, I deliberately offered three versions of the site: graphics-intensive (king) (5.2), minimal graphics (knight) (5.3), and text-only (pawn) (5.4). The folder hierarchy reflected this before I even launched BBEdit (5.5). In this case, designing the site to be viewed in three ways was the same as designing three separate sites, and the file hierarchy mimics this. The king, knight, and pawn are really subfolders that required their own image folders (5.6), which helped avoid spidery URLs in relative links such as `<a href"../../bob/eatsfish.html">`. Planning the directory structure in advance helps you avoid wasting time correcting things later. It is easy to move files to a new subdirectory, but that means you'll have to update links throughout the site, which is time consuming. You'll need your time and concentration for better things!"

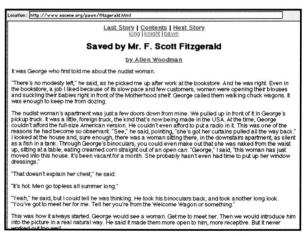

5.4

5.5

Finally, be sure to set up a reliable version-tracking system! "I have a copy of the whole Web site structure marked with '.old' or the date at the end of the folder's title on a Zip. If I accidentally apply changes to the wrong file and save it, I can go back and grab a fresh copy from the backup directory." This, of course, is in addition to a regularly scheduled backup system.

NAMING CONVENTIONS AND CONSISTENCY

Naming your files correctly and consistently will help you avoid problems with some browsers, servers, and within your own workflow, especially if you are working in a production team. A safe rule of thumb is to use all lowercase with the DOS *eight-dot-three* (8.3) format (such as Coffeemn.htm). "Most people do tend to fudge on the 8.3 issue, especially Macintosh aficionados since 8.3 filenames can be cryptic. To play it safe, check with the ISP that will be hosting the site to see if they have a preference based on what type of machine will be serving the site. Every standard needs to be bent a bit, and you will notice that most Web designers use the suffix .html rather than .htm when saving their HTML pages."

When naming files and links, don't use spaces. For example, when writing HTML, the filename Hot_drinks.html is preferred over Hot Drinks.html. "You won't realize the headaches you'll prevent. It's more universal to use underscores in place of spaces or use no space at all in filenames. Most importantly, develop and use a consistent naming scheme, especially if you are a part of a larger production team."

GETTING INTO THE CODE

The best thing about learning HTML is that the resources can be found on every single Web site you visit. When you are surfing and find a page you admire, look at the HTML structure by viewing the page's source (5.7). Notice we say "look," not "copy" and substitute your own graphics into already written code. Writing clean code that structures effective Web sites is an art form. Learn from it and take that knowledge further, knowing that the next person will be looking at your HTML, too (5.8).

5.6

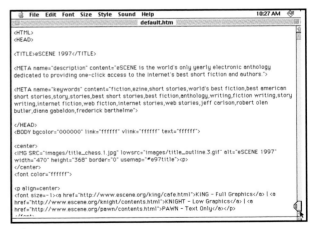

5.7

5.8

As Jeff explains, "In the past, collaboration was key. Looking at people's HTML is how most people initially learned how to design Web sites. Now that the Web is more commercial, people are worrying about having their HTML code stolen. The way I see it, the designer goes into this knowing that her source code will be visible to all. Specialized code, such as JavaScript, should include a copyright notice. Someone may steal your table layout, but it's not the layout that necessarily makes the design succeed. That's just the mortar. It is your design and images that make the table really work.

"If I have a set of Tinkertoys, I can build lots of different things. Someone else can come and use my Tinkertoys to build their own creation, even if they retain 80 percent of my structure and build their own on top of that. I don't own the copyright to those Tinkertoys, just my creation in that particular manifestation. Tinkertoys and HTML are shared tools. Often I'll view a site's source and have the browser window open at the same time (5.9). That way I can scroll through the code to find the part of the site that I like, study the HTML, and be inspired to try new things."

CLEANLINESS IS NEXT TO . . .

To be a happy coder, write HTML you can skim through quickly by using spacing and line breaks. Browsers will ignore spaces, color (if your HTML editor supports text coloring as BBEdit does), and line breaks. But that doesn't mean you have to, since

they will help you organize your thoughts and the structure of the Web site. "I designed the Movie Maven site but I do not maintain it. It was imperative that the Webmaster could easily find the spot to place the latest reviews, so writing clean code with comment tags was essential. From the browser software point of view, both examples of HTML are identical, but from the Webmaster's point of view, the well-spaced version is much easier to get oriented in and work with (5.10 and 5.11)."

WHAT EVERY WEB PAGE NEEDS

From the simplest to the most complex, every Web page has certain attributes in common. Notice that HTML tags always appear in pairs. For example, `<title>eSCENE 1997</title>` translates to "display page name 'eSCENE 1997' stop display page name" (5.12). The angle brackets (`<>`) are the open or start tag and the forward slash brackets (`</>`) are the closing tag. Everything has a beginning and everything must end prior to continuing.

In the following few pages, we walk you through some basic aspects of HTML. You can work along in either SimpleText or BBEdit Lite, save the HTML file, and then preview it by opening it with your browser. Consider this a sip of what you can create with HTML. We hope to show you that HTML isn't overwhelmingly complex or cryptic. To create the absolute minimalist page, open a new page in BBEdit or SimpleText and type the following tags:

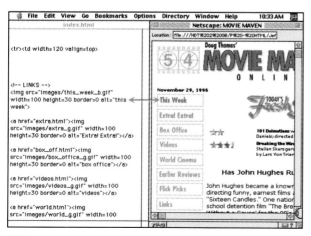

5.9

5.10

1. <HTML> — Tells the browser that it is looking at an HTML document to display.
2. <HEAD> — Defines the title of the Web page.
3. <TITLE> — The name of the Web page, not the URL. In any site you may have a number of pages: opening page, index, products, reviews, and so on. Each one of those pages can display its own name in the title bar. The <TITLE> </TITLE> must be enclosed within the <HEAD> and </HEAD> tags.
4. </TITLE> — Closes the page name.
5. </HEAD> — Closes the heading section.
6. <BODY> — Contains the page's content, including text, images, links, and all page formatting.
7. </BODY> — Closes body content and attributes.
8. </HTML> — Tells the browser that the HTML document has ended. To see what the file looks like, save it and open the file via your browser or use BBEdit's preview function to load the file into your browser. Sadly, the above HTML will result in a gray Web page with absolutely nothing on it (5.13)!

<BODY> ATTRIBUTES

The body attributes define the most important parts of the Web site, including the color of backgrounds, text, and links, and placement of images, tables, and frames. This is where you do the bulk of your work.

5.12

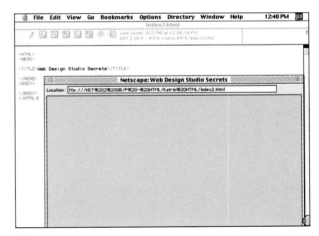

5.13

5.11

5.14

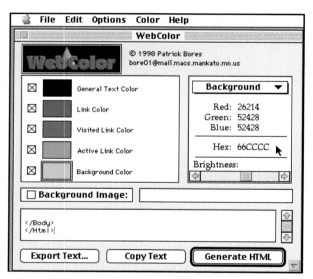

5.15

00FFFF	00FFCC	00FF99	00FF66	00FF33	00FF00
00CCFF	00CCCC	00CC99	00CC66	00CC33	00CC00
0099FF	0099CC	009999	009966	009933	009900
0066FF	0066CC	006699	006666	006633	006600
0033FF	0033CC	003399	003366	003333	003300
0000FF	0000CC	000099	000066	000033	000000
33FFFF	33FFCC	33FF99	33FF66	33FF33	33FF00
33CCFF	33CCCC	33CC99	33CC66	33CC33	33CC00
3399FF	3399CC	339999	339966	339933	339900
3366FF	3366CC	336699	336666	336633	336600
3333FF	3333CC	333399	333366	333333	333300
3300FF	3300CC	330099	330066	330033	330000
66FFFF	66FFCC	66FF99	66FF66	66FF33	66FF00
66CCFF	66CCCC	66CC99	66CC66	66CC33	66CC00
6699FF	6699CC	669999	669966	669933	669900
6666FF	6666CC	666699	666666	666633	666600
6633FF	6633CC	663399	663366	663333	663300
6600FF	6600CC	660099	660066	660033	660000
99FFFF	99FFCC	99FF99	99FF66	99FF33	99FF00
99CCFF	99CCCC	99CC99	99CC66	99CC33	99CC00
9999FF	9999CC	999999	999966	999933	999900
9966FF	9966CC	996699	996666	996633	996600
9933FF	9933CC	993399	993366	993333	993300
9900FF	9900CC	990099	990066	990033	990000
CCFFFF	CCFFCC	CCFF99	CCFF66	CCFF33	CCFF00
CCCCFF	CCCCCC	CCCC99	CCCC66	CCCC33	CCCC00
CC99FF	CC99CC	CC9999	CC9966	CC9933	CC9900
CC66FF	CC66CC	CC6699	CC6666	CC6633	CC6600
CC33FF	CC33CC	CC3399	CC3366	CC3333	CC3300
CC00FF	CC00CC	CC0099	CC0066	CC0033	CC0000
FFFFFF	FFFFCC	FFFF99	FFFF66	FFFF33	FFFF00
FFCCFF	FFCCCC	FFCC99	FFCC66	FFCC33	FFCC00
FF99FF	FF99CC	FF9999	FF9966	FF9933	FF9900
FF66FF	FF66CC	FF6699	FF6666	FF6633	FF6600
FF33FF	FF33CC	FF3399	FF3366	FF3333	FF3300
FF00FF	FF00CC	FF0099	FF0066	FF0033	FF0000

5.16

COLOR

The Web started out as a gray, desolate place. Early browsers used the default gray as the only color. Now colors have all but eradicated the old gray. As discussed in Chapter 3, working with the Web-safe palette is imperative to avoid banding and dithering. Since browsers can only recognize and display hexadecimal color values, you'll have to use any of a number of hex calculators on the Web that convert RGB values into hex values (unless you want to do the math yourself). Another possibility is to go to sites such as *www.hidaho.com/colorcenter/cc.html* (5.14) to select the hex values for background, text, active, and visited links (5.15). Some great utilities include WebColor 2.2 (go to *www. shareware.com* and search for Web color to download it), and AcmeWidgets ColorFinder (*www.acmetech.com*), a Mac OS 8 Contextual Menus add-on that allows you to choose any color from any pixel on your screen with an eye-dropper and then paste the resulting hexadecimal value into your HTML document. On the *Web Design Studio Secrets* CD-ROM you'll find a Photoshop document with 216 Web-safe color patches, complete with hexadecimal values (Hexchart.pct) (5.16) you can use to see and select Web-safe colors.

The body tag defines the color of background, text, and links by enclosing the attributes within the tags brackets, like so: `<body bgcolor="#C6EFF7" text="#000000" link="#00D500" alink="#299C39" vlink="#8FF6342">`. In this case the background (`bgcolor`) will be light turquoise, the text (`text`) will be black, an active link (`alink`) will be green, and a visited link (`vlink`) will be a muted red. As you can see in the Netscape Navigator preview from the BBEdit source file, the only thing that has changed about the test Web page is the background color (5.17), even though we defined the color for text and links. The browser, of course, doesn't have anything to display until we add text.

BACKGROUND

As discussed in Chapter 3, you can create patterned backgrounds on a Web site using small GIF or JPEG files. These files can be any variation of a rectangle. Working with a narrow file (5.18) allows you to create backgrounds that mimic a notepad or open book (5.19).

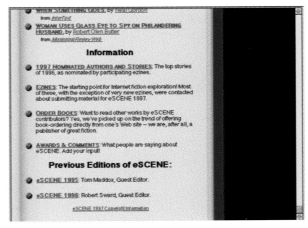

5.19

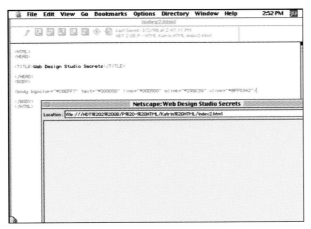

5.17

![5.18 gradient bar]

5.18

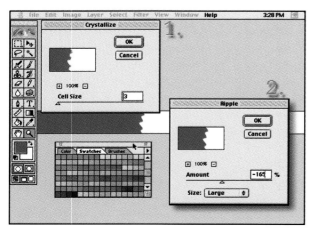

5.20

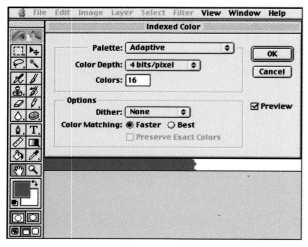

5.21

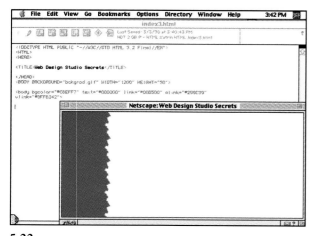

5.22

Follow these steps to create the side-strip look that is currently so popular on the Web:

1. Create a new Photoshop file that is 50 × 1,200 pixels. The extreme width ensures that the strip will not wrap around.

2. Do the creative work. "In this case, I started with a blue and white file and used the Ripple and Crystallize filters to break up the edge (5.20)."

3. Index the file and save it into your Projects folder (5.21).

4. To assign this tile as a background, go to the beginning of the body tag and type in `<BODY BACKGROUND="filename.gif">` (5.22).

THE ESSENTIAL TEXT TAGS

"HTML is a language created to work with text. The fact that one could display inline images was a nice added bonus. From those basic beginnings, designers have come up with ways to stretch HTML into a vehicle for visual delivery of information, and browser developers contributed by creating tags to facilitate the designers. But it's important to remember that text lies at the root of all HTML. Although the visual limitations of HTML have caused designers to bemoan the lack of control that they have over the final appearance of a Web site, there are ways to use HTML's text foundation to create good design."

<HN>

The headline tag `<Hn>` tells the browser to display the enclosed text in large type, just like the headline in a newspaper. The lowercase *n* is reserved for a number between 1 and 6 that denotes the headline size (5.23). Because headings are treated hierarchically (like an outline), 1 is the largest, while 6 is the smallest. The following HTML generates these results (5.23):

```
<H1>
The Designer's Guide to HTML
</H1>
```

Keep in mind that due to the way operating systems assume which types of monitor you use, text will usually display larger on the PC than on the Macintosh. (Macs always assume 72 pixels-per-inch (ppi) resolution, whereas PCs can range from 90 ppi to 120 ppi, regardless of the actual physical size of your screen.) There is no way to control this except by checking your Web pages on both platforms and then fixing extreme problems right away, which is part of the entire Web design process.

`<BASEFONT SIZE>`

This tag defines the size of the body text, not the headlines of a Web page. The size ranges from 1 (small) to 7 (large). Yes, the sizing is the opposite of the sizing for the headlines.

`<FONT FACE>`

The `<FONT FACE>` tag allows you to list which font the browser should use to display the body text. The only caveat is that the font must be installed in the viewer's operating system. To guarantee the viewer will see a font change, select typefaces that are bound to be preinstalled on her system. For sans serif fonts, you'll usually see `<FONT FACE="arial, helvetica">` because Arial (under Windows) and Helvetica (on the Mac OS) are installed by default. Serif font specifications usually read `<FONT FACE="times new roman,times">`. You can, however, include any number of typefaces, depending on what you think

viewers may have installed on their systems. The browser will start at the beginning of the list and continue down the list until it finds a font name that matches a font loaded in the operating system.

If your Web site audience includes graphic designers, you can have fun and use a number of creative fonts such as `<FONT FACE="caflisch script web, hobo,sanfrancisco,tekton,helvetica, arial">` (5.24). The browser will go down the list of fonts and use the first one it finds installed on the viewer's system. In this example, the first font listed, Caflisch Script Web, was also in the system folder. If the viewer possessed only the default typefaces, the browser would go down the list and finally display the text in Helvetica on a Macintosh and Arial on a PC. In the last example, although Caflisch Script Web is listed in the font face tag, the browser found a font that was listed and in the system folder before it read Caflisch Script Web (5.25).

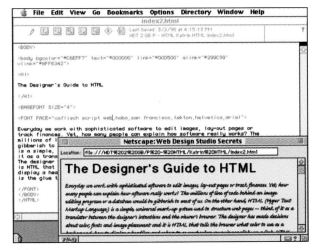

5.24

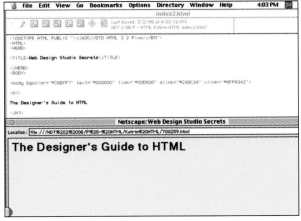

5.23

Microsoft offers a collection of free fonts designed to display well onscreen: for the Macintosh go to *www.microsoft.com/truetype/fontpack/mac.htm*; if you work on a PC go to *www.microsoft.com/truetype/font-pack/win.htm*. Adobe also sells a package of a dozen "Web" fonts that read well onscreen. If everyone surfing the Web had at least one of these packages on their machines, the Web would be a prettier and more legible place to be! Although several options for automatic font display — such as OpenType and TrueDoc — are in development, for now most designers are sticking with the <FONT FACE> tag.

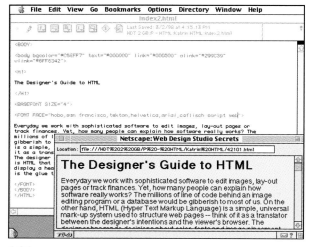

5.25

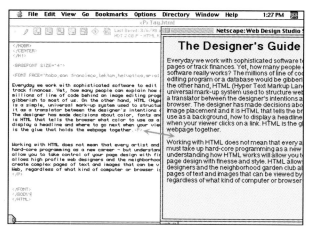

5.26

FORMATTING TEXT

HTML was never designed to be an accurate page layout tool such as PageMaker or QuarkXPress. For the most part, accurate spacing and indenting is achieved through hacks and work-arounds, unless you are using Cascading Style Sheets.

<P>

The <P> tag is unique in that it doesn't require that the tag include "open" and "closed" versions for it to work. To add a double carriage return, just insert <P>. Formally, the HTML specifications state that <P> and </P> be used together (surrounding a paragraph, for example). Although more people and software are implementing the full-tag option, most HTML coders just use <P> to make a paragraph break (5.26).

<P ALIGN>

ALIGN is an attribute of the <P> tag, so you can specify the position of a paragraph of text by typing <P ALIGN=RIGHT>, <P ALIGN=LEFT>, and <P ALIGN=CENTER> (5.27). You can also control centering of objects (not just text) by enclosing them within <CENTER> and </CENTER> tags. Notice that the second paragraph does not have the alignment attribute and the paragraph is automatically aligned left.

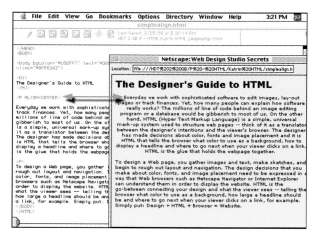

5.27

The `<P>` tag is inconsistently spaced in different browsers and for many designers the space is visually too large (5.28). Often designers will use one or two `<BR>` tags in place of one `<P>`. Use the line break tag of `<BR>` to create a single carriage return between paragraphs (5.29).

<NOBR>

By default, resizing a Web browser window causes the text to rewrap to fit in the new size. If you want to make sure a line doesn't wrap when the window size is adjusted, use the `<NOBR>` tag. (We cover other methods for controlling text wrapping when we talk about tables later in this chapter.) You do not always want a headline or a sentence to be broken up (5.30). Using the no line break tag forces the browser to keep the text together. Notice in the illustration that although the browser window is narrow, the headline does not break (5.31).

<SPACER>

Once again, browsers do not recognize spaces and tabs in HTML documents, but you can add a horizontal spacer to create an indent (5.32). Spacers can also come in horizontal and block forms, and you can control their height, width, and alignment: `<SPACER TYPE="horizontal" SIZE="48">`.

5.29

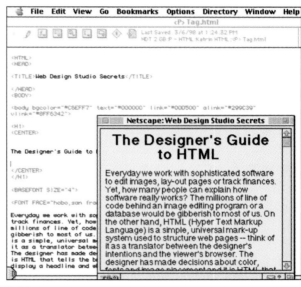

5.30

5.28

LISTS

Working with lists is an easy way to organize text on the page. You can create plain, numbered, and bulleted lists through *ordered* or *unordered* lists. Unordered lists allow you to indent blocks of text without using table elements or invisible GIFs (5.33). Be warned, unordered lists add fairly ugly bullets unless you leave off the <LI> tag before each item. Paragraph spacing is likely going to be less than ideal. Using the <BR> tag helps keep things together.

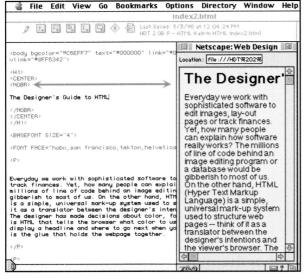

5.31

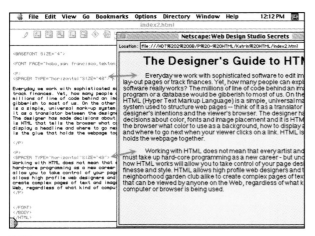

5.32

Start the unordered list with the <UL> tag, paste the item in to be listed, and end the section with the </UL> tag. Add the paragraph tag <P> or line break tag <BR> after every list item to control the space between the lines. Different browsers and browser versions handle spacing differently, so you may have to experiment.

Ordered lists (<OL>) differentiate themselves from unordered lists in that you can assign a counting system to them: numbers, Roman numerals, or alphabetic notation order (5.34) (both lowercase and uppercase). To define the type of list, use <OL TYPE=X> where X can be 1 for numbers, I for capital Roman numerals, i for lowercase Roman numerals, A for capital letters, and a for lowercase letters.

HTML TEXT VERSUS GIF TEXT

All of the font, alignment, and list tags discussed to this point are used to format HTML text. As you have probably noticed, HTML text is not a typographer's or designer's dream, but it has one redeeming feature—speed. Browsers can display it quickly, and the page's file size remains small. Use HTML text when you require speed and don't require a specific, nonstandard typeface for body text, navigation links, and text-only pages. The glaring disadvantage to HTML text is its lack of aesthetic control—you cannot directly control kerning, leading, tracking, or word spacing.

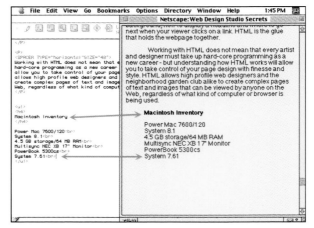

5.33

So what's a designer to do? Design type in Illustrator or FreeHand and Photoshop to be a GIF when you want stylized text and typographic effects such as drop shadows, glows, kerning, leading, letter spacing, and so on. As Jeff illustrates, "On the ZAP site, the long quotes from reviews are ideal as HTML text while the quotes from the book needed a specific typeface that fit into an area of fixed dimensions. GIF images were the best choice (5.35)."

LINK ME UP

All link tags begin with `<A HREF="xxxxx">` where the xxxxx is either a local file, Internet URL, e-mail address, and so on.

A link to a fictitious e-mail address would look like this: "For more information, please e-mail me at `<A HREF="mailto:myhouse@mytown.com">myhou se@mytown.com</A>` (5.36)." When the viewer clicks the link, the e-mail interface appears and they can write you e-mail (5.37).

To create a link to another part of the site, start with `<A HREF="http://www.NAME OF WEBSITE.com">Text to be Displayed</A>` and the text to be clicked. "The literary index of eSCENE links to short stories and the author biographies. To create the link for Lucy Harrison's story 'Just Another Night and Day,' I started with `<a href=" nightandday.html">`

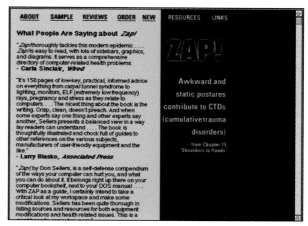

5.35

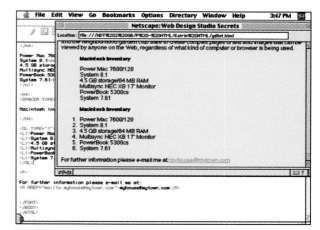

5.36

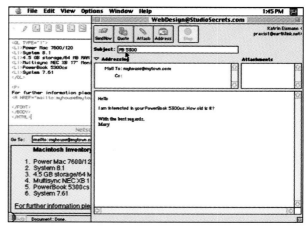

5.37

5.34

which is the actual Web page containing the story (5.38). Then I typed in what the viewer sees, ANOTHER NIGHT AND DAY, to signify the text to be clicked (5.39). Finally, I wanted to link the author's name with her biography, so I typed `<a href="authors.html#harrison">Lucy Harrison</a>`. In this case, the browser loads the author's page, then jumps to the tag named `harrison` (5.40)."

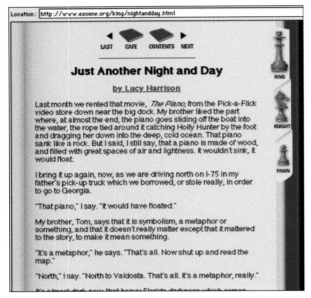

5.38

5.39

ABSOLUTE VERSUS RELATIVE URLS

URLs can be either *absolute* or *relative*. Absolute URLs reflect the entire file path, and relative URLs show where the file is in relationship to the file location. "My opinion is that relative URLs are better because you can set up a test site on your own computer and have the links work. A link will look for File.html instead of wanting to go to a whole server on the Web someplace." The syntax for writing relative URLs is: If the linked file or image is in the same folder as the current HTML file you're working on, the filename is just referenced straightforwardly.

```
<a href="bob.html">
```

If the file exists in a subfolder of the folder your active file is in, you list the folder name, then the filename:

```
<a href="images/bob.html">
```

If you have more than one directory, you can dig down through the hierarchy with slashes, such as

```
<a href="family/events/picnic/
images/bob.html">
```

If you need to go up a level in the hierarchy, you use two dots and a slash. Given the URL here, suppose you're in the Images directory and want to get a file in Events:

```
<a href="../../hiking_trip.html">
```

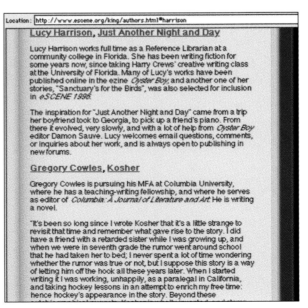

5.40

WORKING WITH IMAGES AND HTML

For an artist, designer, or photographer, the greatest appeal of having a Web site is to display images. Images can be as simple as a company logo or a family portrait, or they can serve to set the entire tone of the site. To insert an image requires that you define the image source, placement, and alignment. The tag is `<IMG SRC="file/location of file">`. Using BBEdit to insert images is the easiest method since it automatically writes the image path plus the width and height attribute tags (5.41), and gives you an opportunity to add an image `<ALT>` tag right away. (Note that you'll need to install HTML Extensions to add this functionality to BBEdit Lite.)

When an image comes into an HTML document, the image and text do not interact. This doesn't look very good, does it (5.42)? To wrap text around an image use `<IMG SRC="file/location of file" ALIGN=left or ALIGN=right>`. As you'd expect, setting the alignment to the left or right positions the image to the left or right of the text (5.43).

To make an image be a link or hot spot, start with `<A HREF="url.address">`. The URL is the actual address the user goes to when he clicks the image. After the `<A HREF>` tag you need to insert the image with `<IMG SRC="imagefile.location">`. "In the eSCENE site, the home page and the Cafe can be reached by clicking on the red and blue books, or a viewer can go to the less graphics-intensive versions by clicking on the knight or pawn icons on the right (5.44). This allowed me to create attractive links that are more than just boring colored text."

To create a link to eSCENE's home page, Jeff used the following HTML:

```
<a href="../default.htm">
<IMG SRC="images/home_nav.gif"
ALT="Home" WIDTH="46" HEIGHT="36"
BORDER="0"></a>
```

Unless you want a 2-pixel blue line surrounding your linked image, make sure to specify a zero border in the image tag, like so: `<IMG SRC="name of file" border="0">`.

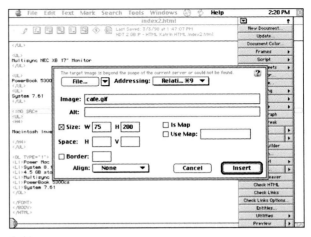

5.41

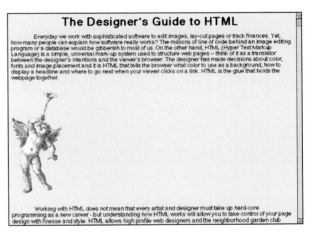

5.42

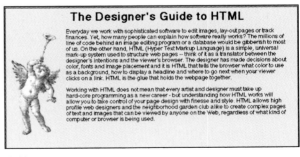

5.43

PLEASE LEAVE THE LIGHTS ON!

Imagine walking into a dark and unfamiliar room. You orient yourself by feeling your way around to 'see' how big the room is and what is in it. At the same time you try to avoid stumbling into the furniture. Now imagine walking into that same unfamiliar room with the lights on. It is a completely different experience as you quickly orient yourself, see exactly how large the room is and where the furniture is. Web browsers do the same thing! When the lights are off (in other words, when you do not include width and height tags for images), the browser must load all the images before it knows where to place them. Using width and height attributes in the <IMG SRC> tag is like leaving the lights on. The browser can read the size and dimensions of the image and block out the appropriate amount of space without actually loading the image. This way, the browser can display the page more quickly and then go back to grab the images.

Using the width and height attributes also maintains the integrity of the page in case the viewer is surfing with graphics turned off. If the ZAP site did not have any image attribute tags and a viewer came to the site with graphics off, they would see a jumble of image icons (5.45). With the image tag attributes, at least the browser will know how large a certain image is supposed to be, and it will display a properly sized box (5.46).

The <ALT> tag is text that is displayed when the viewer is surfing without graphics or using a slow modem connection. Rather than seeing an empty box, the viewer can read a description of the image (5.47), and when they want to actually see the file they can click it and the image will load. The image attribute tags are as follows:

```
<IMG SRC="name_of_image.gif"
WIDTH="200" HEIGHT="100" ALT="Text
you want the viewer to read goes
here!">
```

Give the viewer that browses without graphics as much information as possible by using <ALT> tags so that they read what the image represents. This is especially important when an image is a link. Rather than seeing the generic image icon, the viewer could see the word *Order* or *Info*. If the viewer is intrigued by what the <ALT> tag says, and they want to see the image, they can click it and the image will load (5.48). Or the viewer can load all the images at once (5.49 and 5.50). "On the ZAP site, the image is so large that I could type in the entire quote from the GIF file. On the links, the image <ALT> tag really makes a difference, since the viewer can see what the button would do even when graphics are turned off."

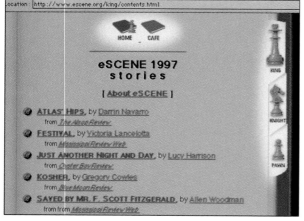

5.44

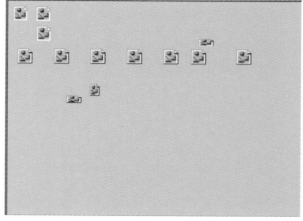

5.45

WORKING WITH NOTHING
TO DESIGN THE PAGE

Massaging a page with the use of tags and attributes only works to a point. Using invisible images to create space of any size and dimensions — also referred to as the "single-pixel GIF trick" — allows you to position images and text wherever needed. "Some designers scoff at using the single-pixel GIF technique, referring to it as a design kludge, but the fact remains that it works and it's simple to use. In Photoshop, create a 1 pixel × 1 pixel file, index it, and export via the Gif 89 Export command. Specify the one color as transparent, and save the file in your images folder as something like Spacer.gif."

Combining this file with an image tag that specifies the size of the empty space allows you to create empty boxes that serve as blank place holders to position images and text. Start by defining the image source with `IMG SRC` and then by defining the width and height of the space you need. In this case, by aligning the text left, the text aligns flush left to the Spacer.gif file: `<IMG SRC="spacer.gif" WIDTH="50" HEIGHT="200"ALIGN=left>` (5.51). If no alignment is defined, then Spacer.gif serves to create vertical space between blocks of text or images.

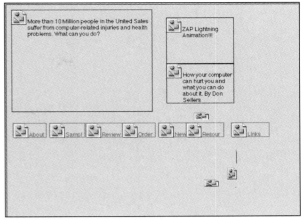

5.47

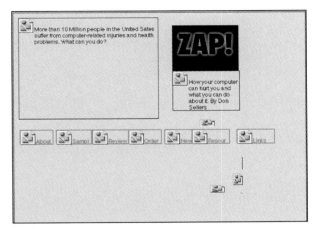

5.48

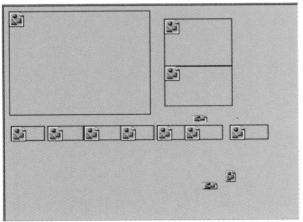

5.46

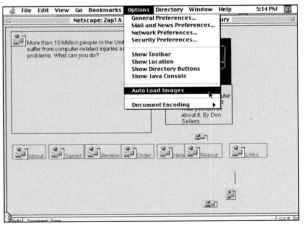

5.49

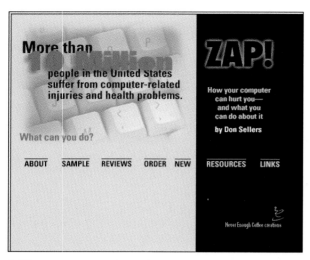

5.50

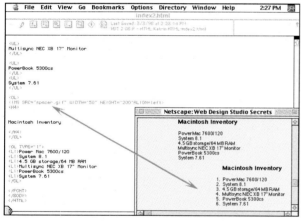

5.51

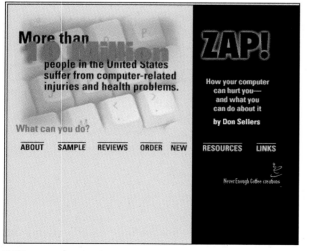

5.52

"On the ZAP site, I wanted the links and my logo to be 'pushed' down a bit. Instead of trying to experiment with `<P>` or `<BR>` tags, I added the spacer file with the image attribute tag of a 1 pixel width and a 50 pixel height: `<img src="images/spacer. gif" width=1 height=50 border=0>` (5.52 and 5.53)."

USING THE LOWSRC TAG

The `LOWSRC` (low source) image tag is good for large images when you need the viewer to get an impression of an image quickly. "You're actually loading two images on top of one another, but one is usually created as a low resolution version — perhaps a sketch or black and white version (5.54) — that gives an impression of the final image (5.55). Using low source actually increases the load time because an extra image is being fetched, but the perceptual effect is that the viewer sees an image quickly. Low source is especially good for image maps, where you want the visitor to see the navigational options immediately."

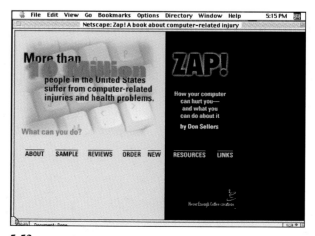

5.53

The low source tag resides in the `<IMG>` tag. `SRC` defines the main full-resolution file, while `LOWSRC` points to the low-resolution file. The `LOWSRC` image loads first when the tag is present: `<IMG SRC=" images/title_chess.1.jpg"lowsrc=" images/title_outline.3.gif">`. Make sure your `LOWSRC` image is the same size as your main image because otherwise the height and width tags that describe the image will be applied to the low source image, as well:

```
<IMG SRC="images/ title_chess.1.jpg"
lowsrc="images/  title_outline.3.gif"
alt="eSCENE1997"width="470"
height="368" border="0">.
```

5.54

5.55

5.56

5.57

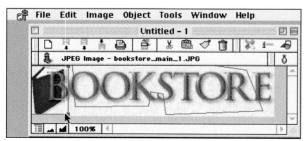

5.58

IMAGE MAPS

Links are what make the Web the Web! It's like going into a good bookstore to buy a travel book for your next vacation, and within a few minutes you are flipping though a book about the history of Super Heroes. One thing leads to another just as one link leads to another. As discussed above, text and individual images can be links to another page or to a completely different Web site.

Image maps offer an intriguing method of creating links that don't shout "click me" since they are a part of a larger image — subtle, yet active. Building image maps begins by mapping out where you want clickable parts of the image to be, noting the coordinates, and using these coordinates in the HTML document to define where the active part of the image is. The three shapes that image maps recognize are rectangles, circles, and polygons (for irregularly shaped areas).

A number of tools, such as MapTool and ImageMapper 3.0 (5.56 and 5.57), which generate all the required coordinate information for you (5.58 – 5.61), are available to help you determine coordinates.

Of course, working with the Info palette in Photoshop does the trick, too! In Photoshop, set the Info palette to read out in pixels. Use the marquee tool to select the area to be mapped (5.62) and note the upper-left and lower-right coordinates of the marquee selection (5.63).

After noting the coordinates of the area to be mapped out, type in the image map tag of <MAP NAME="XXX">, where the XXX reflects the name of the file being mapped (in this case, Cupid). Following this tag comes the area shape tag: <AREA

5.59

SHAPE="xxxx"COORDS="xx,xx,xx,xx" HREF="name of link or url that opens when the viewer clicks">. The area shape equals either rectangles abbreviated as *rect*, circles abbreviated as *circle*, or polygons abbreviated as *poly*. Then come the coordinates. For a rectangle, use the upper-left XY coordinates and the lower-right XY coordinates, separated with commas and no spaces. For a circle, the coordinates are X, Y, and R, where X and Y are the center of the circle and R equals the radius. Polygons require all coordinate points X1, Y1, X2, Y2, X3, Y3, X4, and Y4 that identify all points of the polygon. Here's an example:

```
<MAP NAME="cupid">
<AREA
SHAPE="rect"COORDS="29,106,64,130"
HREF="http://www.escene.org">
</MAP>
<IMG SRC="cupid2.gif" ALT="Angel
Blowing Horn" ALIGN=left WIDTH="116"
HEIGHT="248" BORDER="0"
USEMAP="#cupid">
```

After the coordinates have been placed in as attributes and the HREF tag has been inserted, close the map tag with </MAP>. Identify the image source (in this case, Cupid2.gif) and include the alternative tag and image attribute information (5.64). Finally, type in USEMAP="XXX">, where the map used refers to the map name (in this case "cupid"). Clicking the cupid now opens up the link to the eSCENE Web site (5.65).

5.61

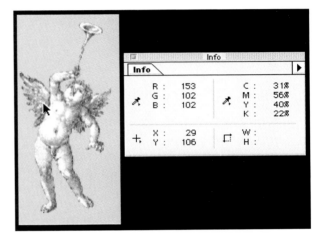

5.62

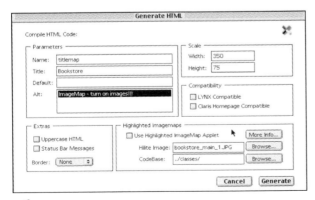

5.60

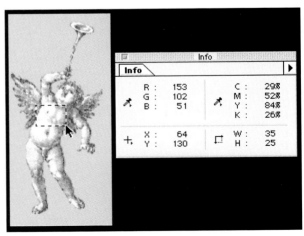

5.63

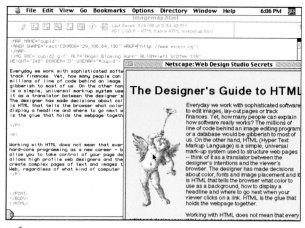

5.64

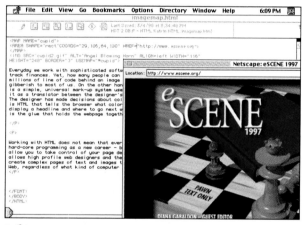

5.65

SETTING THE TABLE

You may find it frustrating that text and images get repositioned whenever the viewer resizes the browser window. What is a designer to do? Tables to the rescue. A *table* is a grid with rows and columns in which you place text and images that always stay in relationship to one another. Using tables creatively allows you to design sites that offer sophistication without complex coding. Each table cell is an opportunity to be creative with file formats and the roles that each table cell can play.

The Meany Theater of Washington University Web site (*www.meany.org*) has a beautiful opening page that effectively implements a table (5.66). The image has been cut into five pieces: the navigation bar on the left (5.67), three smaller files with a GIF animation in the middle (5.68–5.70), and then one large file to the right (5.71). By cutting up the image in Photoshop and placing the separate elements into a table, the site designer has the opportunity to treat each element differently. In this case, the important elements include the navigation bar with a seven-hot-spot image map and the GIF animation that radiates a ripple pattern out from Seattle.

Start a table with the <TABLE> tag and then define the basic table parameters. Consider if you need table borders around each frame, how much padding or space the contents of the cell should have from the cell wall, and how much space there is between cells. These attributes are usually zero when stitching images back together. In the case of the Meany Theater site, the designer also specified the width of 673 pixels that the browser was to reserve for the table.

Although the HTML code for tables looks daunting, it's really quite simple if you remember the following rules. Build across, then down. Once you've set up your table with the <TABLE> tag, the next step is to create a row using the <TR> tag. Rows seldom need any additional attributes, so leaving it like this is fine.

Once your row is specified, you then start filling it with table cells, which get specified across the table from left to right. Table cells are created with the <TD> tag and can contain attributes such as width, alignment (which affects the alignment of elements within the cell), and vertical alignment. After you've placed your content in the cell, close it by using the </TD> tag. If there are more cells in that row, repeat

5.66

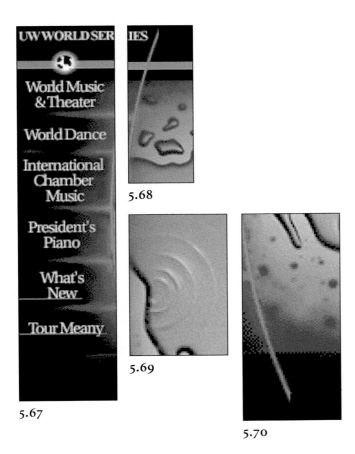

5.67

5.68

5.69

5.70

5.71

the cell-creation process; if not, close the row with `</TR>` and move down to the next row. At the end, close the table with `</TABLE>`. The following code generates a basic table with one row and two cells, and illustrates the "build across, then down" concept:

```
<TABLE WIDTH=100 BORDER=2>
    <TR>
            <TD WIDTH=50>
            First Table Cell<p>
            </TD>
            <TD WIDTH=50>
            Second Table Cell<p>
            </TD>
    </TR>
</TABLE>
```

One powerful feature of tables is the ability to set the width of the table cells. Similar to the `<NOBR>` (no break) tag mentioned earlier, you can include text in a table cell whose width has been fixed. Changing the browser window's size won't affect text wrapping. Widths can also be specified in percentages so the table will shift in size according to the window's dimensions. This comes in handy when designing a site that needs to be readable on small screens as well as larger ones.

You can also stretch cells across other cells if you want. Obviously, you won't always want an even grid of cells, so the designers of the HTML table specs added the `<ROWSPAN>` and `<COLSPAN>` tags. `<ROWSPAN>` literally causes a cell to "span" across a certain number of rows. `<COLSPAN>` spans cells across columns. The following table is a slightly more advanced version of the table above, incorporating cell spanning and dynamic widths:

```
<TABLE WIDTH=100% BORDER=2>
    <TR>
            <TD WIDTH=50%>
            First Table Cell in First
    Row.<p>
            </TD>
            <TD WIDTH=50%>
            Second Table Cell in First
    Row.<p>
            </TD>
    </TR>
```

```
    <TR>
            <TD WIDTH=100% COLSPAN=2>
            Spanned Cell in Second
    Row.<p>
            </TD>
    </TR>
</TABLE>
```

COMMENTING ABOUT <!-- COMMENT TAGS -->

Working HTML to bend to your design wishes requires experimentation, patience, and a good dose of caffeine. Before you upload your Web site to the server there are a few modifications you can make to the HTML document that will make the site easier to maintain. Think of the comment tag like flags or notes, inserted into the HTML document for you to reference when working in the HTML. Since comment tags are invisible to the browser, they won't be displayed.

"Many clients want to be able to add or change site content themselves once the design is finished. Comment tags are invaluable for pointing out elements in the HTML such as `<!-- BODY TEXT BEGINS HERE -->`. This makes it easy for them to navigate the HTML, and goes a long way to preserving the HTML as I created it, without chunks of important code being mangled or deleted. The secret is in the comment tags `<!--` and `-->`. Whatever is inside the bracket/exclamation point/double-dash, and double-dash/close bracket will not be displayed by the browser. On the Movie Maven site, the client maintains the site by updating it with weekly reviews. Rather than teaching the client all the HTML required, Jeff used comment tags to point out to the client where the new movie titles and reviews would go (5.72).

In the following example, Jeff uses the comment tag and all caps to help his client find the right spot to insert the movie title into the HTML (5.73).

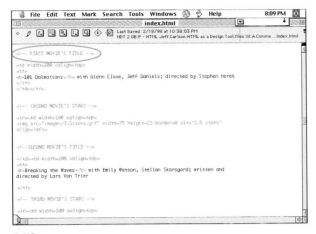

5.72

5.73

```
<!-- FIRST MOVIE'S TITLE -->
<td width=200 valign=top>
<tt>
<b>101 Dalmatians</b> with Glenn
Close, Jeff Daniels; directed by
Stephen Herek
</tt>
</td></tr>
```

One additional use of the comment tag is that, "You can store frequently used strips of code in one HTML file. The Movie Maven home page includes the code for each variation of rating star animation (5.74). The client just has to copy and paste the correct rating for the week's review in the appropriate place. The increase in file size in this case was minimal."

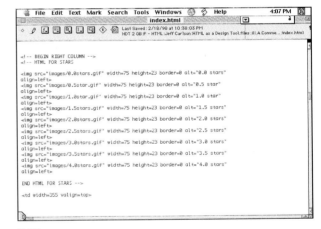

5.74

METATAGS

Once you've built a site, how will viewers ever find you? Designers are finding themselves taking on the roles of marketers, as clients not only want great design, but hits and traffic, too. When search engines index Web sites, they look for keyword *metatags* to store in their databases. If you created a site for a museum, for example, the metatag description keywords could include the name of the museum, the city that the museum is located in, art, names of artists in the collection, culture, painting, sculpture — anything associated with the specific museum.

Please do not type in the same word over and over again so that your site is the first 30 matches for a search. Using the word *sex* to get hits is pretty low, too. Interestingly enough, debates are raging about whether you can include the name of a competitor in your metatag. For example, if you made Coca-Cola, should you be able to use the word *Pepsi* in your metatag?

The description metatag is the sentence that comes up when the browser displays the search results (5.75). The eSCENE metatag is a clear example that uses both description and keywords to aid the search engines in finding the site for viewers interested in short fiction.

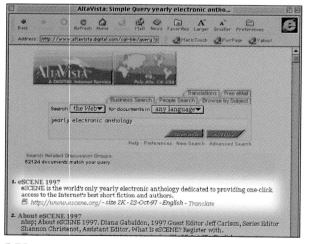

5.75

```
<HTML>
<HEAD>
<TITLE>eSCENE 1997</TITLE>
<META name="description"
content="eSCENE is the world's only
yearly electronic anthology dedi-
cated to providing one-click access
to the Internet's best short fiction
and authors.">
<META name="keywords" content="
fiction, ezine, short stories,
world's best fiction, best american
short stories, story, stories, best
short stories,best fiction,
anthology, writing, fiction writing,
story writing, internet fiction, web
fiction, internet stories, web
stories, jeff carlson, robert olen
butler, diana gabaldon, frederick
barthelme">
</HEAD>
```

<THE END>

Finally, you need to tell the browser that the body of the page is complete, and that the HTML document is done by typing the following:

```
</BODY>
</HTML>
```

AND IN THE END . . .

The site is done! An important step before uploading the site for the entire world to see is to have as many people as possible test the site on different computers and with various connection rates. The people who test your site should be looking for links that don't work, interface that is not clear, and image files that are missing. Once you are happy that the site is ready, you can upload it to your Web server. If you have direct access (usually requiring a password) to your server directory, you can use a program such as Fetch or Anarchie to copy the files directly. Some hosting companies prefer that they do the uploading, in which case you can send the files to them by e-mail or on disk.

The best and worst thing about Web design and Web publishing is that you are never done and can always improve a site. If you like to tweak and experiment, then page layout with HTML is right for you. As the Web tools get better, and WYSIWYG becomes more than an odd term, the need to write your own HTML will decrease, but knowing how it all works and what is and isn't possible will make your Web pages more exciting and unique.

the Davis GROUP

Our firm produces effective and
exciting graphic design solutions for
a diverse group of clients, including
web sites, printed materials, and more...

Portfolio

web design

who are we?

CHAPTER 6
CONSTRUCTING PAGES USING TABLES

The term *table* is one of our least favorite words in the dense and ravenous computer lexicon. For us, it conjures up images of tedious spreadsheets sporting column after rigid column, chock full of insider gibberish, and formatted by a middle manager who wouldn't know one font from another if the letters leapt off the page and impaled him with their serifs. Tables hold price lists, comparative data, amortization payments, and a bunch of other bottom-line dreck that make us wish to heck computers had never been invented.

But HTML tables are different. While you certainly *can* use a <TABLE> tag to house something as mundane as an online spreadsheet (though we naturally shudder at the thought), its primary value to designers is something altogether different. Tables bring order to the otherwise unstructured world of the Web. They hold text blocks, permit columns, and align graphics. Simply put, tables in HTML are the equivalent of snap-to guides in electronic page design.

Tables involve remarkably little coding. You frame the table with <TABLE> and </TABLE>. Within that, <TR> denotes a row and <TD> (table data) marks an individual cell. From a designer's perspective, a <TD> cell is equivalent to a column. So you start by breaking up the table into horizontal rows and then dividing the rows into vertical columns. You always have to work in that order, and that's all the control you have.

If you want to go any further—by, say, dividing a column into additional rows—you have to start a new table inside the <TD> cell. A table inside a table is said to be *nested*, and while it might sound weird, nesting is a commonplace convention. In fact, a typical Web page

It's amazing how much you can do with this one tool. If there's a more versatile tag than <TABLE>, *I'd like to know about it.*

BRETT DAVIS

design may require you to nest tables four or five levels deep. For example, you might create one table to establish the page margins, another inside that to hold two or three columns of text, another inside that to hold a graphic with a caption, and another inside that to align a row of buttons below the caption.

As you can imagine, nesting requires a stout heart and keen attention to detail. Setting up the proper tags, editing them when things don't go according to plan, and recognizing which tags go with which table is enough to test the resolve and the patience of the most even-tempered Web designer.

BRETT WAXES TABLES

That's why we brought in Brett Davis, a guy who eats tables for breakfast. "I wouldn't go so far as to say tables are bucketloads of fun. The interesting part of designing a Web site is creating and experimenting with the look and feel in Photoshop. Coding the site is pretty boring. The biggest joy of tables is the moment when you see the site in a browser and everything fits together perfectly.

"But just because tables are dull doesn't mean they're hard to use. They're really not. I mean, there are some weird things you have to remember about setting column widths and alignment, but once you get that down, it's simple stuff.

"Here you have this old tag that dates back to the earliest days of the Web. It was designed to be easy to use, so you could throw some data into a spreadsheet without thinking. But then it dawned on designers how much control this simple tag gives you. You can put anything inside a table, you have all kinds of alignment options, you can color cells, you can nest tables inside tables — it's just incredible how many different designs you can create.

"In fact, in my opinion, tables are the number one tool for getting a precise layout on the Web." Really? But what about frames? "Well, frames are fine. They let you scroll different areas inside your pages, which you can't do with tables. But some older browsers don't support frames. Even though they've caught on more lately, there are still a few people with old browsers out there. And if your page includes frames and the browser doesn't support them, you've got a big problem. If you want to be universally compatible, tables are the way to go.

"Another advantage to tables is that they don't have to look like tables. A frame is always a frame, but a table can be invisible. You can set up a rigid structure for a page without anyone seeing that it's there. To the user, it looks like a straightforward page design (6.1), but the HTML code may really be a complex network five or six tables deep (6.2)."

Davis uses a WYSIWYG program to set up his basic designs and then edits them in HTML. However, the program he uses — the $25 shareware PageSpinner (*www.algonet.se/~optima*) — boasts a modest feature set. "PageSpinner helps me when I'm picking colors and importing images." But does PageSpinner do

ARTIST:
Brett Davis

ORGANIZATION:
The Davis Group
14730 NE Eighth
Bellevue, WA 98007
425/641-5758
www.groupdavis.com
brett@groupdavis.com

SYSTEM:
Power Mac 7300/180
System 8.0
6GB storage/96MB RAM

CONNECTIVITY:
28.8 Kbps modem

PERIPHERALS:
Sony 17-inch 200SF monitor, Epson ES800C scanner

PRIMARY APPLICATIONS:
Optima PageSpinner, Adobe Photoshop, Macromedia FreeHand

WORK HISTORY:
1986 — Experimented with color animation on a Commodore Amiga as high-school sophomore.

tables? "No, when it comes to tables, I type in all the `<TABLE>` tags with the `<TD>`s and `<TR>`s and all that good stuff." Why not use a program that automatically creates tables, such as NetObjects Fusion? "I've tried out a demo of NetObjects. I don't have anything against it, but I'm doing fine without it. And ultimately I feel like I have more control working manually. I don't need to spend $100 or $300 on all these other applications when I'm meeting my clients' needs with PageSpinner."

So here's a guy who routinely creates nested tables five and six levels deep, he constructs every table by hand, and he thinks it's easy. Either he's completely out of his mind or he's onto something. You'll have ample opportunity to make up your own mind on this and other burning topics in the next few pages.

MAKING GRAPHICS THAT STRETCH

To see a creative use of HTML tables, you have only to follow Davis to work. In constructing the home page for his employer, The Davis Group (*www. groupdavis.com*), the unrelated artist Davis wove a tapestry of invisible tables to create an open, uncluttered design that adapts perfectly to the viewer's screen.

"The idea behind The Davis Group page was to establish some structure while keeping the text at the top of the page loose with a lot of white space (6.3). The words look like they're floating in space, but if you size the browser window, the title always stays

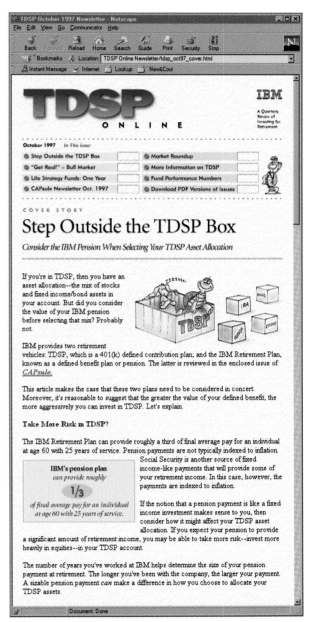

6.1

1992 — Rescued from selling shoes by designer friend who needed temporary substitute; ended up taking over job permanently.

1994 — Hooked up with The Davis Group design firm (no relation to Brett).

1995 — Designed first online project before he had even tried out America Online. Never got paid.

FAVORITE FABRIC SOFTENER:
The Downy Ball ("It's a little ball that pops open in the spin cycle and gives you freshness.")

6.2

centered, and the text along the left and right sides of the page stay toward the outside (6.4). The purple line under the word *Group* stretches as well.

"The thing that I see people getting out of this example are a couple of tricks that work reliably and look great. One of them is object alignment and the other is graphic stretching. Tables are perfect for both."

Like so many Web artists, Davis mocks up his basic page design in Photoshop. He uses Photoshop's guides to divide the page design into separate rows and columns (6.5). "The guides show me where to crop the GIF files. This way, I can make sure the heights add up and that all the graphics line up just right."

After cropping and saving the individual GIF images, Davis begins work on his first HTML table, which describes the overall structure of the page. He divides the table into three columns using a trio of <TD> tags (6.6). The two outer columns (highlighted in green) serve as page margins; the middle column (in blue) will hold the contents of the page. Notice that for the present, the middle column is only partially coded. If

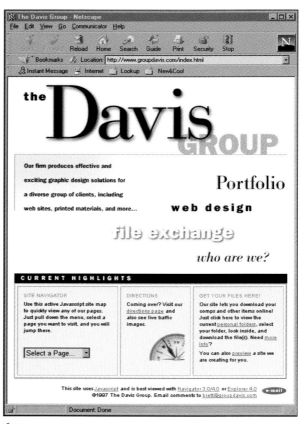

6.3

we were to see every tag for the type and graphics that fit in this area, the code would not only be confusing, it would fill several pages.

"To keep the table invisible — so the page doesn't have a bunch of lines going through it — I set the `cellspacing`, `cellpadding`, and `border` attributes to 0. Then I set the left and right columns to 20 pixels wide using `<TD width=20>`. The cells need to have something in them, so I put transparent GIF spacers in both the outside columns. For the middle column, I entered `<TD width=100%>`.

"Now if you think about it, setting the middle column to 100 percent doesn't make any sense. How can you take 20 pixels on one side and 20 pixels on the other and add it to 100 percent? I mean, 100 percent is everything. But it's not. Anything with a real pixel width takes up the exact amount of room you specify and the percentage value takes up the rest. So the 100 percent value stands for 100 percent of what's left." The upshot is that the left and right columns never vary from 20 pixels wide. Only the middle column expands and contracts to accommodate the size of the browser window.

THE EXPANDING LINE

"I leave the left and right columns empty so nothing gets too close to the outside of the page. From now on, everything is happening in the middle cell" (in the space marked with green asterisks in 6.6). After opening a `<CENTER>` tag, Davis adds a nonbreaking

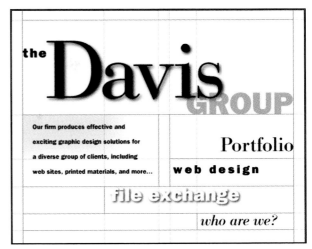

6.5

```
<TABLE cellspacing=0 cellpadding=0 border=0>
<TR>
    <TD width=20 valign=top align=left>
        <IMG SRC="gifs/spacer16.gif"
        WIDTH="20" HEIGHT="63"
        HSPACE="0" VSPACE="0">
    </TD>
    <TD width=100% valign=top>

        ************************
    </TD>

    <TD width=20 valign=top align=left>
        <IMG SRC="gifs/spacer16.gif"
        WIDTH="20" HEIGHT="63"
        HSPACE="0" VSPACE="0">
    </TD>
</TR></TABLE>
```

6.6

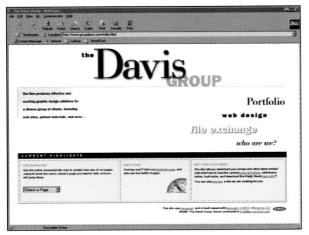

6.4

space ( ) followed by a line break (6.7). This results in a top margin that approximately matches the empty side columns.

Davis then inserts the Davis Group's logo. "The logo graphic is nearly 500 pixels wide (6.8), but the GIF file is less than 10K. Just 32 colors, no dithering. But I still get smooth letters and a soft drop shadow because there are really just two colors, black and purple." And thanks to the <CENTER> tag, it always appears centered on the page.

"Now notice the <BR> that appears at the end of the <IMG SRC> tag (6.7). This ensures that the next item—the purple line—lines up directly beneath the logo graphic without any gap. If I didn't have the <BR> tag, the browser would insert a space."

```
<CENTER>
 <BR>
    <IMG SRC="gifs/dglogo_big32.gif"
    WIDTH="492" HEIGHT="146"
    HSPACE="0" VSPACE="0" BORDER="0"
    ALT="The Davis Group"><BR>
```

6.7

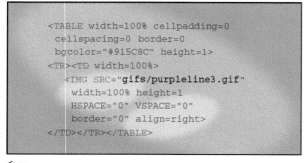

6.8

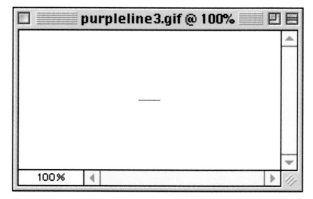

```
<TABLE width=100% cellpadding=0
  cellspacing=0 border=0
  bgcolor="#915C8C" height=1>
<TR><TD width=100%>
    <IMG SRC="gifs/purpleline3.gif"
    width=100% height=1
    HSPACE="0" VSPACE="0"
    border="0" align=right>
</TD></TR></TABLE>
```

6.9

Next, Davis adds a new <TABLE> tag to create a nested table below the logo. But this time, the table includes only one row and one column set to 100 percent (6.9). Davis also adds a height attribute set to 1 pixel. So what in the world is the purpose of a one-cell, 1-pixel tall table set to 100 percent of the column in which it's nested? Why, to hold the expanding and contracting purple line, naturally.

"If you look at the code, you'll see that I've got an image called Purpleline3.gif in the Gifs folder. This is the line that stretches. In reality, that purple line graphic is just 20 pixels wide (6.10). But because I include width=100%, the line stretches to fit the entire table, which stretches to fit the column." But there's one caveat. "You have to say align=right. I know, it doesn't make a lot of sense, but if I didn't right-align the graphic, it wouldn't stretch. It would just appear 20 pixels wide. All the way back to Netscape 2, it works this way. Don't ask me why. But if you use width=100% with align=right, you can stretch graphics.

"I had been using this trick for a while when Netscape 4 came out and, suddenly, it stopped working. But then I found a great way to force the stretching line to display, without losing anything in other browsers. I simply added background="gifs/purpleline3.gif" to the existing <TABLE> tag, right before the first <TR> tag."

This trick works so well with the purple line because the line is a single color. "If the line had a texture, you could see the graphic stretching. It would look pretty awful. But because I'm using a solid color, you can't tell that it's being stretched out."

6.10

ALIGNING THE BUTTONS

Not surprisingly, the next item in The Davis Group home page is another nested table. This time, the table contains a total of four elements — the corporate quote aligned to the left, two buttons aligned right, and a spacer graphic in the middle (6.11). All are GIF images created in Photoshop.

"I start with my standard `<TABLE>` tag, again set to `width=100%`. Like usual, I use just one row. And then there are three columns, set to `width=50%`, `width=4%`, and `width=46%`, which add up to 100 percent (6.12). The middle column is a spacer, just to make sure that the words from the quote never touch the Web Design button." Davis used a single `<TD>` tag to house both the Portfolio and Web Design buttons. A line break `<BR>` divides the two GIF images so they're flush, one directly on top of the other. And the `align=right` attribute assigned to the `<TD>` tag keeps the buttons aligned to the outside of the page. "I guess I could have made a nested table with two rows just to hold the buttons, but I didn't need it, so what's the point? With practice, you learn to recognize when you need a table and when you don't."

The last two buttons — File Exchange and Who Are We? — are flush right with no elements to the left of them (6.13). This time, Davis codes a simple table with two rows consisting of one column each (6.14). "The table has a `width` of 100 percent all the way around, and I'm simply aligning everything to the right. One row contains the File Exchange graphic, the other contains 'who are we?'. Couldn't be much easier."

So why use a table at all? "Actually, I'm not sure if I could get these two graphics to line up without a table. As I recall, you can end up with one graphic slipping to the left of the other. It's weird. A table is just more predictable. By giving each button its own row, I know nothing can go wrong."

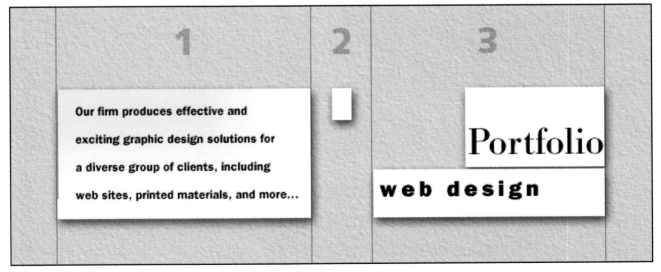

6.11

```
<TABLE width=100% cellpadding=0
 cellspacing=0 border=0>
<TR>
   <TD valign=top width=50% align=left>
   <A href="whoarewe_capabilities.html">
      <IMG SRC="gifs/dg_quote3.gif"
      width="248" height="134"
      hspace="0" vspace="0" border="0"
      </A><BR>
   </TD>

   <TD valign=top width=4% align=left>
      <IMG SRC="gifs/home_spacer19.gif"
      width="19" height="32"
      hspace="0" vspace="0"><BR>
   </TD>

   <TD valign=top align=right width=46%>
   <A href="portfolio_brochures.html"
      onMouseOver = "imgOn('img1')"
      onMouseOut = "imgOff('img1')">
      <IMG SRC="gifs/home_portfolio5_off.gif"
      width="136" height="80"
      hspace="0" vspace="0"
      border="0" name="img1"></A> <BR>

   <A href="webdesign_websites.html"
      onMouseOver = "imgOn('img2')"
      onMouseOut = "imgOff('img2')">
      <IMG SRC="gifs/home_webdesign3_off.gif"
      width="226" height="48"
      hspace="0" vspace="0"
      border="0" name="img2"></A>
   </TD>
</TR></TABLE>
```

6.12

```
<TABLE width=100% cellpadding=0
 cellspacing=0 border=0>
<TR>
   <TD valign=top align=right width=100%>
   <A href="exchange_yourfiles.html"
      onMouseOver = "imgOn('img3')"
      onMouseOut = "imgOff('img3')">
      <IMG SRC="gifs/home_exchange_off.gif"
      width="344" height="51"
      hspace="0" vspace="0"
      border="0" name="img3"></A><BR>
   </TD>
</TR>

<TR>
   <TD valign=top align=right width=100%>
   <A href="whoarewe_capabilities.html"
      onMouseOver = "imgOn('img4')"
      onMouseOut = "imgOff('img4')">
      <IMG SRC="gifs/home_whoarewe4_off.gif"
      width="177" height="28"
      hspace="0" vspace="0"
      border="0" name="img4"></A><BR>
   </TD>
</TR></TABLE>
```

6.14

6.13

THE EXPANDING TITLE BAR

The final item on The Davis Group page is a traditional table — albeit colored in a nontraditional shade of lavender — with an expanding title bar along the top (6.15). "The part of the table that looks like a table is pretty predictable. This is one of the few cases that I use borders, just like a spreadsheet-type table. I set the `width` attributes for the columns to 37 percent, 26 percent, and 37 percent. That adds up to 100 percent, so no surprises there. I also set the `cellpadding` to 11 pixels, which makes a nice margin around the text inside each column. The `cellspacing` is 4 pixels and the `border` is 2."

Davis uses `bgcolor="#ECE8F9"` to give the cells their color. "The `bgcolor` command doesn't work inside tables in all browsers — including Netscape 2 — but who cares? Most people don't use Netscape 2, and if you do, you'll get a white background. But when it does work, I think it looks good. The purple helps the table stand out from the white page. And it echoes the other purple elements on the page."

The unusual part of the table is the header. Like the purple line below The Davis Group logo, the title bar automatically expands and contracts to fit the size of the browser window. Better yet, the stretching is isolated to the black portion of the title bar; the title itself never changes. Davis accomplishes this feat by using two separate GIF files. One contains the Current Highlights title, the other is a random-sized chunk of black that doesn't even match the height of the title (6.16). Then, as is so frequently the case in this chapter, Davis binds the two GIFs together in a table.

"I set the `width` of the table to 100 percent and I set the `height` to 17 pixels (6.17). The next part is just a variation on the purple line trick. The table contains just one row with two columns. I put the Current Highlights graphic in the first column and the black bar in the second. I set the first column to a fixed `width` of 254 pixels, which is the width of the Current Highlights graphic. Then I set the second column to `width=100%`. Again, that's 100 percent of what's left over after the 254 pixels of the first column. Finally, I enter `align=right`, which makes the black spacer stretch out and fill all the remaining room on the page. And though I don't have it here, if I want the graphic to stretch in Netscape 4, I'd also have to add `background="gifs/blacknav_spacer.gif"` right before the first `<TR>` tag."

6.15

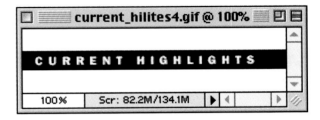

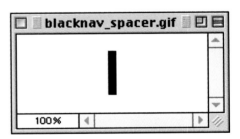

6.16

```
<TABLE width=100% cellpadding=0
  cellspacing=0 border=0
  bgcolor="#000000" height=17>
<TR>
  <TD valign=top align=left
    width=254 height=17>
    <IMG SRC="gifs/current_hilites4.gif"
      width="254" height="17"
      hspace="0" vspace="0"> <BR>
  </TD>

  <TD width=100% height=17
    valign=top align=right>
    <IMG SRC="gifs/blacknav_spacer.gif"
      width="100%" height="17" hspace="0"
      vspace="0" align=right> <BR>
  </TD>
</TR></TABLE>
```

6.17

The black bar stretches and the title does not. And because the black bar is a solid color, it can scale to any size without the slightest trace of stretch marks. This is the kind of basic effect that works all the better because it doesn't attract attention to itself. Visitors to *www.groupdavis.com* haven't the slightest idea that they're looking at a complex network of no fewer than a half dozen tables. All they know is that this is an elegant page design that looks just as sleek and orderly on one screen as it does on the next.

CONSTRUCTING COMPLEX PAGE DESIGNS

Davis also designs and maintains the Web site for Thunder Lizard Productions (*www.thunderlizard. com*), an organization that conducts a series of top-flight conferences on subjects near and dear to the hearts of designers, including Web design, QuarkXPress, and Photoshop. (This same company has generously cooperated in the production of this book—as well as another in this series that will go unnamed (6.18)—a fact which I'm sure you recognize to be a matter of the purest coincidence.)

By comparison to The Davis Group's page, the home page for the Thunder Lizard site is packed to the gills (6.19). Every conference has to be available from page one, a terrific design challenge whether you're working in print or on the Web. But with the help of tables, Davis manages to organize the wealth of information into tidy visual containers that are always at least partially visible regardless of the size of the browser window (6.20).

"Looking at the home page, we have an expanding width, as always. But we also have a strip of red buttons along the left side of the screen, a green strip of

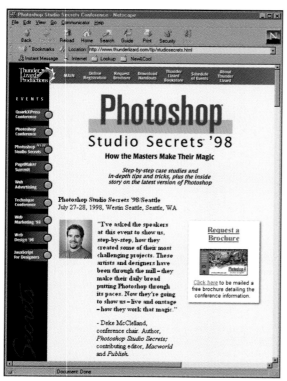

6.18

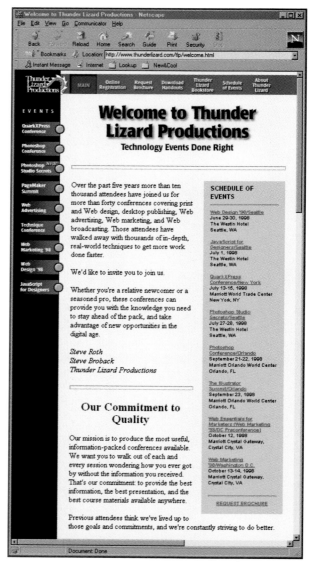

6.19

buttons along the top, and a floating gray Schedule of Events. That's a lot of stuff to try and stick in a single massive table. So this time, I work incrementally, one group of elements at a time."

TABLE 1: THE GREEN BUTTONS

Davis begins by coding a table to hold just the top strip of green buttons. But as he works, he has to bear in mind how the green buttons at top will align with the red buttons along the side. "The first two columns hold an invisible spacer GIF and the Thunder Lizard logo (6.21). The spacer GIF is set to a `width` of 10 pixels, the logo is set to `width=96`. The red buttons below the logo are also 96 pixels wide, but the dinosaur tail sticks out an extra 10 pixels beyond the buttons, so I need the 10-pixel spacer to make everything line up right.

"After that, I code each of the green buttons across the top of the screen using a separate `<TD>` tag. The Main button gets a `width` of 57 pixels, the Online

Registration button is `width=66`, all the way along until About Thunder Lizard, which is `width=64` (6.22).

"Now for the last column, which holds a gradient that fades out to the right. So far, I've coded everything in pixels. But I want this gradient to stretch to

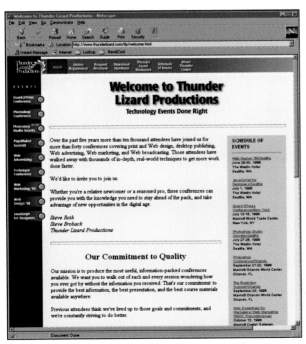

6.20

```
<TABLE width=100% border=0
 cellspacing=0 cellpadding=0>
<TR>
   <TD width=10>
      <IMG SRC="gifs/spacer.gif"
      width="10" height="15" hspace="0"
      vspace="0" border="0">
   </TD>

   <TD width=96 valign=top>
      <A HREF="menu.html">
      <IMG SRC="gifs/logo_tlp2.gif"
      width=96 height=45 hspace=0
      vspace=0 border=0></A>
   </TD>
```

6.21

```
<TD width=57 valign=top>
   <A HREF="menu.html">
   <IMG SRC="gifs/anew_main_off.gif"
   width=57 height=43 hspace=0
   vspace=0 border=0></A>
</TD>

<TD width=66 valign=top>
   <A href="register.html">
   <IMG SRC="gifs/anew_onlinereg_off.gif"
   width=66 height=43 hspace=0
   vspace=0 border=0></A>
</TD>

                    *

                 *

              *

<TD width=64 valign=top>
   <A href="about_tlp.html">
   <IMG SRC="gifs/anew_abouttlp_off.gif"
   width=64 height=43 hspace=0
   vspace=0 border=0></A>
</TD>
```

MAIN

Online Registration

About Thunder Lizard

6.22

```
<TD width=100% valign=top align=left>
  <TABLE width=100% cellpadding=0
  cellspacing=0 border=0>
  <TR>
    <TD width=100% valign=top align=left>
      <IMG SRC="gifs/finishband.gif"
      width=100% height=43 hspace=0
      vspace=0 border=0 align=right>
    </TD>
  </TR></TABLE>
</TD>

<TD width=15 valign=top align=left>
  <IMG SRC="gifs/spacer.gif"
  width="15" height="15" hspace="0"
  vspace="0" border="0">
</TD>
</TR></TABLE>
```

6.23

fit the window. So I set the last column to `width=100%`. Even though there are nine columns before it with specific pixel widths, I still set this last one to 100 percent.

"To keep the gradient aligned with the buttons, I set the column to `align=left`. But as you may remember, the graphic will stretch only if `align=right`. So I put a new table inside the column, put the gradient inside that table, and add `align=right` at the end (6.23). That's all it takes—now the gradient will stretch across the page."

TABLE 2: THE RED BUTTONS AND TEXT

"My next table holds all the rest of the stuff. The table is divided into four columns (6.24). The first column contains the red side buttons, the next column contains a 15-pixel spacer, the third column contains all the body copy, as well as the Schedule of Events, and the fourth contains another 15-pixel spacer."

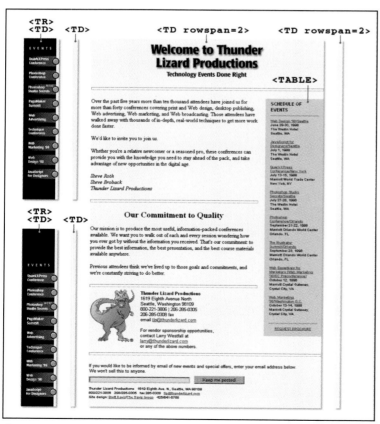

6.24

But Davis has another special concern that complicates the table. "The page is so long that you have to scroll to get to the bottom of it. So to avoid having to scroll up and down to get to the buttons, I decided to repeat the buttons at the bottom of the page. This means adding another row to the table just to house the second set of buttons."

Meanwhile, Davis needed the body text and Schedule of Events sidebar to flow all the way down the page, beyond the point at which the second row of buttons begins. The solution is rowspan, which tells the browser to continue a column across a specified number of rows. "I add rowspan=2 to the third and fourth columns so that they both stretch all way to the bottom of the page (6.24). I also add valign=bottom to the <TD> tag for the second row of buttons. That way they align to the bottom of the screen, which turns out to be wherever the body copy ends. The background pattern is a 10-pixel-tall, 1,200-pixel-wide image that includes 95 pixels of black on the left side of it. So the black area fills in the region between the top and bottom buttons. The result is a vertical stretching effect, with the black area from the background pattern growing and shrinking according to the length of the page. You can only do that with rowspan — I couldn't have gotten the columns to align any other way."

"Otherwise, the code for the red buttons is really simple. I list each of the nine buttons inside the column, divided with a <BR> so one button is flush up against the next. Because I created each button to be the exact same size — 96 pixels wide — they line up just right."

THE NESTED, FLOATING TABLES OF THE GRAY SIDEBAR

"The only other item of interest on this page is the Schedule of Events sidebar, which is actually a floating table inside the third column — the same column that contains the body text. At the top of this column, I center the Welcome to Thunder Lizard Productions headline, which is a GIF graphic. Then I enter <HR size=7> for a horizontal rule (6.25).

"Next, I script the sidebar. The code for the sidebar follows the headline, so it will appear below the headline in the browser. That much makes sense. But here's the weird part: even though the sidebar appears to the right of the copy, I have to put it *before* the copy in the HTML file. Then whatever text comes after the table will wrap around to the left of it."

```
<TD width=100% valign=top rowspan=2>
   <CENTER>
   <IMG SRC="gifs/headline_main2.gif"
   width="367" height="106" hspace="0"
   vspace="17" border="0">
   </CENTER>

   <A name="schedule">
   <HR SIZE="7">
    <BR>
```

Welcome to Thunder Lizard Productions
Technology Events Done Right

6.25

```
<TABLE cellpadding=0 cellspacing=0 border=0
width=190 align=right>
<TR>
    <TD width=15 valign=top align=left >
       <BR>
    </TD>

    <TD width=170 valign=top align=left>
        <TABLE cellpadding=3 cellspacing=0
        border=0 width=170 align=right
        bgcolor="#C0C0C0">
        <TR>
            <TD valign=top align=left width=5>
             <BR>
            </TD>

            <TD valign=top align=left>
            <IMG SRC="gifs/spacer.gif"
              width="4" height="4"
              hspace="0" vspace="0"><BR>
            <FONT size=-1 face="helvetica">
            <B>SCHEDULE OF EVENTS</B></FONT>
            <HR>
            <FONT size=-2 face="helvetica">
            <B><A href="webdesign.html">
                Web Design '98/Seattle
                </A></B><BR>
                June 29-30, 1998<BR>
                The Westin Hotel<BR>
                Seattle, WA<BR>
                 <BR>
                    *
                    *
                    *
            </TD>

            <TD valign=top align=left width=5>
             <BR>
            </TD>
        </TR></TABLE>
    <TD width:h=5 valign=top align=left>
      <BR>
    </TD>
</TR></TABLE>
```

SCHEDULE OF EVENTS

Web Design '98
June 29-30, 1998
The Westin Hotel
Seattle, WA

JavaScript for
Designers/Seattle
July 1, 1998
The Westin Hotel
Seattle, WA

QuarkXPress
Conference
July 13-15, 1998
Marriott World Trade
New York, NY

Photoshop Studio
Secrets/Seattle
July 27-28, 1998
The Westin Hotel
Seattle, WA

Photoshop
Conference/Orlando
Sept. 21-22, 1998
Marriott Orlando
Orlando, FL

The Illustrator
Summit/Orlando
September 23, 1998
Marriott Orlando
Orlando, FL

6.26

The sidebar is actually two tables, one embedded inside the other. "I start with a fixed-width table of 190 pixels (6.26), with `align=right` so it floats along the right side of the page. This first table is actually a container for the sidebar; it determines the amount of standoff between the sidebar and the body copy. That's why the first column and the last one just contain non-breaking spaces (`     `). They're buffers between the sidebar and the body copy to keep the text legible.

"The table nested in the second column (green in 6.26) is the actual sidebar. It has three columns. The outer two columns are margins, the middle column contains the text.

"And that's it. After I closed the sidebar tables, I entered the body copy. The text is aligned left by default, so I don't have to give it any special instructions. It automatically fills the area to the left of the floating table. When the sidebar ends, the text fills the area beneath it. It's like a wraparound graphic, all done with `<TABLE>` tags."

THINKING IN TABLES

"As a designer, I don't relish the idea of coding tables for hours or days in a row. The real excitement for me is sketching the site in Photoshop. But if I want to get my sketch to work in a browser, I have to use tables. The great thing about them is that they always work, regardless of what kind of screen or browser the page is viewed in.

"If you understand how I put together The Davis Group and Thunder Lizard sites, you know everything I'm doing with tables. It's really just a matter of being able to see a page and deconstruct it with `<TR>`, `<TD>`, and a few nested tables. Tables are also a great way to divide buttons inside a graphic. Where one designer might use an image map, I use a table instead."

The graphic treatment Davis did for *www. premedical.com* is a good example. The home page features a series of buttons built into a title graphic with a photo montage (6.27). Davis could have saved the entire graphic as a single GIF file and then painstakingly scripted image map coordinates around each of the buttons in HTML. But instead, he divided the site title, montage, and each of the seven

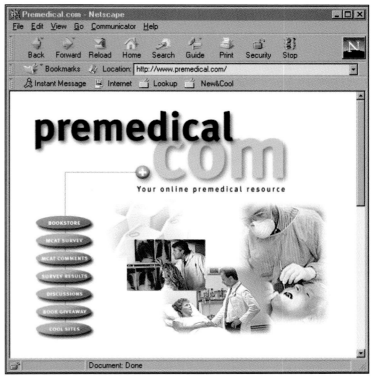

6.27

buttons into separate GIFs. Then he constructed a two-level table with the title in the first row, the buttons assembled into a single-column table nested in the second row, and the montage in a second column in the second row (6.28).

"I know designers who say HTML doesn't give you precise enough layout options. I agree with them to an extent, but I also think a lot of them are missing the potential of tables. Here's a tool that provides incredible control, and it's been around since the very beginning of the Web. What other HTML tag lets you build page designs, piece together image maps, or simply pour text into columns? It's amazing how much you can do with this one tool. If there's a more versatile tag than <TABLE>, I'd like to know about it."

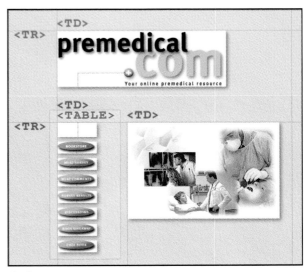

6.28

NEIL ROBERTSON
Senior New Media Designer

If Martha Stewart was a cyber-hip, way-cool, super multimedia designer guy, she'd be Neil. Seriously designer can cook. He'll fillet a Web site, sauté a CD-ROM, steam some interface, and bake a big ol' int known to make holiday wreath disks and fresh-from-the-garde Martha, this guy has a following circuit educating the droves ab and the secrets of keeping your course.

Take a trip with Neil to Disney

ABOUT PBDH
WHO'S THAT CAT?
E-MAIL
HOME

ABOUT PBDH
WHO'S THAT CAT?
E-MAIL
HOME

ABOUT PBDH
WHO'S THAT CAT?
E-MAIL
HOME

NEWS
PORTFOLIO
PEOPLE
ABOUT PBDH
WHO'S THAT CAT?
E-MAIL
HOME

Web Design '97 Speaker

Phinney/Bischoff Design House - Netscape

File Edit View Go Communicator Help

Back Forward Reload Home Search Guide Print Security Stop

Bookmarks Location: http://www.pbdh.com/

Instant Message Internet Lookup New&Cool

PHINNEY/BISCHOFF DESIGN HOUSE
SCRATCHINGPOST

NEWS
PEOPLE
PORTFOLIO
ABOUT PBDH
WHO'S THAT CAT?
E-MAIL

PBDH HOSTS
AIGA SEMINARS...

Copyright © 1997 Phinney/Bischoff Design House - 614 Boylston Ave. E., Seattle, Washington 98102, USA
(206) 322-3484 - Fax (206) 322-3590

Meet Ruby!

PBDH!
NEWS
PORTFOLIO
PEOPLE
ABOUT PBDH
WHO'S THAT CAT?
E-MAIL
HOME
Document: Done

NEWS
PORTFOLIO
PEOPLE
ABOUT PBDH
WHO'S THAT CAT?
E-MAIL
HOME
The latest news from PBDH

NEWS
PORTFOLIO
PEOPLE
ABOUT PBDH
WHO'S THAT CAT?
E-MAIL
HOME
Browse though our work

NEWS
PORTFOLIO
PEOPLE
ABOUT PBDH
WHO'S THAT CAT?
E-MAIL
HOME
Meet the people here at PBDH

CHAPTER 7
CREATING ROLLOVERS WITH JAVASCRIPT

H TML is the one necessary evil on the Web. Like it or not, you can't make a Web site without it. As a result, hundreds of thousands of designers have had to resort to entering and editing computer code, a task they never in a million years wanted to perform.

But while HTML is an inescapable part of the online landscape, every other online language is optional. And as a result, these languages are widely regarded as tools for engineers, programmers, and other propeller heads.

Take JavaScript, for example. Just mention the word and a typical artist will make the sign of the cross and reach for the garlic. In many minds, JavaScript is part of the same crowd as CGI, Active X, Perl, and a whole host of other arcane Internet terms. No doubt you've heard of these things, but you haven't the vaguest idea why you'd ever want to integrate them into your Web site. And even if you knew a reason, you're quite certain you'd never be able to pull it off.

If that describes your opinion of JavaScript, then Neil Robertson has news for you. A relatively recent convert to the Web, Robertson regards many elements of JavaScript as every bit as essential to online design as HTML. "Just as HTML lets you get your pages up on the Web, JavaScript lets you make your pages dynamic. JavaScript is what distinguishes Web pages from traditional printed documents — it makes your site interactive."

JavaScript is what distinguishes Web pages from traditional printed documents — it makes your site interactive.

NEIL ROBERTSON

NEIL WELCOMES YOU TO ROLLOVERS

Let's start at the beginning. What exactly is JavaScript? "Well, for starters, JavaScript has absolutely nothing to do with the Web language Java. It's purely a licensing ploy from Netscape. Java was getting really hot and some guys at Netscape thought, 'Oh, we've got this little thing called LiveScript that we're going to incorporate into our browser. Let's license the name Java from Sun and call it JavaScript and that way we'll ride Java's coattails.'

"So, okay, the licensing thing is dumb, but JavaScript is actually great. It's a way to make online pages more intelligent and dynamic and interactive without having to rely on a lot of server-based CGIs and stuff. For example, let's say you have a form and

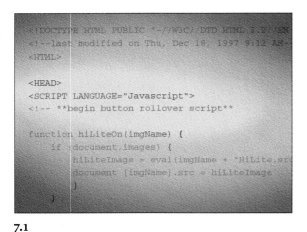

7.1

you want the user to be able to type in his e-mail address. Before, you would have to make a CGI script to confirm the e-mail address, and the CGI would send back a separate page saying, 'No, that's not an e-mail address,' or, 'Swell, got it, thank you for answering.' With JavaScript, you can create an intelligent form that prequalifies the address and other data before anything gets sent to the server. And best of all, you don't have to create a separate document. You just enter the commands directly into your HTML file. You start the code with a single line `<SCRIPT LANGUAGE="JavaScript">` and you're set to go (7.1)."

Sounds great. But let's say you don't know squat about servers or forms or any of that techie stuff. What can a designer do with JavaScript? "One of the coolest functions of JavaScript started with Netscape 3.0. Version 1.1 of JavaScript was the first to let you swap out one image with another according to the user's mouse actions. So if the user clicks on a button or moves the cursor over a link, you can have that image change. This is called a JavaScript *rollover*. It's actually not excessively hard to do, and you don't need to worry about using a plug-in or a Java applet or any of that weird stuff.

"I like to use rollovers because they make the page more responsive. It gives people a good clue as to what's clickable. I think a lot of Web pages err on the side of making their buttons too obscure. Making a 3-D button is good, but if the button actually highlights, it

ARTIST:
Neil Robertson

ORGANIZATION:
Phinney/Bischoff Design House
614 Boylston Avenue E.
Seattle, WA 98102
206/322-3484
www.pbdh.com
neilr@pbdh.com

SYSTEM:
Power Mac 8500/180
Mac OS 8
2GB storage/96MB RAM

CONNECTIVITY:
ISDN

PERIPHERALS:
Sony 17-inch monitor, Wacom ArtPad II, UMAX S12 scanner, and Fuji DS-7 digital camera

PRIMARY APPLICATIONS:
Symantec Visual Page, BB Edit, Adobe Photoshop, Extensis PhotoTools, Macromedia FreeHand, KPT Vector Effects, and Microsoft Personal Web Server

calls attention to itself and invites the user to interact with it (7.2). The button is saying, 'Hi, I'm an active element. Click me!'

"You can also preview links to lead the user through your site. When the mouse moves over the link, you can supply information about that link in the status bar (7.3). Instead of simply listing the URL for the page where the link is going to go, which is the way it works by default, you can tell the user, 'Check out the latest news from So-&-So Design,' or whatever. You can spell out the destination in plain English with JavaScript."

Naturally, like any relatively recent advancement, rollovers are not compatible with all browsers. "What I'm doing with rollovers is applicable to Netscape 3.0 and 4.0, as well as Internet Explorer 4.0. Earlier browsers are spotty. Internet Explorer 3.2 for Windows doesn't support rollovers, but Internet Explorer 3.1 for the Mac (which came out later) does. The good news is that JavaScript is officially standardized and all the new browsers support rollovers and all the rest."

MOUSE OVER AND OUT

A basic example of rollovers at work is Robertson's home page for Teledesic, a company involved in laying the groundwork for high-bandwidth, satellite-based Internet access (7.4). Most of the page is static, run-of-the-mill HTML. But stretching along the bottom is

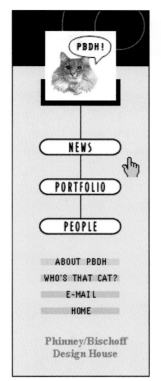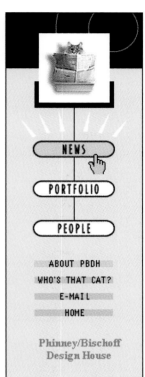

7.2

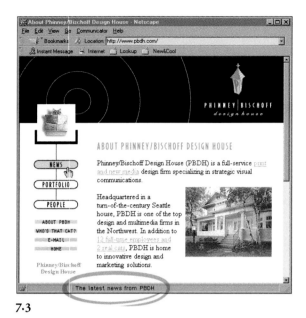

7.3

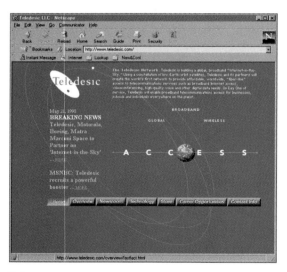

7.4

a row of interactive buttons, each of which highlights — from dull blue to bright green — when you hover your cursor over it (7.5). The button changes back to blue when the cursor moves away.

Because this page is so simple, it serves as an excellent introduction to both rollovers specifically and JavaScript in general. So I asked Robertson to bare all, starting with the basic structure of the page and working up to the way he makes the buttons highlight.

GIVING JAVASCRIPT THE GAS

"I start with the `<SCRIPT LANGUAGE>` tag. Everything after that is identified by the browser as JavaScript code. Immediately after that line, there's an HTML comment `<!--` (7.6). This tag hides all the JavaScript code from a browser that doesn't understand JavaScript at all. If I didn't have that comment tag in there, all that script would be displayed as text on the page in an old browser.

"The bit after the comment tag `-- **begin button rollover script** --` doesn't really matter; that's just a note to me so I remember what I'm doing. But the comment tag `<!--` is important — HTML thinks everything after the tag is a comment; JavaScript just ignores it and interprets the code as always.

"At the end of the JavaScript code, I have to close the HTML comment tag with the standard `-->`. Now, JavaScript ignores the opening HTML comment tag, but it gets confused by this closing tag. So I have to add JavaScript's comment tag `//` before the HTML closer. As a result, I end up with `//-->` (7.7)."

PRELOADING THE IMAGES

"Before you script your rollovers, you want to preload all the images for the buttons so that they're all in cache, ready to go, when requested by the browser. If the images aren't preloaded, the user would have to wait for a new image to download every time the cursor moves over a button. And by the time the image finally downloads, the user may have moved the cursor elsewhere. There would be a string of lags and it would get pretty ugly.

"With JavaScript, you can preload any graphic as an image object. Do you see `overviewOn = new Image` (7.8)? That creates a new image object called `overviewOn`, which represents the highlighted Overview button. I don't have to call it `overviewOn`, of course — I'm making up a variable, so I can call it anything I like. The next line, `overviewOn.src`, puts the actual GIF button in the image object. So now whenever I ask for `overviewOn`, I get that specific GIF file."

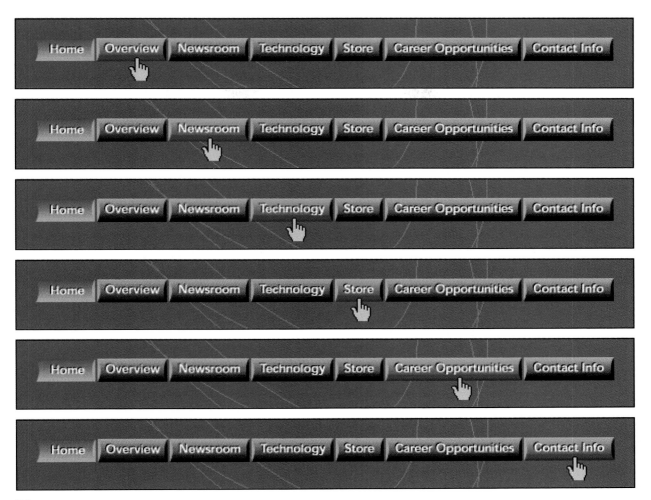

7.5

```
<HEAD>
<SCRIPT LANGUAGE="Javascript">
<!-- **begin button rollover script**

function hiLiteOn(imgName)
    if (document.images)
        hiLiteImage = eval(imgName + "On.src")
```

7.6

```
    contactOff = new Image()
    contactOff.src = "gifs/2contact.gif"


    }

//-->
</SCRIPT>
```

7.7

```
if(document.images)

    overviewOn = new Image()
    overviewOn.src = "gifs/2overOn2.gif"
    overviewOff = new Image()
    overviewOff.src = "gifs/2over.gif"

    newsroomOn = new Image()
    newsroomOn.src = "gifs/2newsOn2.gif"
    newsroomOff = new Image()
    newsroomOff.src = "gifs/2news.gif"
```

7.8

Memorizing which browsers support JavaScript and which specific versions of JavaScript they support is a nearly impossible task. Luckily, you don't have to. "I set up my code so it automatically sorts out whether the browser can handle rollovers or not. And the line of code that's doing this is `if (document.images)` (7.9). This tests if the browser can handle image objects, in which case it can do the rollovers. If it can't, then `if (document.images)` returns a 'no,' and the browser skips the function."

```
function hiLiteOn(imgName) {
    if (document.images) {
        hiLiteImage = eval(imgName + "On.src")
        document [imgName].src = hiLiteImage
    }
}

function hiLiteOff(imgName) {
    if (document.images) {
        originalImage = eval(imgName + "Off.src")
        document [imgName].src = originalImage
    }
}

if(document.images) {
    overviewOn = new Image()
    overviewOn.src = "gifs/2overOn2.gif"
    overviewOff = new Image()
    overviewOff.src = "gifs/2over.gif"
```

7.9

"(If you want, you can insert an `else` script that points people to a different page that says something like, 'To see all the functionality of this page, download a new version of the browser.' But I'd rather just make it seamless. When I'm surfing the Web, I don't want to have to download new browsers and plug-ins. I feel like, show me the page or shut up.)"

"You have to run this test each time you define a new function and when you preload the images. That way, you aren't wasting time preloading when the browser's not going to see the images anyway. With `if (document.images)`, nobody will notice that they're missing anything if they use a browser that doesn't support rollovers."

"Next comes `overviewOff`, which is the blue Overview button as it looks when it's not highlighted. Here I repeat the process—I make a new image object and put a GIF image inside it.

"Each time I create a new image object, I'm actually accomplishing two things. I'm defining my variables, so I can call them up later in my script. And I'm telling the browser to store the image in cache. The caching occurs automatically whenever I define a new image object."

CREATING THE ROLLOVERS

After you assign the image objects and cache all the buttons, it's time to script the rollovers. "The row of buttons on the Teledesic page are essentially just a series of `<A HREF>` and `<IMG SRC>` tags. The first image is the Home button, so it doesn't even have an `<A HREF>` link. It's a dead button that's there to show that we're already on the home page (7.10).

"So far, this is all the same kind of stuff you'd do if there weren't any rollovers. The only difference is that I've added the JavaScript commands `onmouseover` and `onmouseout`. These are called *event handlers*. JavaScript is driven by events, whether it's a timed event or an action initiated by the user. If the user moves the cursor over a button, that gets picked up by `onmouseover`. When the cursor moves away from the button, that gets picked up by `onmouseout`. Both of these commands are associated with links, so they have to be inside an `<A HREF>` tag."

```
<CENTER><PRE>
<IMG SRC="gifs/2dhome2.gif"            Home
   width="58" height="23"
   align="bottom" alt="home"
   border="0" name="home">

<A HREF="../finalSite/overview.html"
   onmouseover="hiLiteOn('overview')"
   onmouseout="hiLiteOff('overview')">
   <IMG SRC="gifs/2over.gif"           Overview
      width="70" height="23"
      align="bottom" alt="overview"
      border="0" name="overview"></A>
```

7.10

"To let the browser know what to do when the cursor moves over an image, I say `onmouseover=
"hiLiteOn('overview')"`. This is where it gets kind of tricky: `hiLiteOn` isn't a JavaScript command — it's a function that I made up at the beginning of the script in the initial JavaScript section. And `hiLiteOn('overview')` sends `overview` to the function `hiLiteOn`, then the browser looks back to my earlier definition to figure out what it needs to do (7.11).

"Let's go back to the top. At the outset of my script, I have a `function` command. This lets me define my own function, in this case `hiLiteOn`. I also introduce a variable `imgName` which gets replaced by whatever I put in parentheses. So when I call `hiLiteOn('overview')`, the browser places `overview` into the variable `imgName`. Wherever you see `imgName` in this definition, the browser is thinking `overview`.

"The next line in the definition — `if (document.images)` — just checks to see if the browser understands the image object. If it does, it goes to the line after that. Starting on the right-hand side, I have `(imgName + "On.src")`. In this case, the browser adds `On.src` to `overview` and gets `overviewOn.src`. This is that same image object that I discussed earlier, the one that contains the green Overview button (7.8). So the browser puts `overviewOn.src` — the green button — into `hiLiteImage`, which is the variable on the left."

At this point, Robertson has called up the green button. But he still needs to tell the browser to replace the "off" blue button with the "on" green one. And this is exactly what the line `document
[imgName].src = hiLiteImage` does. "With JavaScript, every object gets an address. `document` is the address of the document that's open in the current window — in this case, the Teledesic page. The `<IMG SRC>` tag for the Overview button includes the line `name="overview"` (7.10), which tells the browser that the name of the button is `overview`. So the address of the button is `document overview.src`. The line `document [imgName] .src = hiLiteImage` just tells the browser to replace the source of the object called `document overview.src` with `hiLiteImage`, which is the green Overview button."

```
<A HREF="../finalSite/overview.html"
  onmouseover="hiLiteOn('overview')"
  onmouseout="hiLiteOff('overview')">
  <IMG SRC="gifs/2over.gif"
  width="70" height="23"
  align="bottom" alt="overview"
  border="0" name="overview"></A>

function hiLiteOn(imgName) {
  if (document.images) {
    hiLiteImage = eval(imgName + "On.src")
    document [imgName].src = hiLiteImage
    }
  }

function hiLiteOff(imgName) {
  if (document.images) {
    originalImage = eval(imgName + "Off.src")
    document [imgName].src = originalImage
    }
  }
```

7.11

The `onmouseout` line does the opposite, switching out the green button for the blue one when the cursor moves away from the button. This command relies on another function defined by Robertson, this time called `hiLiteOff` (7.12). "As you can see, `hiLiteOff` is more or less identical to `hiLiteOn`. The only difference is that it puts `overviewOff.src` — the blue button — into a variable called `originalImage`. But the basic workings are the same."

THE POWER OF FUNCTIONS

Could Robertson have pulled off his rollovers without defining the custom functions at the beginning of his script? "Well, yes and no. You can put some of that function code directly inside the `<A HREF>` tag, but not all of it. For instance, it's a pain in the neck to run an `if` statement inside an `<A HREF>`, so it would have been harder for me to test browser compatibility.

"But even if I could, I wouldn't have done it. It would have involved a lot more work. What makes the functions useful is that they work regardless of how many images you have highlighting on the page. For each highlight, I can call up a single function instead of entering several lines of code again and again and again. If I want to add another highlighted button, I just add the image names to the preload list, and then call the functions inside the <A HREF> tag."

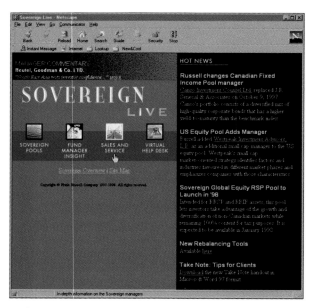

```
<A HREF="../finalSite/overview.html"
    onmouseover="hiLiteOn('overview')"
    onmouseout="hiLiteOff('overview')">
    <IMG SRC="gifs/2over.gif"
    width="70" height="23"
    align="bottom" alt="overview"
    border="0" name="overview"></A>

function hiLiteOn(imgName) {
    if (document.images) {
        hiLiteImage = eval(imgName + "On.src")
        document [imgName].src = hiLiteImage
    }
}

function hiLiteOff(imgName) {
    if (document.images) {
        originalImage = eval(imgName + "Off.src")
        document [imgName].src = originalImage
    }
}
```

7.12

7.13

ROLLING IMAGE MAPS

Robertson's next project is a private site he created for Frank Russell Company, an investment consulting firm. The opening page to the site, dubbed Sovereign Live, features an animated GIF title and a group of four rollover buttons (7.13). The border of each rollover button highlights when you move your mouse over it.

But for a more interesting rollover element, you have to surf to the Sales and Service page (7.14). This page features a large image map boasting five rollover buttons (7.15). "The tricky part when working with an image map is that you have to swap out the entire image. You can't snip out little parts of the image, you have to load the whole thing. That means I have to create a different image for each of the highlighted buttons—five in all—plus a sixth that shows all buttons off."

That's a lot of data. Is any browser smart enough to know which pixels it has cached so it can load only the new ones? "Nope, it has to load each and every pixel. That's why it's a good idea to keep your graphics as small as possible. In the case of the Sovereign Live graphic, I was careful to fill the buttons with flat colors. So while the image map takes up a lot of space on the page, each variation is only about 8K on disk."

THE ROLLOVER FUNCTIONS

"I start my HTML code with a <SCRIPT> tag just as before. Then come the functions, hiLiteOn and hiLiteOff, similar to before (7.16). The main difference is that in the hiLiteOn definition, I use a new variable which I call areaName. The way I use this variable tells the browser to evaluate the specific area of the image map that the user has moved the cursor over and then display the proper graphic. Also, I add ".src" to the end of the image object name instead of "On.src".

"Then in the function hiLiteOff, I switch everything back to the same image. I don't have to build the name, I don't have to send a parameter—whenever the user moves the cursor outside of a hot spot, the image changes to Base.src, which is the graphic where no button is highlighted."

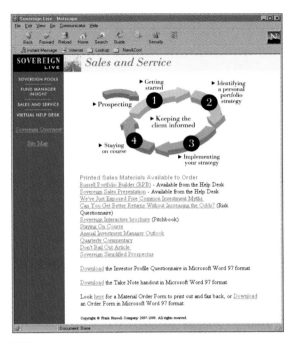

7.14

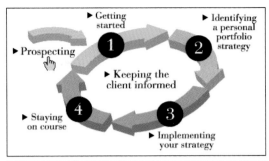

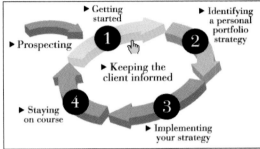

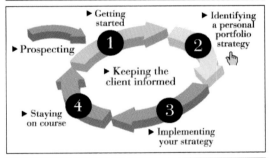

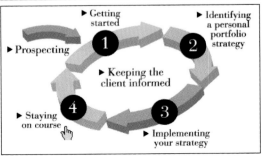

7.15

```
<HTML>

<HEAD>
<SCRIPT LANGUAGE="Javascript">
<!-- **begin button rollover script**

function hiLiteOn(areaName) {
   if (document.images) {
      hiLiteImage = eval(areaName + ".src");
      document.arrows.src=hiLiteImage
      }
   }

function hiLiteOff() {
   if (document.images) {
      document.arrows.src=Base.src
      }
   }
```

7.16

Next, Robertson defines and preloads his image objects (7.17). "You can see Base.src, which points to the graphic with all buttons off. Then it's one.src, two.src, and so on for each of the five highlighted buttons. The browser loads all six GIF files into RAM so they're ready to go."

```
if(document.images) {

    Base = new Image(407,241);
    Base.src = "serviceGifs/arrowsBase.gif"

    one = new Image(407,241);
    one.src = "serviceGifs/arrows1.gif"

    two = new Image(407,241);
    two.src = "serviceGifs/arrows2.gif"

    three = new Image(407,241);
    three.src = "serviceGifs/arrows3.gif"

    four = new Image(407,241);
    four.src = "serviceGifs/arrows4.gif"

    five = new Image(407,241);
    five.src = "serviceGifs/arrows5.gif"

    }

//-->
</SCRIPT>
```

7.17

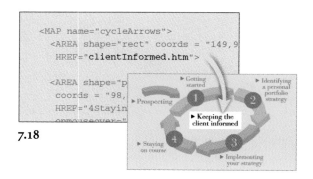

7.18

SCRIPTING THE IMAGE MAP

"The image map starts off with the standard HTML `<MAP>` tag (7.18). The first button—the one that starts out `<AREA shape="rect">`—surrounds the central area of the graphic that reads 'Keeping the client informed.' This is the only button that's not a rollover.

"The other buttons start out `<AREA shape="polygon">`, then I name each area `five`, `four`, `three`, `two`, `one`. These names don't go with the numbers in the graphic, they're just the names I assigned the image objects that contain the highlighted buttons (7.19).

"At the end of each of button, there's an `onmouseover` and an `onmouseout` command. Here's where I call up the `hiLiteOn` and `hiLiteOff` functions. Notice that I have to put a name in the `hiLiteOn` function so it loads the right image object. But I don't need a name for `hiLiteOff`, because there's just the one `Base.src` image."

ADVANCED ROLLOVERS

Like many electronic design firms, Robertson's employer—Phinney/Bischoff Design House—shows off its best scripting techniques at its own Web site (*www.pbdh.com*, 7.20). The site features scads of highlighting buttons, (7.21) as well as a couple of extra ingredients.

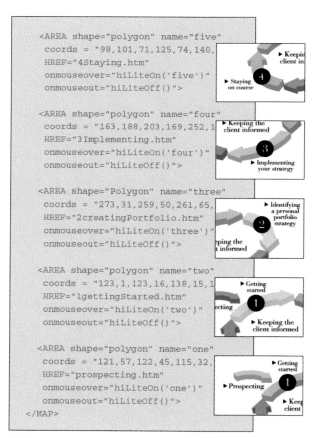

7.19

7.20

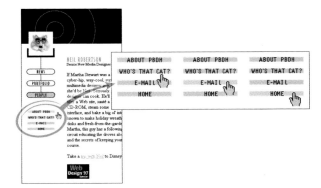

7.21

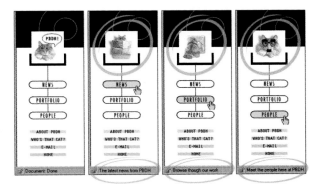

7.22

"When you move your cursor over one of the three main buttons—News, Portfolio, or People—the browser swaps out two images at the same time. One image is the button itself, which changes from white to yellow. The other is an icon that has no connection to the buttons—namely, that picture of the cat (7.22). The changing cat doesn't really serve any purpose, but it's fun and it adds a little extra visual interest to the page."

The browser also displays a special message in the status bar at the bottom of the window. For example, when you hover the cursor over the Portfolio button, the status bar reads, "Browse through our work." Robertson pulls off this little trick with JavaScript as well.

THE DOUBLE-SWAP FUNCTION

"At the outset of the script are the same `hiLiteOn` and `hiLiteOff`—no big deal. After that, there's a new function called `switchIcon` (7.23). It's basically similar to the others, but notice that the `document` line is a little different. In the case of the

```
<HTML>

<HEAD>
<SCRIPT LANGUAGE="Javascript">
<!-- **begin button rollover script**

function hiLiteOn(imgName) {
  if (document.images) {
    hiLiteImage=eval(imgName+"HiLite.src")
    document [imgName].src=hiLiteImage
    }
  }

function hiLiteOff(imgName) {
  if (document.images) {
    originalImage=eval(imgName+"White.src")
    document [imgName].src=originalImage
    }
  }

function switchIcon(imgName) {
  if (document.images) {
    iconImage=eval(imgName + "Icon.src")
    document.Icon.src = iconImage
    }
  }
```

7.23

buttons, the document line includes an `[imgName]` parameter because I can't be sure exactly which button on the page will change out. It could be the first one, it could be the third one. But in the case of `switchIcon`, I'm always swapping out the cat icon. So instead of inventing a special parameter, I refer to it by the fixed address `document.Icon.src`, which refers to the image called `Icon` on the page."

And refresh our memory: how does the browser know that `Icon` is the cat? "Because later in the HTML file, when I first place the cat icon on the page, I say `name="Icon"` (7.24). This tells JavaScript that this image is called `Icon` so it can replace it using the `switchIcon` function."

```
<TABLE
  border="0" cellpadding="0"
  cellspacing="0" width="575">
    <TR>
      <TD width="21"
      rowspan="2"> </TD>
      <TD width="100" valign="top"
      rowspan="2">
        <P><IMG SRC="images/pbdhicon.gif"
           width="96" height="229"
           align="bottom" border="0"
           name="Icon"><BR>
```

7.24

```
<A HREF="news.htm"
   onmouseover="hiLiteOn('News');
     switchIcon('News');
     window.status= 'The latest news
     from PBDH'; return true"

   onmouseout="hiLiteOff('News');
     switchIcon('PBDH');
     window.status = ' ';
     return true">

<IMG SRC="images/newswite.gif"
  width="96" height="20"
  align="bottom" alt="news"
  border="0" name="News"></A><BR>
```

7.25

THE DOUBLE-IMAGE SWAP

You may have noticed that the cat icon is part of a table (7.24). Directly following the cat, in that same column, is the News button. "Because it's a link, I script the news button using an `<A HREF>` tag, which includes our old friends `onmouseover` and `onmouseout` (7.25). The `onmouseover` command calls `hiLiteOn`, just like always. I also call the `switchIcon` function, which replaces the cat with the News icon, which shows the cat reading a newspaper in a litter box.

"In that same `onmouseover`, I'm also changing the message in the status bar. JavaScript thinks of the status bar as the `status` object of the window, so the script is `window.status= 'The latest news from PBDH'`. Notice that the text is surrounded by single quotes. That's one thing about JavaScript—nested quotes have to follow a double/single/double/single pattern. The whole `onmouseover` script is in double quotes, so anything that needs to be in quotes inside of that goes in single quotes.

"After that is a semicolon and `return true`. This is necessary for the `window.status` line to work." Why is that? "Don't ask me why. It just has to be there. I think JavaScript needs to send back `true` because you're calling . . . you know, I really don't know why. It just does." But it works. "Yes, it does work, and it won't work without it." Well, then, we know all we need to know.

"On the `onmouseout`, I again call multiple functions. I call `hiLiteOff` to reset the button to the plain white version. I call `switchIcon` and change the cat back to the PBDH version. Then I say `window.status=' '` to set the status bar back to empty.

"Incidentally, JavaScript lets you change a lot of different `window` objects. By saying `window.location=` and then entering a URL, you can tell the browser to go to a different page. For example, you might check with the user to find out what operating system they're using. If they're using Windows, you can switch to one page; if it's a Mac, you can go to another."

MAKING ANIMATED ROLLOVERS

"By the way, since you can use any GIF or JPEG image in a rollover, you can animate a button by calling up an animated GIF (7.26). For example, you can make a button jump up and down when the cursor moves over it and then make it stop when the cursor moves away.

"One caveat, though: Any time you're doing a rollover — whether it's animated or not — the images that you're swapping out have to have the exact same dimension. If they're not the same dimension, the browser will make them the same dimension. So if you try to swap a 50 × 50-pixel button with one that's 100 × 100, the browser will squeeze the second button down to 50 × 50. This means if you want the effect of a button growing and shrinking, you'll want to make sure you build that effect into your original images."

RANDOM ROLLOVER NOTES

With so many scripting languages available to Web designers, why did Robertson take up JavaScript? "I was looking for something beyond flat HTML text on a page. I considered taking up CGI scripting, but CGI is very definitely server-specific. A lot of the Web sites for our clients are hosted on NT boxes or UNIX boxes, and we just don't have those here for me to play around with. I needed a language that I could work on locally, using a typical desktop computer. JavaScript was something manageable that I could pick up and learn on my own and start integrating into my pages right away."

Are rollovers one of the easier elements you can create with JavaScript? "Not really — at least, not the way I do it. There are easier ways to make rollovers, but the way I do it makes them easier to maintain and adapt to different kinds of uses. My way also makes the rollovers easier to test, so the user isn't met with an annoying error message when an image object doesn't work."

How does Robertson code his pages? "I use Symantec's Visual Page to set up the basic layout of the page. Remember that image map example? I made all those polygon buttons with Visual Page. But I hand-code all the JavaScript. And the great thing about Visual Page is that it doesn't mess up my JavaScript code when I put it in, unlike some versions of PageMill, which will totally chew up the code.

"There are programs out there like Macromedia Dreamweaver that do JavaScript for you. But it's just like any HTML editor — it's really a good idea if you know what's going on under the hood so you can look at it and say, 'Okay, this is right,' or, 'Gee, I need to fix this.' I've used Dreamweaver a little bit, and while it seems pretty good — it's actually amazing what it does — like all the visual editors, it generates a lot of unnecessary code. So there's always a trade-off."

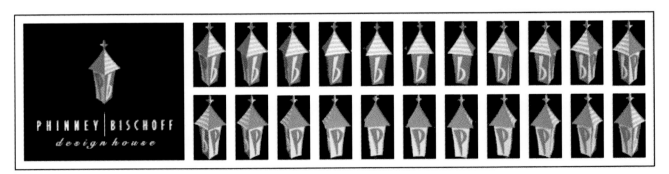

7.26

MI CODA ES SU CODA

I suspect our last question is the one that will most interest readers of this chapter: Is your code sufficiently adaptable that other designers can lift it and integrate it into their own pages. "Oh sure, feel free to copy my functions verbatim and use them any way you want to. For what it's worth, I didn't write this code from scratch. I've looked at the various ways that other people have done rollovers, tested out a few different refinements, and boiled down the code to get it as tight as I could. But like everyone else out there, I'm standing on a lot of other people's shoulders. If you want to jump on board, that's fine by me."

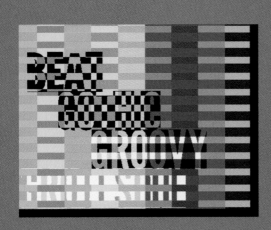

PART II
SPECIFIC
APPLICATIONS

DEMO SPOT

STAR TREK
VOYAGER

LEGEND

Introduction

Identity

Campaigns

Demo Spots

Timeline

Exit

Paramount
EXPEDITION
1995

CAMPAIGNS

CHAPTER 8
SITE MANAGEMENT AND WORKFLOW TECHNIQUES

Welcome to the second half of the book. We thought we were going to lose a couple of you during the intermission, but here you are. Hope you managed to snag one of the free cocktails that were making the rounds. Participants in our focus groups tell us they enjoyed the book much more when they were looped.

Now that we've examined some of the more fundamental principles of electronic design, we thought we'd kick off Part II with a chapter that divides the amateurs from the pros. In the following pages, we learn the answers to two important questions: what does it mean to "produce" a site, and why should you care? This chapter tells how one producer brings together diverse talents to create great on-line content, while making sure the client falls madly in love with the results. Or as this chapter's artist puts it, "I make sure everyone's on the same page at the same time."

The producer in question is Kelly Goto. A graduate of UCLA's earliest multimedia program, Goto has produced and designed some of the most ambitious multimedia projects published to either CD-ROM or the Internet. Her clients range from the usual media titans (8.1) to button-down corporate interests in the banking and healthcare industries (8.2). She routinely handles big budgets and manages large teams of designers and programmers.

It's all about effective communication. You have to develop ways to communicate with all the different players in the process.

KELLY GOTO

8.1

On first blush, the art of Web site production may strike some as a wee bit esoteric. But if you're looking to attract higher-profile clients or simply to work more efficiently with the clients and coworkers you have, then this information should be right up your alley.

So again, welcome to the second half of the book, where general design techniques run head long into the real world.

WHAT IT MEANS TO PRODUCE

The producer is the person who supervises the artists, manages the costs, meets the deadlines, and keeps the client happy. According to Goto, "The first job of a good producer is to find out what the client needs from a site. Clients often have unrealistic expectations of what you can do. They know they want all the bells and whistles, but they don't know what it takes or how much it costs. It's my job to educate the client and tell them how much technology they need to meet their goals. After a careful survey of the client's needs, I help them figure out what they want to do, how much it will cost, and how their decisions will impact their users."

If Goto could sum up what she does in one word, it would start with a capital *C*. "It's all about effective communication. You have to develop ways to communicate with all the different players in the process. In this day and age, we communicate with groups of people, not just individuals. So I think the most important thing is to establish methods of communication that work with the different groups. Some of these people are left-brainers, some are right-brainers. We have artists talking to designers and designers talking to programmers. Then we have the client who doesn't understand any of them.

"I have to talk to everyone. If I can communicate the key issues — urgency, priorities, and all the specifics of when the project needs to completed and how it needs to look — to all parties, then I've done my job. That's the secret. You can put together schedules and programs and budgets. But it's when you convey the necessity of meeting the schedule — when someone looks up and says, 'Oh, my god, this is due next week! I've got to jam!' — that's when you know that you've got everybody's attention and they're on track."

What kind of background does it take to be a good producer? "You have to be able to put yourself in other people's shoes, so you know the way they think and you know what they need. In the past, I did jobs without a separate producer. I just did the whole thing myself, starting from scratch from concept to design and final production. So I've worn the hats of the designer and the artist. And though I'm not a technical expert, I know enough so that I can go in and fix somebody else's code. I've also hired people to create elements for me, so I know what it's like to be the client. You want to know what's going on — good or bad, you just want to know.

ARTIST:
Kelly Goto

ORGANIZATION:
Gotomedia
San Francisco: 415/957-7701
Los Angeles: 310/915-3141
www.gotomedia.com
kgoto@aol.com
kelly@gotomedia.com

SYSTEM:
PowerBook 1400c/166
Mac OS 8.0
2GB storage/64MB RAM

CONNECTIVITY:
33.6Kbps modem, ISDN

PERIPHERALS:
Viewsonic 21-inch monitor
Epson ES-1200C scanner

PRIMARY APPLICATIONS:
Microsoft Word, Symantec Visual Page, Equilibrium DeBabelizer, Adobe Photoshop, Macromedia FreeHand, QuarkXPress, GifBuilder

WORK HISTORY:
<u>1988</u> — Participated in first multimedia program at UCLA; created first project in Macromedia Director.

8.2   *©1997 Phinney Bischoff Design House*

<u>1990</u> — Hired at Marina Del Ray-based design firm; art directed photography and layout for entertainment clients and Infinity Car collateral.

<u>1994</u> — Started own business, Goto Design/Media, with clients Gramercy Pictures, Paramount Domestic Television, and Warner Bros.

<u>1995</u> — Became Senior Producer at Warner Brothers Online; launched sites for *Babylon 5* and Rosie O'Donnell.

<u>1997</u> — Began freelancing in the Bay Area, producing sites for National Geographic and Wells Fargo Online.

FAVORITE X-MEN CHARACTER
Kitty Pride, a.k.a., Shadow Cat ("She can move through walls, but her best power is that she's really, really smart and she can solve problems.")

"Anyone with skills in a variety of different areas can be an effective producer. You just have to find ways to communicate with people who are thinking in different ways than you are. Clients, programmers, designers, CGI and JavaScript guys, the ISP — everyone has needs that have to be met. And you're the one who has to meet them, every step of the way."

THE FIVE PHASES OF WEB DESIGN WORKFLOW

Short of hiring Goto and having her take care of your site for you, what steps can you take to produce an effective site that meets your client's realistic expectations? And more important, how do you do it on budget and on time?

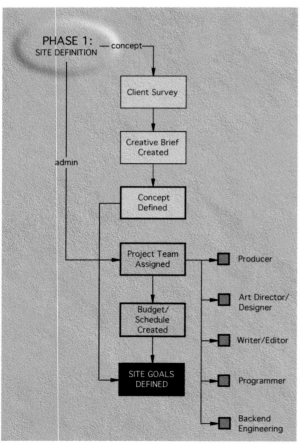

8.3

"Although every Web project is going to differ in content, size, and functionality, there's a basic structure that I always follow. From large to small sites, you can work through them in this same way. First you develop the site, then you define the structure, then you create the interface, then you get the technical specifics in order, and finally you publish it online. I call these the 'Five Phases.' Follow these steps, make sure that you keep a running dialog with your team and your client, and you'll get through the experience in one piece."

PHASE 1: SITE DEFINITION

The first step is to define the site. Goto's flow chart of the process shows two tracks, one conceptual and one administrative (8.3). "The conceptualization of the site begins with the client. Once a project has been assigned, you need to sit down with the client and define the goals. What is the overall concept? What is the purpose — what kind of message do they want to convey? What kind of content do they want to include? How do they want to see it organized? What kind of visual style are they looking for? What are their technical needs? You also need to work out the budget, the timeline, when they want what, and the schedule.

"At this same time, you're assembling your project team. You need to decide what people you need, what kind of programmer, a writer, an editor, what kind of back-end engineering you're going to have, the artists, and designers." But Goto cautions that you shouldn't feel compelled to pigeonhole each member of your team in a specific slot. "Collaboration is the secret to a great Web site. Because of the changing nature of roles as we know them, many individuals wear multiple hats when working on projects. You may find it very helpful to allow and even encourage roles to overlap. You need to make your people feel creative and engaged, so they're all partners in the outcome.

"Phase 1 is the preplanning stage, where you get everything together. A lot of people don't take the time to do this because they don't think they *have* the time. But you've got to build the initial planning into the process. Otherwise, you're going to suffer in the end, when you can least afford it. Proper planning and organization from the outset is the most important part of creating an effective site."

FRASIER'S CRANIUM

Goto thoughtfully provided us with several examples of her trade. While no one project absolutely sums up her style or the way in which she works — after all, every project is different — many of the examples help to demonstrate the various phases in action. To start with, we'll look at a promotional CD-ROM for the television show *Frasier* that Goto produced for Paramount Pictures.

"The *Frasier's Cranium* CD was designed to promote the rerelease of *Frasier* into syndicated television. It went out to all advertisers and affiliates around the country. The CD is really just a collection of promotional photographs and audio clips, which you access by clicking on different parts of Frasier's forehead (8.4). It's a fun, fully interactive piece. There are random audio clips from the show and theme music and graphics that help to create the environment. We created the interface in MTropolis. Even though this is a CD project — it was never intended for the Web — the basic approach is the same.

"Normally, I like to get involved in the creative end of things. But some projects take so much time and require so many people that you have to step back and work strictly as a producer. That's what I did with *Frasier*. This means that I'm working directly with the client, putting together which information needs to go where, what buttons need to be active, what kind of action has to take place, what sound bites they need, and so on. I'm also in charge of putting together schedules and budgets that work, and then getting everyone — both the client and my team — to stick to them.

"A project like this starts with a simple interface, but putting it all together is a complicated task. The first thing is to create the site map to show everything that the client wants to show. I have to map it all out so an artist can take it and know what needs to appear on each screen. There are a lot of pieces involved — and, of course, the content is the one thing that always lags. It doesn't matter what the project is, getting content from the client takes forever. They're often creating the content at the same time you're building your project, so you have to figure that into the schedule."

FROM SURVEY TO SIGN OFF

"When you begin putting together a site for a client, it's a good idea to make up a survey to find out what kind of site the client wants. It doesn't say, 'What do you want your Web site to look like?' It asks who their target audience is, what kind of visual sense does the company already have, what message do they want to convey? This gives you a sense of their expectations and what kind of audience they're trying to reach.

"From all these questions, you put together a 'Creative Brief.' Take what you perceive to be the client's expectations and put it in your own words. Then have the client sign off on it. When I talk to the client, I frequently use print media terms. A lot of people come from a print background, so they can relate. When I have clients sign off on each phase, I say things like, 'This is the comp, this is the blueline, this is the finished piece.' Most clients already understand that once they sign off on the blueline, it becomes their responsibility. They can't blow off the blueline; they have to take a close look at it.

"After they've signed off, we have change orders. I try to keep people in line and not let them ask for impossible things. If you set the standard right at the beginning — this is when you sign off, this is what was sent to you, this is what you accepted — then they understand they have to accept responsibility for further changes."

8.4

NW FEDERAL CREDIT UNION

Few of us can attract clients with quite as much profile as Paramount Pictures. So in the interests of providing some balance and transitioning our attentions to the Web, Goto also walked us through a site she created for a local banking firm, NW Federal Credit Union (*www.nwfcu.com*) (8.5).

"This is a great site. It's not high profile and it's not glamorous. It's a medium-sized project with a small budget. It really demonstrates how you can be a Web producer on a modest, local scale. Most producers are working in small to medium-sized companies. They have limited means to add multimedia elements, CGI scripts, and that kind of thing, so they have to choose wisely. And they have to get the site done in a certain time frame. The NW Federal Credit Union site came in on time and on budget, and the client was really happy with it.

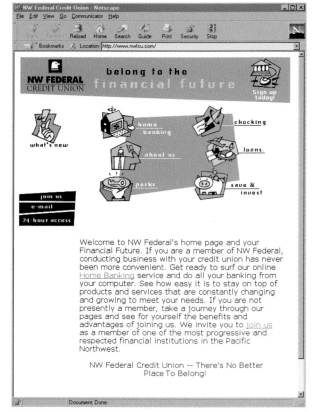

8.5

*Design Firm: Phinney Bischoff Design House, www.pbdh.com
Designer: Dean Hart*

"The client's goal for this site was to create something that was completely antitechnical. The credit union wanted to encourage their current members to get in the habit of doing their home banking on-line. So we had to come up with something that was fun, friendly, and easy to interact with."

But as with most companies who are itching to make a splash on the Web, NW Federal Credit Union required some education. "The credit union was not at all technically savvy. They had seen all these new fancy things on the Web and they wanted to do everything. It was up to me to explain what was possible and what was simply beyond their means."

From a programming perspective, the most complicated aspect of the credit union site was the CGI scripting, which was required to process the electronic bank forms (8.6). "There was a lot of back-and-forth work with the CGI. We ended up using the CGI programmers that were available at the hosting site. When working with CGI scripters, it's almost always better if you hire folks that work at the ISP. That way, they have direct access to the servers. It makes it easier to test out the scripts and make sure there are no problems. Plus, a lot of times the CGI stuff you're doing is common enough that the ISP guys can repurpose stuff they've already done. You pay less money because they don't have to write the whole thing from scratch."

PHASE 2: DEVELOPING SITE STRUCTURE

"During the second phase, you meet with your team to map out how the site is going to work and what it's going to look like (8.7). The first step is to develop a 'site map,' which is basically a big flow chart that shows how the content will be organized. I use a program called Inspiration. You can get a demo at *www.inspiration.com*. Inspiration is fantastic — you can whip site maps out fast and it's really easy to use.

"Your site map should show every key page in the site and how it relates to the others. Technical notes and main links should appear here as well. It's important to have the client sign off on the site map and note any changes — like taking away or adding pages — that might have an impact on the budget.

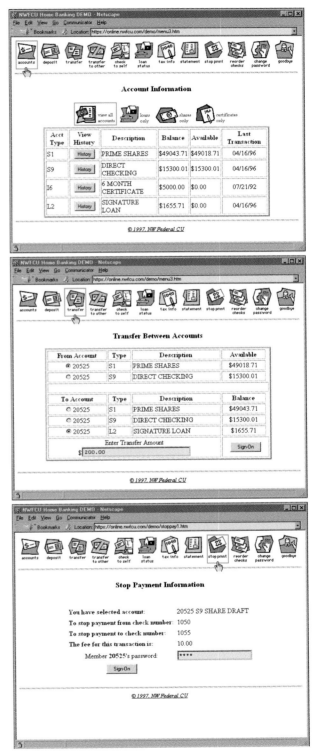

8.6

"If the client is providing all the content, you need to schedule the transfer of materials. This always takes longer than you think. There are usually several people who you have to get the content from, even in a small company. If you're responsible for some of the content, you need to meet with your writers and editors and get them on a tight schedule as well. This is also the time to discuss the site's technical needs with your artists and programmers.

"Next, you want to decide how the navigation is going to work. How will the user flow through the site? Which pages are accessible from where? You also need to decide what kind of naming conventions you're going to use. What is the folder structure for the files? The naming convention is the secret code that gets used by programmers and artists alike. You don't want each member of the team naming files and sticking them in folders without any direction. It'll turn into a mess fast and you'll have to rename everything at the end. The navigation and naming conventions make up the backbone that the rest of the project builds from."

THE ROSIE O'DONNELL SHOW

An example of a project that required special attention to structure is *The Rosie O'Donnell Show* on America Online (keyword: Rosie) (8.8). "Rosie O'Donnell was a good challenge for me. I took it from start to finish. I designed and produced the site and put together the content. All the while, I was relying heavily on a remote staff. We had about 30 remote staffers in all."

Goto's biggest challenge was developing a site where a community of home workers, children, and other computer novices could take root and flourish. "I had to organize a community for the AOL site that ran parallel to the TV show. In reality, communities create themselves, but controlling them is difficult. AOL is more limited in the ways you can kick disruptive

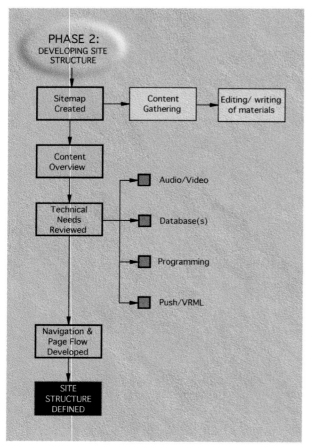

8.7

8.8

©1996 Warner Bros. Online
Design/Art Direction: Kelly Goto

people out of a chat room. And that was a problem, because everyone's a Rosie fan. We had to think about both kids and adults coming to this site," most of whom are used to the relative structure and safety of network TV.

"But if you create the proper guidelines up front and you assemble a staff who knows what they're doing, then you can accomplish anything. Create a chain of command and it runs a lot smoother. We started off with six chat hosts and ended up with 30, most of whom were voluntary. Every host was an adult who was trained in how to control a room.

"We developed software to say hello to every person entering the room. We had different themes—a Saturday morning cartoons chat, sing-alongs, even a virtual-reality room. One room had bean bag chairs on one side, vending machines on the other, and you could interact with it, like a real rec room. People who are very, very used to chats are familiar with these things, but newbies aren't at all. They don't know how to interact or talk. But with proper super- vision, the site just grew and grew. It turned into one of the biggest successes that AOL has ever had. Her AOL Live chats were incredibly popular, with thou- sands and thousands of people."

GO WEST WITH LEWIS AND CLARK

To communicate how she wants the individual pages in a site to look, Goto creates what she calls a "content bible." The bible contains placeholders for text and graphics so that the artists and programmers have a sense of the finished appearance of the site. "When I was creating the Lewis and Clark site for National Geographic (*www.nationalgeographic.com/features/97 /west*, 8.9), I created a content bible to show everyone

what they were working toward (8.10). Obviously, it was just for internal purposes, something that I handed out to members of my team. The bible showed the pixel dimensions of each element on the page, from the frames down to the National Geographic Kids logo. I also included naming conventions."

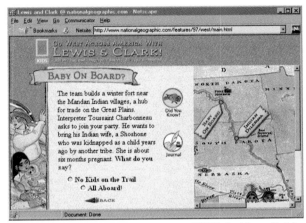

8.9

©1997 National Geographic Online
Design Firm: Electravision, LLC, www.electravision.com
Designers: Kelly Goto, Val Casey

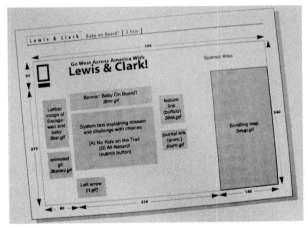

8.10

QUICK SITE SKETCH

Goto's prototypes are just sketches of the final site, designed to make sure everything's in order. A prototype is not supposed to be the real thing, so you cut corners when you can. "First of all, in my prototypes, the graphics haven't been optimized. I make sure the client understands that the final graphics will suffer a little when we compress them down to the right size.

"Also, where I might use tables or some other HTML tool in the final page design, I'll whip together an image map for the prototype. You're not concerned with all the different parameters you are when getting the final site up on the Web. The prototype just has to look right in one browser on one screen."

Goto is sometimes prepared to go to extremes to save time on the prototype. "Here's a little secret thing I do: I throw together the whole page design in FreeHand really quickly, then I save it as an EPS file. I bring it into Photoshop and change it to a GIF. Then in Visual Page, I make it into an image map. I have created a nice fake, full page that works just like the final HTML in no time at all."

"The site came out at the same time as the Ken Burns PBS documentary. The illustrations come from a book by Rosalyn Schanzer. Kids explore with Lewis and Clark and make decisions on each page. The map on the right builds itself as you go on your journey, so you can scroll through it and look where you've been. Because Lewis and Clark didn't have any maps, the map gets made as you go along—you can't see any further than you've been. The map is actually a bunch of GIF images arranged in vertical strips. I hired out CGI and JavaScripters to piece them together. Because the map gets filled out incrementally, kids can go through at their own pace, make choices and see the consequences, just like Lewis and Clark did."

PHASE 3: INTERFACE DESIGN AND PRODUCTION

"The next step is to define the basic interface of your site (8.11). A lot of designers start at this point, but then you run the risk of making your content fit the interface. It's better to work the other way around. After you've finished Phases 1 and 2, you know every-

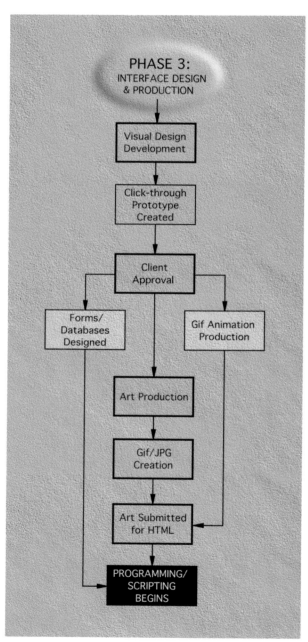

8.11

thing you need to know to do the interface right. You know the goals of the site, you know the navigation, and you know the content. Now you're ready to put together the graphic 'look and feel.'

"Teamwork becomes very important at this point. You have to work closely with your artists and programmers to come up with design elements that work within Web standards. You have to work as a unit to keep file sizes down, come up with efficient uses of color, and establish a clear and consistent visual direction. It's tempting to go nuts with the graphics, but you have to reign it in. A good rule of thumb is to figure that 1K of data takes about a second to download. So a 30K image takes 30 seconds to draw on the user's screen. That's about as much patience as anyone has on the Web. So a single page —the whole thing, including graphics, everything— should be less than 30K.

"I think it's also a good idea to create a 'click-through prototype,' which is a working HTML mock-up of the site that you can test in different browsers and show to the client. Make sure the client takes time to experiment with the prototype. Get them to sign off on it. It's very important that they understand that the prototype represents the actual interface for the site."

EXPEDITION '95

A project that resonates with purposeful interface and strong visual design is a CD-ROM that Goto produced for Paramount Domestic Television. The project, called Expedition '95 (8.12), was a multimedia mock-up of ad campaign ideas and identity treatments for Paramount's budding television station, which eventually became UPN.

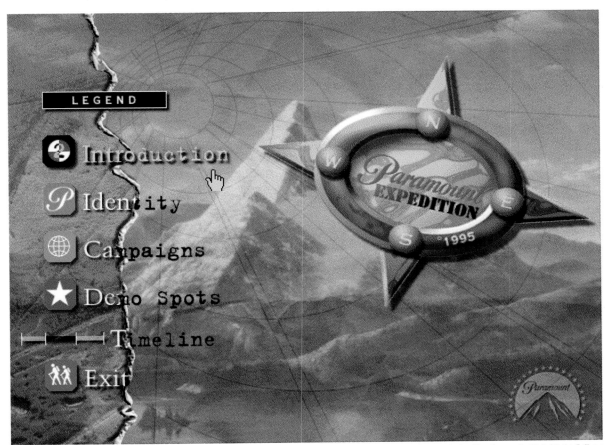

8.12

©1995 Toolbox Productions. Design Firm: Gotomedia. Digital Artist: TcChang

"We created Expedition '95 to show that the company I was working for could do the naming, advertising, and on-air promotions. This was before there was a UPN. The executives at Paramount Television were still trying to decide if they wanted to get involved with a new television network. For the presentation, we bound the printed notes in a metal book that I had cast, bound, and fired. All the advertising and sales materials were inside. Then at the back of the book was the CD-ROM. We had to put the whole thing together in two weeks. It was one of the slickest presentations I ever worked on.

"The CD contained a series of suggested logos, ad spots, and marketing timelines. The flagship of the new network was *Star Trek: Voyager*. They hadn't started producing the series yet, so there was no real material to work from. We just had this concept of a woman captain, so we came up with promotional storyboards from that. I decided to animate them, so at the bottom of the Campaign screen there are three icons that turn yellow when you mouse over them (8.13). If you click on a button, it tells a story. I had an illustrator draw a series of sketches on paper. To animate the sketches, I took a video camera and moved the paper under the camera. Then I edited the video, added sound, and put together a moving storyboard.

8.13

"Another area shows a color demo spot for *Voyager* (8.14). We hired an artist to put it together on an SGI machine. It has lots of explosions and planets flying around. The voice-over is by the same man they later hired for the real on-air commercials.

"I really like to create prototypes for my clients. For Paramount, we could have put together storyboards. And in the old days, we probably would have. But prototypes are better. The client gets a better sense of how the project will look on screen."

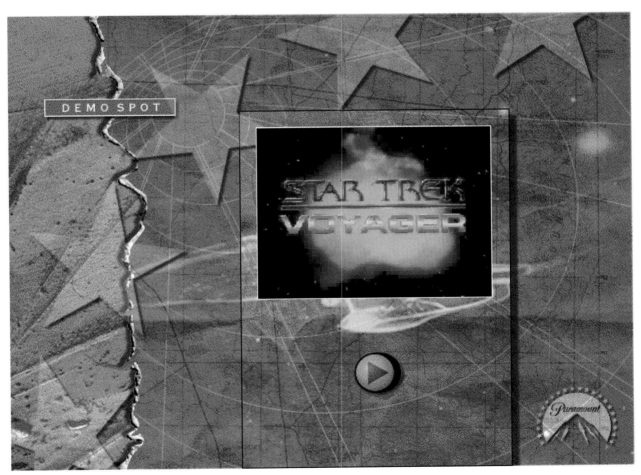

8.14

UCSC NETTRAIL

Another advantage to putting together a prototype is that it permits you to perform quick-and-dirty usability studies. A prototype can even come in handy when trying to demonstrate how something *shouldn't* be done. Consider the case of one somewhat recalcitrant client, the University of California at Santa Cruz.

"The UCSC NetTrail was a four-part modular training system for freshmen coming into the University of California system (8.15). It's a secured, Intranet site that teaches students how to use e-mail, how to use their browsers, how to search, and how to use the library research resources. It is a big on-line tutorial so every freshman can become fluent in UCSC's computer system.

"The idea was to come up with a basic template that they could then use for each branch of the university. Then all of the UC schools will have their own proprietary on-line education system for students."

But conflicts arose. "I had a few problems with the content. The professors wrote the material and they didn't think that they needed any designers messing around with it. They didn't even like the idea of a graphical interface. The professors wanted to write the content and have it be from their school and that was it. It turned into an us-versus-them thing.

"But after we put together a prototype and they tested the site on a few students, they realized that they needed to make some changes. The students couldn't get through it; they would get to certain parts and stall out. And the content was confusing. The content was not action-oriented. It didn't explain what the student was supposed to do in simple terms — what you were supposed to do next. When the whole thing was put together, they realized that the style of content and the interface really did matter after all.

"The compromise was that we weren't allowed to cut any content, but we did put in markers and graphics to help students know where they were. That's why we came up with the metaphor of the trail (8.16). When the students go through the site, they understand that they're on a trail and here's where they go next."

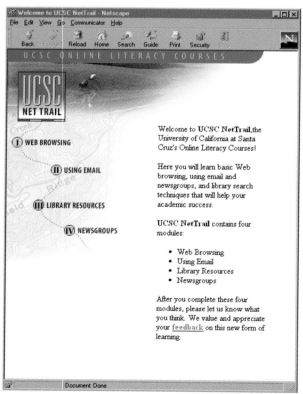

8.15

©1997 Electravision, LLC
Design Firm: Electravision, LLC
Art Director: Lisa Lopuck

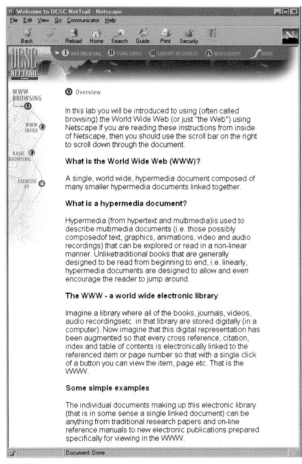

8.16

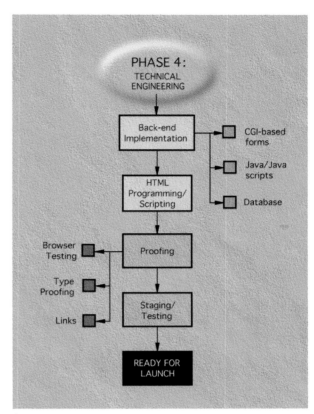

8.17

"What I've found is, people don't have a lot of patience on-line. A lot of people think you can just transfer a brochure directly to the Web, but it's not true. When you're on-line, you expect immediate results. You want to get on and off, not meander through one page after another. There's not a lot of time to explain technicalities or go into philosophy. The Web is not a reading experience. You move through it, you get what you need, and you get off."

PHASE 4: TECHNICAL ENGINEERING

"After you get the design and layout the way you want it, you can start work on the site engineering (8.17). By engineering, I mean all the technical aspects of the site — the real HTML scripting, tables and frames, CGI forms, databases, and all the other programming."

Phase 4 also includes the testing and proofing of the site. "It's critical for everyone involved in the creation of the site — including the client — to be involved in the testing and proofing stage. The more people you get, the more problems you'll catch. I try to make it really clear that problems are going to be found across the board and that no one should start pointing fingers. You want to foster an atmosphere where everyone feels like they're helping each other out.

"The proofing stage is also a great way to get your client involved so that they feel like they're a part of the team. But make sure you give the client some guidelines, preferably a form to fill out. I usually print the entire site out, page by page, and hand the document to each person responsible for proofing. This seems to be the easiest way to take notes and make changes.

"You need to test every browser you can get your hands on. There are some weird ones out there that people don't think of. For instance, Internet Explorer 2 comes preconfigured with a lot of Windows NT machines. You also need to test different platforms, multiple screen sizes, and different modem speeds.

"When testing the site, you can host it from your own computer using a program like Microsoft Personal Web Server, which is available with Internet Explorer 3. You can even password-protect the site to make sure it stays private until the site goes live.

THE VIRTUAL LOT

An example of a project where an interface problem became apparent in the final testing phase is The Virtual Lot (8.18). "The Virtual Lot is an AOL site for Warner Brothers. The idea is that you're on a movie lot where you can check out information about Warner Brothers' TV shows such as *Friends* and *Murphy Brown.*

"The executives in charge of the project wanted an environmental interface, so you felt like you were at a place. You can go down different streets, enter a subway, and visit a theater (8.19). Not only was it friendlier, they felt, but it was an excellent way to go after a new advertising model. They called it 'environmental advertising.' For instance, you're walking down a street and you pass by a store, that store just happens to be 1-800-FLOWERS. It's more clever than a banner ad and it's not just sitting there flashing in your face.

"This premise worked great as an advertising model. They had a lot of high-end advertisers, but it wasn't a completely satisfying user experience because the pages took so long to download. I had a real problem with that. I wanted to develop interfaces that were user friendly, that were easy to interact with, and that downloaded quickly and lent themselves to continuous updating. We're still learning on every project how to better satisfy both users and advertisers on the Web."

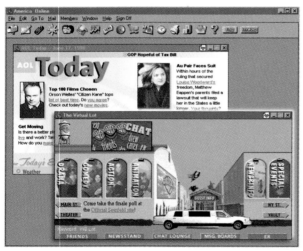

8.18   ©1996 Warner Bros. Online

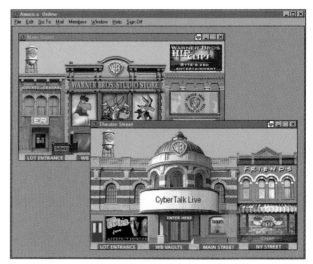

8.19

PHASE 5: PUBLISHING AND MARKETING

By now, Goto has devoted a couple of months of her life to the site. "With a team of two to five artists and programmers, a big project typically takes about eight weeks. I've turned a few around as quickly as six weeks, but that's awfully tight." After the site is complete, Phase 5 kicks in. This is when you publish the site, promote it, and begin planning the updates (8.20).

The marketing process is so important that we analyze it in detail in Chapter 14. But Goto is equally concerned with what happens to the site after she leaves it. "Once the site is up on the Web, it's important to have a maintenance schedule in place for at least six months out. Always make sure that there is a way that the client can perform the updates. You may want to help them put together a maintenance schedule. Make sure they know that it's their responsibility, but try to make it as straightforward as you can. You don't want to leave them with a mess that they can't handle — that generates bad will.

"I also like to include little randomizing elements, so that the site looks a little different every time someone visits it, even if it hasn't been updated. You can create scripts that tell the time and date. You can also make randomized graphics and animations. Most JavaScript programmers can put this stuff together really easily. I know it's somewhat of a gimmick, but it helps keep the site fresh.

"You want your site to continue to look good long after you leave it. You want it to remain something you're proud of. Obviously, you can't make the client keep up the site exactly the way you would. But you can put schedules and conventions in place so that everyone has what they need to do it right."

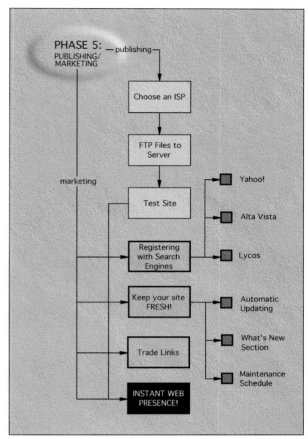

8.20

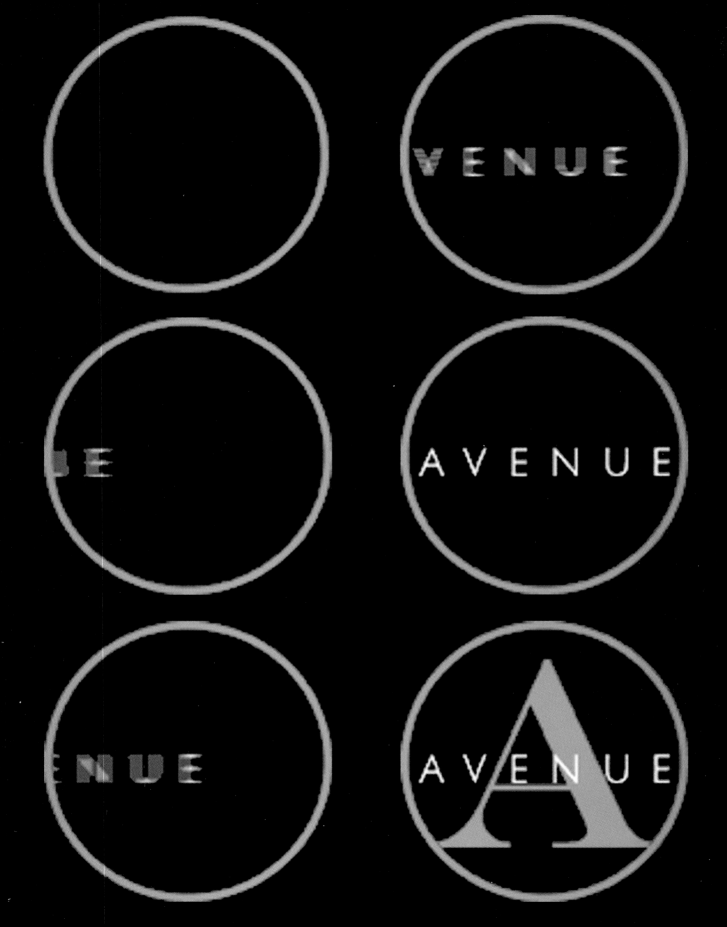

CHAPTER 9
GIF ANIMATION

Steamboat Willie, Bugs Bunny, and Monty Python have influenced generations. All of us have memories of a favorite cartoon character. Some of us may have even found ourselves in the midst of raucous debates over who is really top duck — Daffy or Donald? What does it take to be a professional animator, the kind that can become immortalized in a young generation's mind? Drawing and storyboarding skills plus good connections at Disney or Warner Brothers. What does it take to be an animator on the Web? A few playful ideas, a layered Photoshop file, and basic GIF animation software.

As Yann Oehl, designer and GIF animation specialist at Emergent Media explains, "I love GIF animation! Oh sure it has its limitations but so does doing anything on the Web, and the advantages of GIF animation definitely outweigh the disadvantages. As any Web-savvy designer will tell you, using the appropriate tool and solution for the task at hand, is the name of the game. GIF animation is a great way to liven up a page, increase a Web site's impact, and draw a viewer's attention to an advertisement or logo without taking a huge hit in file size. I like that it doesn't require any plug-ins or heavy-handed programming. It is much easier to learn and work with than Java or Shockwave. Plus GIF animation encourages experimentation due to the relatively simple tools it requires. It's really animation for the masses! The disadvantages to GIF animation are that it doesn't support interactivity or sound, and, admittedly, GIF animations can sometimes look clunky if the connection speeds are too slow. But hey, that's part of its charm!"

GIF animation encourages experimentation due to the relatively simple tools it requires. It's really animation for the masses!

YANN OEHL

ANIMATION 101

Clever animation catches our eye, be it in a feature film or when used as a Web banner advertisement. Whether you are watching a high budget feature film or like the way a logo spins on a Web site, the concepts, terms, and techniques to create either are similar. To create traditional animation, characters are inked onto a sheet of acetate called a *cel*—black line first and then color is added later. Each cel is a picture of the motion stopped at every ⅓₀ of a second and each frame is played twice resulting in a 30-frames-per-second playback. Some of the techniques that professional animators use include only drawing those parts of the figure that change, keeping the figure separate from the background, and more sophisticated techniques such as overlap, squash and stretch, and slow in and out (to create an illusion of motion and believability).

GIF animation also uses cels, where each cel is an individual frame or picture of a stop motion that plays sequentially. The designer can control playback speed and looping, but these controls are not 100 percent predictable since the connection speed does influence playback. The best thing about GIF animation is that it is based on the GIF file format and the great majority of browsers recognize and display them. Netscape Navigator 2.0 and Internet Explorer 3.0 and higher have no problems displaying and playing GIF animation. Once the animations are loaded, they are in the browser cache, reducing bandwidth strain and allowing the designer to use them again on additional pages.

FROM SKETCH TO SCREEN

As Yann explains, "GIF animation is ideal when you need high visual impact in a limited space. The issues to take into account when planning a GIF animation are physical dimensions, color palette, file optimization, looping, and timing. In a nutshell, I start out with pencil sketches, which I scan in and optimize in Photoshop, and then I use ULead GIF Animator to create the animation. (Note that all techniques and concepts discussed here also apply for those using GifBuilder on the Macintosh.)

"I rough out the animation with pencil on a Strathmore artist block (9.1), and then I use tracing paper to ink the individual frames (9.2), experimenting with line weight and progressively changing position, gesture, (9.3) or motion with each new sheet of tracing paper. At this point, I'm still working in black and white. I don't add any color until I get into Photoshop where I can use the Web-safe color palette. When I'm happy with the series, I scan each piece of tracing paper on the flatbed scanner. It helps to place a white sheet of paper behind the tracing paper when scanning. I scan all the frames in as grayscale files at 200 dpi, which is much higher than the required 72 ppi, but the added resolution helps me to clean up the scans. The original images tend to be about 1–2MB for each frame. It's easier for me to clean up the higher resolution file and then size it down. Each frame goes into its own Photoshop layer, and by using layer transparency it's easy to align the

ARTIST:
Yann Oehl

ORGANIZATION:
Emergent Media
1809 Seventh Ave, Suite 908
Seattle, WA 98101
206/292-3990
www.emergentmedia.com
yann@emergentmedia.com

SYSTEM, PC:
P200
Windows NT 4.0
3GB storage/64MB RAM

CONNECTIVITY:
T-1

SERVER ENVIRONMENT:
NT Sequel Server SQL

PERIPHERALS:
CTX 17-inch monitor, Epson 800 flatbed scanner

PRIMARY APPLICATIONS:
Adobe Photoshop 5.02, ULead GIF Animator, Macromedia Flash, and FreeHand 7.0

layers which will later become the separate animation cels (9.4). As you can see (9.5), I like to try out a lot of variations on a theme!

9.2

9.1

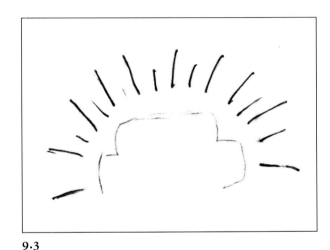

9.3

WORK HISTORY:

<u>1990</u> — Saw Photoshop for the first time — motivated Yann to save and buy his first PC.

<u>1992</u> — Received degree in Psychology and Philosophy.

<u>1992 – 96</u> — Social work.

<u>1996</u> — Designer with Emergent Media.

FAVORITE SNACK FOOD:

Australian candied ginger-and-coconut sorbet

FAVORITE HEXADECIMAL COLOR:

Definitely #996666

9.4

9.5

"The good thing about working with a high-resolution image is that I can adjust the contrast to force the light areas to go white and the darks to go black. Using a contrast adjustment of +30 Brightness and +75 Contrast may seem really extreme, but by working on the hi-res file, once you size the file down, the softening of the interpolation takes care of any jaggy edges like magic! I do make sure to use the same settings for all the layers. By playing with Brightness/Contrast, I can also influence the line weight. If a line is too thin, just drop down the Brightness/Contrast. And if it is too thick, boost the values way up and the lines will become thinner. Of course, you could also achieve the same results by using Levels or Curves, and I wouldn't recommend Brightness/Contrast if my end goal was high-quality print reproduction."

IN LIVING COLOR

"Once I have the series of line drawings, I begin to add color to the image." The most important "secrets" when adding color to a GIF animation are as follows:

- "Never put color directly on the layer that you are coloring. I always use an empty layer that is dedicated to color. This allows me to experiment with color variations and ideas."
- Use the Multiply layer blend mode. That way the color doesn't affect the black lines (9.6).

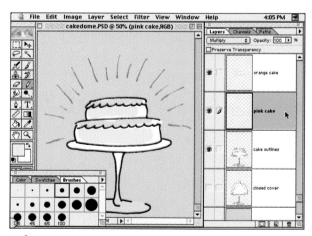

9.6

- Use the pencil tool to add color. This avoids antialiasing, which adds to the final file size.
- Use the Web-safe color palette, except when you need a specific color that is not in the Web palette. For example, "I wanted the apple pie to have a color between a Granny Smith and golden delicious apple color (9.7), so I used BoxTop's Ditherbox to create the hybrid color for the apple pie (9.8). Only use the Ditherbox filter to create colors on the final resolution file. If you create the hybrid color and then size the file down, the interpolation will blend the pixels to become one color that, most likely, isn't Web safe."

You can also animate photographs, QuickTime movies, PICT files, and Adobe Premiere Filmstrip files. The only caveat to working with any of these file formats is you need to keep the colors simple. For the Behold animation, "I started out with three nineteenth-century black-and-white lithographs and used Photoshop Duotones to add the subtle color (9.9 - 9.13). The problem with animating photographs is the animation files can get really large if the photos are saved as PICT files or the photos may visually fall apart in the indexing process. I prefer to work from my own sketches, line art, or vector art from FreeHand and Flash.

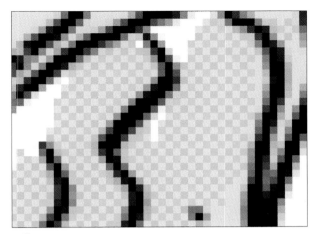

9.8

9.9

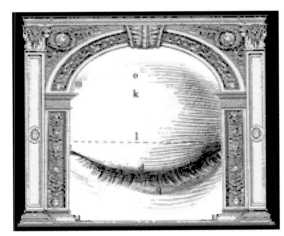

9.10

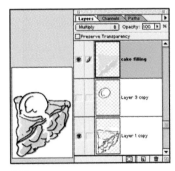

9.7

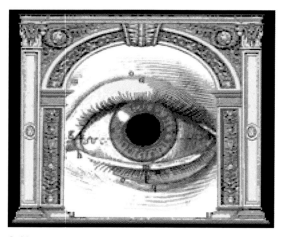

9.11

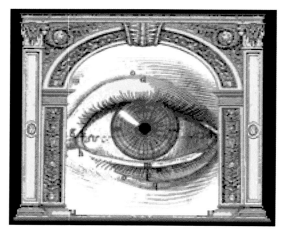

9.12

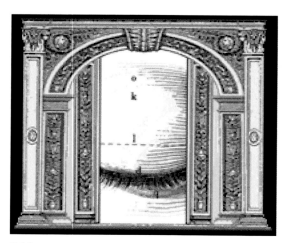

9.13

"Once I have the color right, I can visualize what the animation is going to look like. To check if the animation is going to work visually, I zoom the file out to approximately the size that it's going to be on the Web (9.14) and check line weight and motion. Then I size the file down to the final size of the animation, making sure that the final animation will be at 72 pixels per inch (ppi), also referred to as 72 *dots per inch* (dpi). Sizing the file down tends to soften the black lines and I use Unsharp Mask with settings of Amount 33, Radius 1, and Threshold 0 to bring back the crispness. I like using a low Unsharp Mask setting so that I can use it a few times if need be. Remember, only sharpen the layers that have black lines. Don't sharpen the color layers because Unsharp Mask will create light/dark edges that look ugly, create artificial colors that aren't Web safe, and increase file size — three strikes and you're out!"

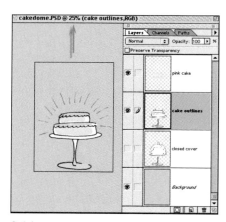

9.14

TIP

When sizing the file to 72 ppi, keep an eye on the Photoshop image title bar to check the view ratio of the file (9.15). For Web graphics and animation, the image needs to be sized to view at 100 percent. After sizing the image, double-check it by pressing ⌘/Ctrl+Option/Alt+0 to zoom to 100 percent view instantly (9.16).

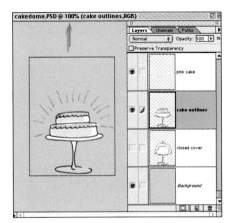

9.15

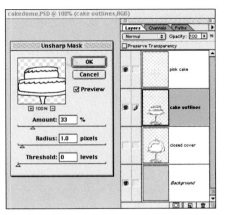

9.16

"In Photoshop, I use Copy Merged to create the individual frames that combine line art and color (9.17). I click on the layer view icons that I need for a particular animation cel. I copy merge and paste and a new layer is created with all the required pieces (9.18). Notice that the cake's background layer is on 75 percent gray, which helps to create neutral antialiased edges without troublesome color fringing. You can also get a neutral background customized for your particular needs by desaturating a sample of your target background and using that gray. Once I have all the required cels on separate layers, I use the magic wand with a tolerance of 1 and no aliasing to select the 75 percent gray areas and then fill the selection with a solid red, green, or blue. Just make sure to use a color that you don't have anywhere else in the image. It is this color that I use to define as transparency in GIF Animator (9.19)." (Note that you can also copy merge the animation layers with a background color similar to the color on top of which the animation will be placed.)

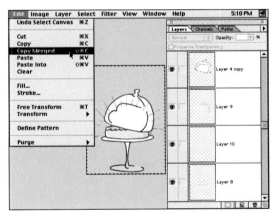

9.17

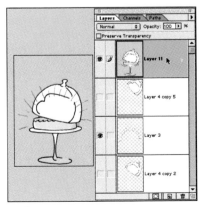

9.18

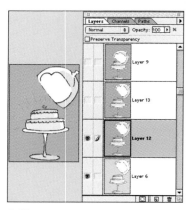

9.19

> **TIP**
>
> A useful feature in Photoshop 5.0 is the ability to create new documents and snapshots with the History Palette. When the layers are visible that make up a specific animation cel, click Make Duplicate document and save that file as your animation cel.

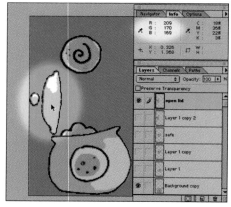

9.20

"After I have all the required cels in the layered Photoshop document, I need to index the files as follows:"

1. Separate the layers into individual files either by copy pasting the layer into a new file or by duplicating the layer into a new document.

2. Choose Image ➢ Mode ➢ Indexed Colors and use the Adaptive palette with the lowest possible amount of colors and no dithering. "Although I never use a dither for flat color areas, I do experiment with a diffusion dither when indexing photographs. You need to experiment with a variety of versions to see what looks best."

3. Convert back to RGB.

4. "I use the free Photoshop filter Web Scrub (*www.verso.com/agitprop/dithering/*) to bring any non-Web-safe colors back into the Web-safe palette. Even though I've been working with the Web-safe palette, indexing the file in Photoshop can cause color shifts which may also cause dithering. I run this filter to ensure that every pixel is Web safe."

5. Choose Image ➢ Mode ➢ Indexed Colors and use the Exact palette.

6. Yann then exports the file via the Export GIF 89a module and does not define (in this case) the green as transparency. Both GIF Animator and GifBuilder will ignore the transparency from Photoshop. "We'll define that later in GIF Animator."

You can double-check that the most important color areas are Web-safe by using the Info palette and seeing if the R, G, or B readouts are in multiples of 51: 0, 51, 102, 153, 204, and 255. "For example, in the Cookie Jar animation, I double-checked the color of the cookie jar lid and by reading the Info palette values I could see that the colors aren't Web-safe — since 209, 170, and 169 are not multiples of 51 (9.20). By running the Web Scrub filter (9.21) I can bring the colors into the Web-safe palette very quickly. Notice that the Info palette read-out for Cookie Jar lid is now in multiples of 51, which means that the jar lid is now in a Web-safe color (9.22).

"Working with Actions is a definite must for this production work! Since GIF Animator 2.0 can read and separate layered Photoshop files, I can quickly rebuild a layered file with all the indexed files. By holding down the Shift key with the move tool, I can drag and drop and center each file very quickly."

9.21

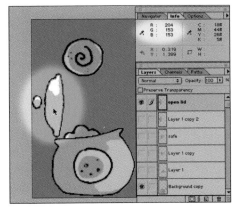

9.22

FOOLING THE EYE

Yann explains, "I experiment with turning layers on and off and try to see if there are frames that the animation doesn't need. Keep in mind, you want to use the minimum amount of frames necessary to convey the sense of motion. Rather than just deleting layers, you can use the Motion Blur filter to take out layers. For the Avenue A logo animation, I initially had the sharp word 'Avenue' on 12 separate layers. By blurring six layers, I could delete six of the layers. The trails of the motion blur help to fool the eye to 'see' motion (9.23 – 9.29). You can also create similar effects by working with layer transparency."

NOTE

Both GIF Animator and GifBuilder accept layered Photoshop files. Any image information outside of the visible layer frame can cause problems when importing into GifBuilder. Before importing layered Photoshop files into your GIF animation program, choose Select ➢ All and Image ➢ Crop, which will trim off any image that extends outside of the Photoshop layer frame.

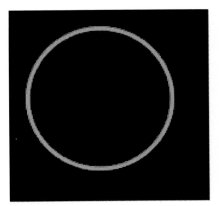

9.23

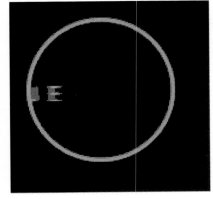

9.24

9.25

9.26

9.27

9.28

9.29

LET'S GET MOVING!

Once all the files are prepped, "I use ULead GIF Animator 2.0 to build the animation. One issue to consider before bringing either the separate files or the layered Photoshop file into GIF Animator is to think about the color palette that GIF Animator will use to optimize the animation. If all the frames use the same colors, then I can continue. But if there are important colors that are not on the first frame but are used later on in the animation, then I recommend building a patchwork file with all of the important colors and bringing that into GIF Animator first, since GIF Animator looks at the first file to build the global palette. When it comes time to actually time and build the animation, you can just throw the patchwork file away."

The most important issues to consider when creating a GIF animation are *looping*, *timing*, *removal method*, and *file optimization*.

■ Looping refers to how many times the animation should play. "When I'm working on a banner ad, the client tells me how often the animation should loop, usually three times (9.30). Make sure that the animation stops on a meaningful frame, such as 'Click Here!,' or on the name of the client or product. In the *www.cookierecipe.com* site, the banner ad starts with the simple logo and then the cookie guy comes out and sneaks up on the cookie. Once he has the cookie, I added a slight delay and the words 'All cookies. . . All the time' blur in from the left and the animation stops on the final site name after playing three times (9.31)."

■ Timing refers to the speed that the animation plays. "GIF animation software measures time in $\frac{1}{100}$ second increments, which is of course an estimate since connection speed influences the playback (9.32). You might be tempted to use a delay of 0, thinking that this would allow the animation to play as quickly as possible — don't. A delay of 0 is not understandable by all browsers and the animation will not play at all. Also, Netscape 3.0 will read any speed under $\frac{10}{100}$ as 'go as fast as possible'

and may move much faster than expected or desired. In the announcement banner for *www.cakerecipe.com* and *www.pierecipe.com*, I wanted to create a bit of excitement by making the cake and pie come in as quickly as possible. I also used transparency and scale on the writing to give the animation some depth (9.33)."

■ "Offbeat timing can also be used in a subtle manner to surprise the viewer. The cookie fellah's eyes move infrequently and that makes him more human. Staggered timing is when two animations never synch, which keeps them interesting even after a few loops."

■ The removal method tells the animation software how to compare one frame to the other. Depending on the desired effect, the two most common removal methods are "do not remove" and "to background color," also known as the disposal method.

9.30

9.32

9.31

9.33

9.34

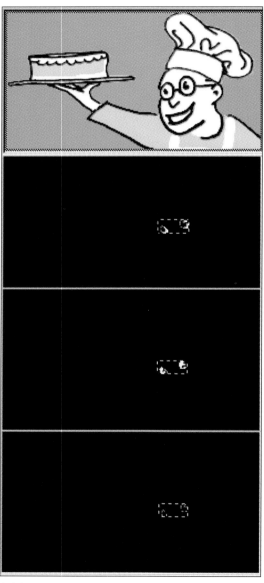

9.35

Which removal method you use depends upon if there is transparency over the animation that will be taking place. The majority of animations do not play over transparency and should therefore use "do not remove" also referred to as the "do not dispose" removal method. In the cookie fellow example, (9.34) only his eyes change and that does not take place over a transparent area. The "do not remove" or "do not dispose" removal will look at each animation cel and only keep those parts that change. "In the cookie fellow animation, by using the 'do not remove' removal option, GIF Animator compared all the files and cropped and kept out only the areas that changed—and to think I used to have to do this by hand and try to align the pieces (9.35)! GIF Animator also allows me to open a preview in Internet Explorer or Netscape Navigator so I can double-check the timing, looping, and removal method (9.36 and 9.37)."

9.36

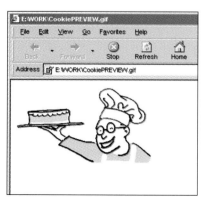

9.37

In cases where an animation will be playing over a transparent area, use "to background color." The first step is to define the transparency color by checking the transparency box (9.38) and clicking the color to be transparent (9.39).

The "to background color" removal method allows animations to play over the transparent area. "For the Cookie Jar animation, I wanted the lid to open and the cookies to come out. In Photoshop, I prepared all the pieces for the animation: jar, cookies, and the motion of the lid on separate layers (9.40). If I had used 'do not remove' removal, the animation would have played like a slide show and the cookie frames would have obliterated the cookie jar. To let the cookies come out of the jar, I used 'to background color,' which allowed the cookies to come out of the jar and be seen over the 'red' transparent image area (9.41).

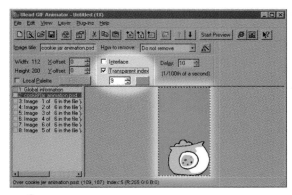

9.38

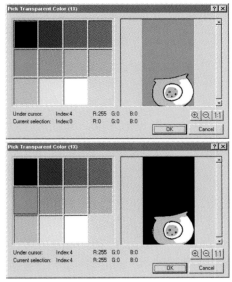

9.39

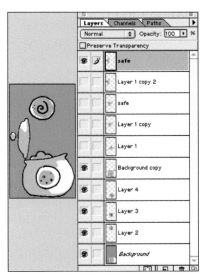

9.40

9.41

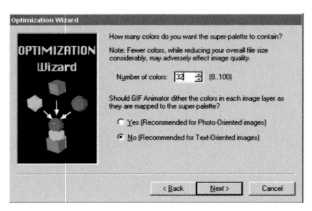

9.42

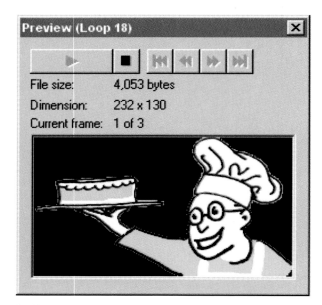

9.43

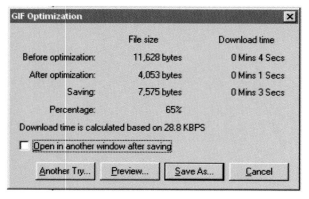

9.44

"Once I have the animation worked out, I run the Optimization Wizard (9.42), which steps me through the final settings with which the animation will be built. I set the colors to 32, do not dither, and never interlace. Interlacing increases file size and the first frame of the animation will look fine, but the subsequent frames will be displayed as chunky interlaced images. Finally, I check the animation in preview (9.43). Before saving the file, I can see how much file size GIF Animator has saved me. In the case of the cookie feller, the file size has been decreased by 65 percent (9.44). The largest I ever want a GIF animation to be is 15K."

BILLBOARDS ON THE INFOBAHN

Banner ads are a great way to reach thousands of viewers. The advantages of banner ads are they can be targeted, response can be measured, and the customer can be just one click away from your product. Using GIF animations for banner ads is popular since the majority of browsers support GIF animation. This allows you to add visual impact without taking a huge file size hit. Including motion in a banner ad has been shown to increase reader response by up to 40 percent.

Before designing a banner ad, establish the following elements:

- **Final pixel dimensions.** Standards are developing and the most popular proportions are 468 × 60 pixels for a full banner. Go to *www.commercepark.com/AAAA/casie/standards/proposal.html* for a complete listing of recommended banner ad measurements.
- **File size.** How many K is the file allowed to be? Banner ads without motion are usually limited to 2 – 4K, and the maximum file size for a banner ad with motion is generally 15K or less.
- **Looping.** How often should the advertisement play? After four loops most viewers tend to ignore the ad.

Effective banner ads combine placement in context, good design, and balanced cost. The average banner ad is priced between $20 and $125 per 1,000 page views.

GIF ANIMATION AND FLASH

"I obviously love to sketch, but our clients also expect different visual solutions. Working with Macromedia FreeHand and Flash allows me to create vector-based graphics that are graphically sophisticated. For the FoodBite logo, I received the initial sketch from a graphic designer who had created the apple and text in Illustrator. I took the initial vector outlines from Illustrator into FreeHand and brought that file into Flash. In each Flash layer, I created masks that were the same color as the backgrounds that the animation was going over. In the process of removing the masks, the effect was created that made it look as if the apple and text were being scripted in. In this case, I exported the animated GIF from Flash. It is meant to be shown on a solid white page. If this animation had required transparency, the file would have been huge (9.45 – 51).

9.45   9.46

9.49

9.47

9.50

9.48

9.51

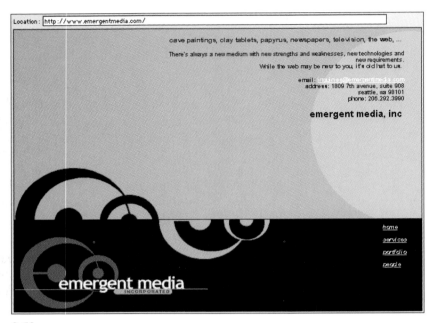

9.52

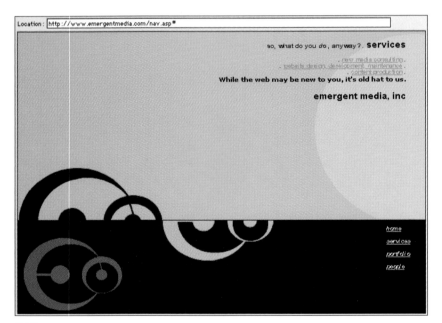

9.53

"For the Emergent Media site, I was challenged to create an animation that was visually intriguing and still small in file size (9.52). I solved this problem by making the animation transparent, allowing the background color of each page to be the color of the animation (9.53). I started by designing the logo in FreeHand, cutting it up, and bringing it into Flash where I used the rotate tool to spin the cels. From Flash I saved the individual layers out as GIFs, which I brought into a layered Photoshop file (9.54) in order to cut up the separate areas that would be put back together with an HTML table (9.55).

"The actual animation is just black and white with a few shades of gray for antialiasing. And by defining the transparency in GIF Animator, I created the illusion that the colored arc was 'cutting' into the black area. The company name that comes in from the left is also a good example of using a blurred layer to fool the eye to see motion as the words zoom in."

NOTE

Macromedia Fireworks will simplify creating tables immensely because it allows the user to work with guides to define and create the table cells. Fireworks also writes the required HTML to build the table.

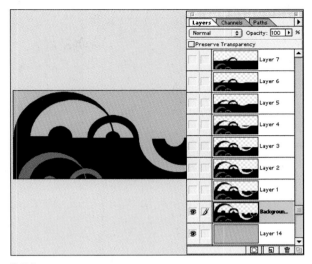

9.54

EMBEDDING ANIMATION

The beauty of GIF animation and HTML is that an animation can be embedded just like any other image using `<IMG SRC="name.gif" ALT="Click Here!" WIDTH=468 HEIGHT=60>`. The HTML defines the image, the `<ALT>` tag, and image size attributes.

"All in all, the merit of GIF animation is that I can animate drawings, photos, logos, and QuickTime movies. I love that I can work with the most sophisticated tools, including Photoshop, FreeHand, and Flash, and still end up with an animation that practically everyone can see without having to download a plug-in. A few Photoshop layers and a creative idea is all I need to be happy for a few hours. . . okay, add a cup of coffee and I'll be really, really happy."

9.55

The AFI ONLINE CINEMA is brought to you by...

INSTRUCTIONS | MOVIE INFO | LOBBY

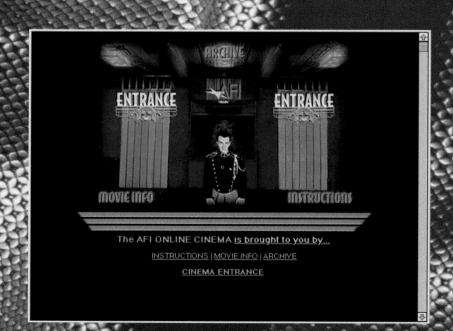

The AFI ONLINE CINEMA is brought to you by...

INSTRUCTIONS | MOVIE INFO | ARCHIVE

CINEMA ENTRANCE

CHAPTER 10
FILMS AND VIDEO ON THE WEB

W e all have fond memories of going to the movies, munching on popcorn, waiting for the house lights to dim, and watching the shimmering screen that transports us into times and places full of fantasy, excitement, and drama. A few short hours later you shuffle out of the theater, eyes blinking as they adjust to the sudden brightness of the lobby or afternoon sidewalk light. Where had you been? To the ends of the universe and back.

Going to the movies is one of our favorite pastimes — but don't you hate it when the film that you wanted to see isn't playing in your neighborhood any longer and you have to wait for it to get to the video store? What about the classic black and white movies that flicker in our memories featuring Buster Keaton, Charlie Chaplin, and Mary Pickford (10.1)? Where can you go to see those classics? Pop the popcorn and point your browser to *www.afionline.org* to see up to 250 movies either in short QuickTime clips or as streaming-video feature films that play up to 20 minutes.

The American Film Institute (AFI) was founded in 1967 by an act of Congress to "advance and preserve the art of the moving image." At that time over half of all movies ever made in the United States had been lost due to environmental damage and sheer negligence. Film stock was deteriorating, nitrate films were literally burning up, and the lack of a comprehensive catalog of the American film was threatening even more losses. The American Film Institute, based in Los Angeles, California, is a graduate school with seven disciplines (10.2), a film preservation center (10.3 and 10.4), and a focal point for film aficionados from around the globe (10.5).

Even though the screen is small, the audience we are reaching is huge.

DAN HARRIES

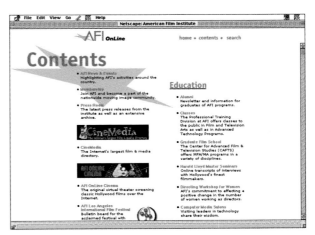

10.1

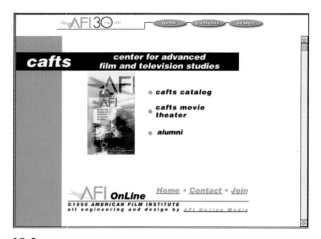

10.2

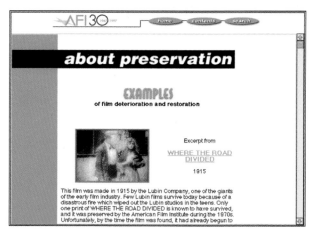

10.4

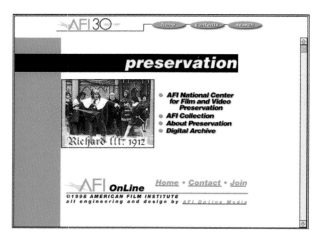

10.3

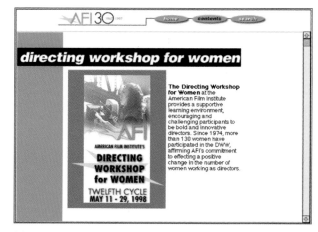

10.5

ARTIST:
Dan Harries

ORGANIZATION:
American Film Institute
2021 N. Western Ave.
Los Angeles, CA 90027
213/856-7630
www.afionline.org
dan.harries@mdx.ac.uk

SYSTEM, MAC:
Power Mac 8500/180
Mac OS 8.0
2GB storage/48MB RAM

SYSTEM, PC:
Intergraph StudioZ

CONNECTIVITY, ISP:
Ethernet to the AFI Intranet to T-1

SERVER ENVIRONMENT:
Compaq NT

PERIPHERALS:
Radius 17-inch monitor and two external
MicroNet 2GB hard drives for processing
video

SMALL SCREEN, HUGE AUDIENCE

"One of the best ways to preserve a film is by having a lot of viewers see it," explains Dan Harries, Director of Online Media at the AFI. "We launched the AFI Web site in 1995. Over half a million people visit the site every month, and in the last year over 500,000 people have watched a movie. In our OnLine Cinema, (10.6) 85 percent of the audience have watched a movie from beginning to end. We're recapturing an audience for films that have rarely seen the light of a projector bulb in over half a century. The best thing is that film fans from all around the world are coming to the AFI site to learn more about a featured director, to see clips from the graduate students' work, or just to spend some time with the classics. In the area of film preservation, the AFI OnLine Cinema is an interesting juxtaposition that advances and preserves the classic films with the newest technology."

It would be great to watch a complete film at your computer anytime you wanted to — making the Internet not only your means of distribution but also your means of exhibition — but the present bandwidth limitations just don't make this feasible. On the other hand, including film clips on a Web site isn't very complex at all. In fact, the simplest type of movie can be a file that the viewer downloads to play whenever they want to. As more and more movies are accessible via the Web, we are actually developing an audience that needs, wants, and expects to see movies within the context of the online experience.

10.6

PRIMARY APPLICATIONS:
Adobe Premiere 4.21, Media Cleaner Pro 2.0, Movie Player, BBEdit 4.5, and Netscape 3.01

WORK HISTORY:
1992 — Ph.D. in film and television, UCLA.
1993 — Professor of Media. Griffith University in Brisbane, Queensland, Australia.
1994 — Designed and launched Cine-Media, the Internet's largest film and media directory.

1995 — Started the American Film Institute's Online Media Department. Designed and launched the Web site of the AFI in Los Angeles, California.
1997 — Launched the AFI OnLine Cinema featuring classic and contemporary movies.

FAVORITE MIDNIGHT SNACK:
Waffles with guava syrup

Very soon, you will see more instances where movies and interactivity are combined. As viewers watch a film, they will be able to click an actor's face and read a biography or listen to an interview with the director. At present, however, we are still in an incubation period as the codecs, file formats, and delivery systems get worked out. The cable companies are looking into delivering on-demand digital video via fiber optics in a way that will creatively combine the cable TV and Internet experience.

NOW SHOWING

"Before a movie goes online we identify two primary factors: who is the audience and what is the function of the film going to be? These factors will influence the editing, digitizing, compression, and delivery method used. What experience do you want to deliver to your audience and what goals do the viewers have for watching these films? If a viewer goes to the trouble of either downloading a clip or getting the required plug-ins, then the movie he ends up seeing needs to be compelling, valuable, and fulfill his expectations.

"The two delivery methods that we feature on our Web site are download and real-time viewing. Each type has its place, depending on the film and target audience. The simplest method is to have viewers download a QuickTime movie and watch it whenever they want to, as many times as they want to."

USING QUICKTIME

Today, location scouts and film production teams are using QuickTime clips to show casting and stock footage to producers and directors around the world. "The benefit of using QuickTime is that in the US alone 60 million computers already have it installed, most viewers won't have to download a separate plug-in, and the quality of a QuickTime clip is usually much better than the streaming video. The drawback is that the delay between the viewer deciding that they want to see a movie and the actual playing of the movie grows in direct relationship to increasing file size. To offset this delay, we use a progressive download scheme that lets the movie start to play before the entire file is done downloading."

> **NOTE**
>
> Apple QuickTime is cross-platform compatible on Macintosh, Windows 95, and Windows NT. The recent release of QuickTime 3.0 adds a bevy of features, including better compression and playback options.

USING STREAMING VIDEO

"The real-time movie experience screens the film in the context of the online experience. These clips are perfect for movie trailers, brief interviews, and often serve as teasers for film festivals. The longest films that we feature have a run length of up to 20 minutes and weigh in at 60MB per film. Using streaming video technology, we screen extended interviews or entire films. As the viewer watches the film, additional footage is being funneled to the browser in the background. The advantage to streaming video is that there is never an actual file downloaded to the viewer's hard drive, allowing more movies to go online since films cannot be downloaded, manipulated, or redistributed. The disadvantages of streaming video are that it requires server support, browser plug-ins, a very fast connection on a clear pipeline, and the quality isn't of the highest caliber — hey, it's a miracle that it's even getting there in the first place." The most common types of streaming video include RealMedia (*www.real.com*), VDO (*www.vdo.net*), Vxtreme, and NetShow (`www.microsoft.com/netshow/vxtreme/`).

CHOOSING THE RIGHT FORMAT

Balancing the function of the film, goals of the Web site, and audience expectations with the pros and cons of QuickTime and streaming video form the foundation for the decision about which format to use. "I've noticed that a lot of Web sites are using videos to catch the viewer's attention when an animated GIF would work much more quickly and easily. We use animated GIFs in combination with our movies to create a setting or convey an atmosphere (10.7 – 10.9). Animated GIFs are a great way to start with motion imaging on a Web site."

FROM CELLULOID TO BITS AND BYTES

"We spend a lot of time shuttling back and forth with the video deck to find the best twenty seconds. We edit with the viewer in mind, looking for the twenty seconds that tell a story. It also helps to select clips that aren't full of frenetic detail and motion, since fine details don't come across well in the small frames that we use on the Web."

CAPTURE

QuickTime and streaming video are captured in the same way, either through a separate capture board—for example, a Radius Video Vision board—or with any AV Power Macintosh 8100 or 8500 in combination with a standard video deck and simple RCA jack connections. "We digitize straight into Adobe Premiere, where we also edit, add simple transitions and titles, and then export to Media Cleaner Pro for fade-ins, fade-outs, and final compression. Our goal is to get the file as small as possible, maintain reasonable image and sound quality, give the viewer a 20-second clip, and come in with a 1.5–1.7MB movie file size."

Setting up the capture preferences correctly in Premiere is essential to getting a good video capture. "We use a letterbox format of 164×124 pixels. This gives the clip the accustomed movie theater aspect ratio. We capture at 15 frames per second and do not apply any compression to the incoming video (10.11). It is better to capture at the final pixel resolution of the file and with the correct sound settings, rather than capturing, reworking, and sizing the file down later. If needed, we correct tonal problems, hue shifts, and contrast issues at the time of capture."

Desktop and digital video professionals often capture at full screen and size the image down in Media Cleaner Pro, but this creates files that are unwieldy. By capturing larger than the final size, you can crop off edge noise without making the video smaller than the final image. Also, by capturing at a larger size and scaling down, the video noise is reduced. For example, if you capture at 640×480 and scale down to 320×240, each pixel in the final image is an average of 4 original pixels. This averaging tends to smooth the image and reduce noise. However, all this being said, it is frequently difficult to capture at full screen because it requires much more hard drive space and a more tightly "tuned" system.

10.7

10.8

10.9

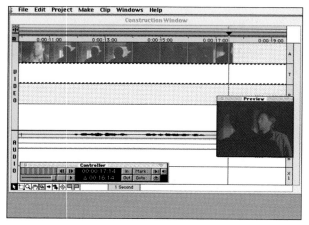

10.11

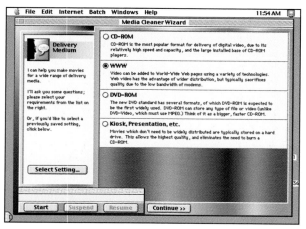

10.12

10.13

"Capture the audio at the highest quality setting of 44.1 Hz with 16-bit sound at mono, since streaming doesn't support stereo sound yet. We put an increased importance on sound—if the sound is really good it will help compensate the experience of the video being jerky, fuzzy, or blurry—to a point! Viewers will put up with less image quality but will not tolerate poor sound. If the sound is ambient sound or background noise, less quality is required than for an interview where the sound is obviously more important."

Queue up the tape and capture the segment with a little bit of buffer at the beginning and end of the clip. Place the raw capture into Premiere's construction window and do any editing required (10.12). "One problem with Premiere is that it has so many easy-to-use transitions—spins, wipes, zooms, fades, peels, and dissolves. If you only have 20 seconds you don't want to waste a lot of time with fancy transitions. Jump cuts and a simple fade-in at the beginning and a fade-out at the end are better. The opening and closing fades set the tone—analogous to the house lights going down in a real movie theater—making the film experience contained and special. We use Media Cleaner Pro to add the final fade-ins and outs."

CLEANUP

After digitizing an video clip, it is necessary to prep it with file efficiency and format in mind. Dan uses Media Cleaner Pro, an encoder software to add opening and closing fades, optimize color palettes, and do the final compression—all with a tab before/after interface which makes making decisions really intuitive. "If you are digitizing video for the first time, using the Media Cleaner Pro wizard is a great way to learn about the variables to take into consideration, such as the final media CD-ROM, WWW, DVD, connection speed, playback options, and so on. The best thing about the wizard is that as you select a certain option it will remove conflicting options further along so that you create the best movie possible (10.13)."

Once the capture is done, do a preview in Premiere in RAM and export the file into Media Cleaner Pro or save the file as a MOV file and open it with Media Cleaner Pro. "When you export the file into Media Cleaner Pro, Media Cleaner Pro has to be running in the background. This may sound odd at first, but it is actually very interesting since a preview in Premiere is just a map of the pieces, and exporting the map allows Media Cleaner Pro to construct the movie file from the map."

Video compression looks at image information in two ways—spatially and temporally. *Spatial* compression removes redundant information row by row. For example, a large expanse of blue sky will compress spatially very well. *Temporal* compression looks at a video frame by frame and removes the information that isn't moving. Imagine a person talking in front of a building. Because the person is moving, he will be left alone and because the building is not moving it will be temporally compressed.

Experimenting with settings and variables is crucial to making movies successful on the Web. This requires editorial decisions, testing, saving and comparing settings, and always checking the final movie on a PC with a 256-color monitor. "Although we do all of our digitizing and creative work on a Macintosh, the great majority of our audience is coming to the AFI Web site via a PC. Our general rule is: Make it look good on the PC and it will look great on the Mac."

SETTINGS FOR QUICKTIME

Here's how the settings that Dan uses to create downloadable QuickTime movies (10.14) work:

- Set the output format to QuickTime and add the file suffix .MOV to the file name by checking the File Suffix box. It is important to add the file suffix so that the server knows how to handle the file.
- *Flattening* is the final pass applied to a compressed movie, which ensures that no edits remain in the movie.
- The "Make cross-platform" option enables both Macintosh and PCs to see the movies.

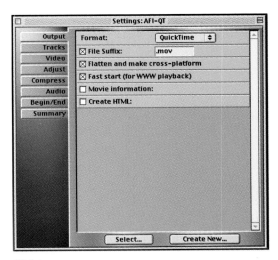

10.14

10.15

- The "Fast start" option enables the very important progressive download in which a movie will start playing before the entire file has been downloaded.
- Selecting "process" means that the track will have all the adjustments and compression parameters applied to it prior to inclusion in the final output movie (10.15).
- Dan maintains his original pixel dimensions of 164 × 124 pixels (10.16).

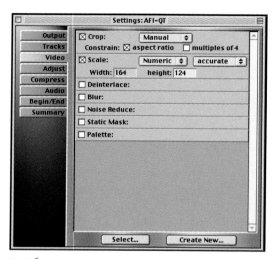

10.16

■ The compression used is very important to the final outcome of the movie quality. "Presently, we are in a transitional period from using Cinepak to using Sorenson Video Compression. Cinepak is a commonly-used QuickTime codec and allows temporal and spatial compression, as well as data rate limiting (10.17)."

■ "We like to play the movies at 15 frames per second, but if the file size becomes too big, we drop down to 10 frames per second."

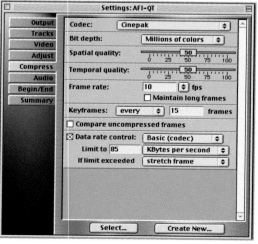

10.17

■ The *keyframe rate* is a safety net in case the movie doesn't download or play quickly enough, then at least every fifteenth frame will be displayed. Especially if you have a slow machine or connection that can't keep up playing the movie, the keyframes will play like a slide show.

■ After the actual pixel dimensions of the frame, the "Data rate control" option is the second most important determining factor that affects playback quality and speed. The *data rate* is the amount of information per second used to represent a movie. "A single-speed CD-ROM movie is usually made at a data rate of 100 Kbps and we try to keep the data rate between 65 and 100." This number does not refer to download speed, which is dependent on a users modem; rather, this is for playback.

■ "Although we capture the audio track at 44.1 kHz, we let Media Cleaner Pro take the audio track down to 22.050 kHz and still get very good results."

■ "Media Cleaner Pro does a great job at doing the fade-ins and outs, and we use the shortest increment possible of one second, fade to and from black (10.18)."

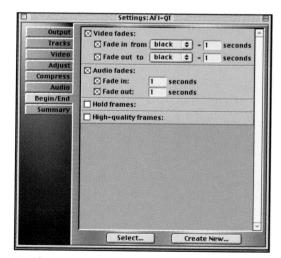

10.18

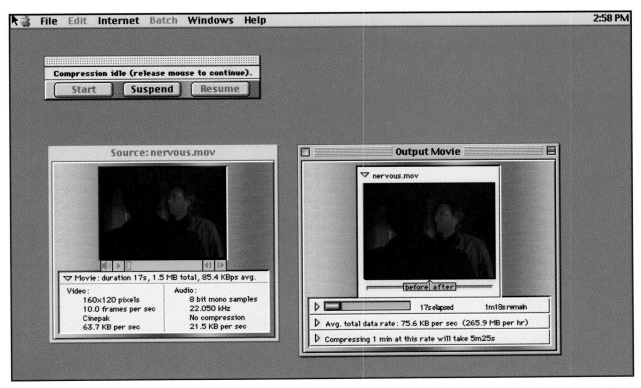

10.19

Once the settings are all determined, save the settings, export the file from Premiere into Media Cleaner Pro, and save the file. Notice the video and audio breakdown. By moving the tab slider to the left and right you can see how the settings are going to effect the final output (10.19).

HTML FOR QUICKTIME

The HTML required to embed a QuickTime file that shows the control strip and starts playing when the download is complete is straightforward:

```
<EMBED src="name_of_movie.mov"
WIDTH=164 HEIGHT=124 AUTOPLAY=true
CONTROLLER=true LOOP=false PLUG-
INSPAGE="http://quicktime.apple.com
/" ALIGN="MIDDLE">
```

BEHIND THE SCENES

When you see a movie you like on the Web, download it, open it in Movie Player, and Get Info to see all the information you will ever need—video tracks (10.20), frame rates, data rates, audio information (10.21), width/height, bit-depth, and so on (10.22). It's a great way to learn. "We rarely use Movie Player to play videos, but we do use it to analyze our clips all the time."

10.20

10.21

10.22

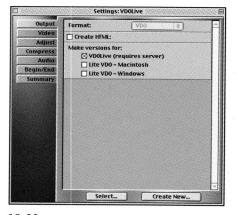

10.23

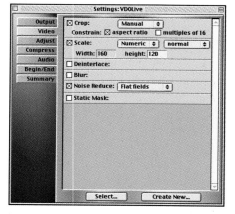

10.24

STREAMING VIDEO

"We currently use streaming video for films up to 20 minutes in length, long enough to screen graduate projects, short films, and in-depth interviews. The difference between a 20-second QuickTime clip and a 20-minute streaming video is huge, but we often grapple with the decision as to which one to use. The quality of the QuickTime movies with progressive download is much higher than the streaming video movies, but the time it takes to download a file can be too long for some viewers. On the other hand, a 20-minute streaming-video movie can balloon to a 60MB file, but it starts to play within seconds."

Viewing a 20-minute movie requires that the server, server software, and the viewer's browser are configured to handle the demands of streaming video. The AFI currently uses VDO — a true streaming, server-based online video architecture created by VDOnet. The biggest advantage to streaming video is that the file is never downloaded to the viewer's hard drive; rather, streaming video uses a buffer that feeds video data into memory — if there was a bandwidth transfer slowdown, enough data should be in the memory buffer to allow continuous play. "We use a VDO codec and server. VDO monitors the connection speed, and if the connection slows down, the server will reduce quality to continue sending frames — albeit blurred frames. If the data flow slows severely, the VDO server will send out a slide show based on your keyframe setting. That way the viewer will always be seeing something."

The capture workflow is similar to that just described here: video deck to Macintosh computer, into Premiere, capture clip, preview, and export to Media Cleaner Pro running the VDO settings in the list that follows. (When working with such large files you'd do best to work with two external hard drives — one for the raw captures and the second for the built files.)

- Output a VDOLive file that is 160×120 pixels (10.23 and 10.24).
- Keyframe every 100 frames at a 15-frame-per-second frame rate (10.25).

Media Cleaner Pro will automatically create an AVI file, which is required with streaming video. An AVI file is a windows-based file that a Macintosh user cannot just double-click to see the movie. Use the program AVI to QuickTime (*pointnet.scoca.ohio.gov/ public/spms/aviqt.sit or ftp://sumex-aim.stanford.edu/ info-mac/grf/util/avi-to-qt-converter.hqx*) to view AVI files on a Macintosh. When viewing an AVI file in QuickTime, the bottom few rows of pixels may be blurred. This is irrelevant since it will not show up in the final presentation, so don't worry about it.

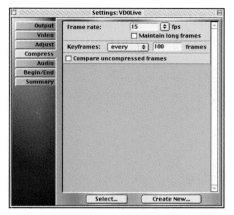

10.25

NOTE

Additional effective streaming video solutions include RealMedia by RealNetworks, Inc., (*www.real.com*) and Microsoft's NetShow (www.microsoft.com/netshow/).

SERVING STREAMING VIDEO

Using VDOnet streaming isn't as simple or inexpensive as linking a QuickTime file in an HTML document. Serving streaming video requires specialized server software that monitors the streaming process, and the viewer must have the appropriate browser plug-ins installed. When a viewer accesses a streaming video file, the VDO protocol in the HTML document redirects the viewer's browser to access the VDO server that has the desired movie file (10.26). Simultaneously, on the viewer's machine, a 3K homing file is created that establishes the IP address that communicates with the VDO server. Using browser cache, the movie immediately begins to screen without ever downloading any of the video.

To embed a VDO file into your Web page use the following code:

```
<EMBED SRC="name_of_movie.vdo"
WIDTH=166 HEIGHT=129 STRETCH=TRUE
AUTOSTART=TRUE ALIGN=MIDDLE>
```

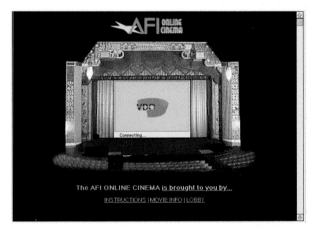

10.26

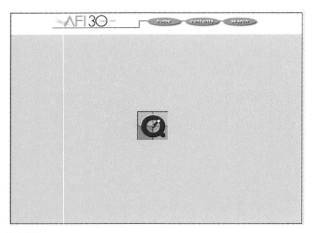

10.27

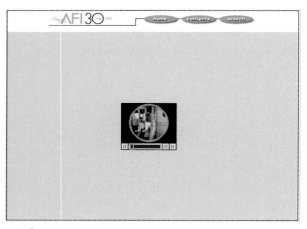

10.28

10.29

FROM NICKELODEON TO MULTIPLEX

The context in which both QuickTime clips and streaming-video movies are presented influences the viewer's experience tremendously. Creating the viewing environment combines HTML, page design, and deciding how much control the viewer has over playback.

The simplest method is to embed a QuickTime movie into an HTML file just like any other image. When the viewer accesses the clip it comes up in a gray default browser page (10.27) and the viewer waits for the entire QuickTime movie to download before the movie plays. With all that gray space around the movie, the clip looks much smaller than it really is (10.28).

The second method used is to have the movie clip play in a separate mini browser (10.29). This keeps the viewer within the context of your Web site and in the online experience. In the example pictured here (10.30), the viewer can read about Robert Wise and Orson Welles and then click See a Clip to watch a scene from *The Magnificent Ambersons*.

Constructing a context for the movie draws the viewer into the moviegoing experience. For example, before you can go into the AFI OnLine Cinema, you see the cinema entrance, enter, and click the usher (10.30) before taking your seat. The surrounding environment, (10.31) beautifully designed by Todd Hughes, the AFI's online media designer, gives the movie clip a grandeur that an isolated QuickTime postage stamp just doesn't have. As the movie starts to play, the viewer has the feeling of being in a classic theater.

10.30

10.31

10.32

IN HONOR OF ROBERT WISE

In 1998, the AFI honored Robert Wise (10.32) with the Life Achievement Award. The AFI Web site has numerous Web pages that feature interviews, film clips, and photo galleries in his honor. Robert Wise directed and won the Oscar for *West Side Story*, and on the AFI Web site you can read about the film's production and how he solved the problem of imparting the feeling that the young lovers were by themselves when they were actually on a swirling school dance floor. After reading about how the problem was solved, you can watch the clip and see the final results.

Strikingly, the frame for the movie clips, again designed by Todd Hughes, is an animated GIF that mimics the flickering light coming out of a projectionist's window in a crowded theater. This sets the tone perfectly for classic American films such as *West Side Story*, *The Sound of Music*, and *The Day the Earth Stood Still*. The GIF animation projectionist is made up of three separate GIF files put back together in a table with the movie clip in the center. (10.33 – 10.35)

10.34

10.33   **10.35**

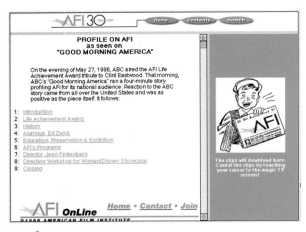

10.36

10.37

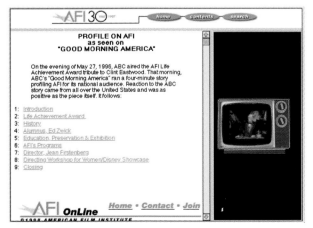

10.38

USING JAVASCRIPT

A variation on the concept of setting the stage is to use JavaScript to target the film to go into a specific frame. The AFI was featured on the morning news program *Good Morning America* (10.36). "The spot was four minutes long, and we edited the highlights and created nine separate QuickTime movies for the best sections. The viewers can choose which clip they want to see, and the JavaScript tells the clip to play within the television frame (10.37 – 10.38)."

FINALLY, WITH OR WITHOUT BUTTER?

"When you go to the movies, you are not responsible for when the movie starts or stops. In our online cinema, we have hidden the controls of the clips since they connote 'computer-ness' and distract the viewer from the entertainment experience. It may be a small cinema, but we are trying to create a complete experience!"

Make sure the viewer has to click to see a movie. "Never embed a movie on a page that starts to download without letting the viewer decide whether he wants to see the clip. Technology makes watching movies on the Web possible, but it is still slow and the unassuming viewer will become very irritated as the browser slows to an imperceptible crawl. Always design the interface so the viewer makes a decision to watch a movie by clicking on a play, select, or load button."

The most important question to ask before putting any video online is, "Is this compelling content?" The technology is fascinating, but it shouldn't usurp a good story or a well-crafted film production. Kevin Thomas, film critic from the *Los Angeles Times* reviewed the revival of Buster Keaton's *The Boat* that AFI featured in the OnLine Cinema. In the review, he did comment on the fact that the film was on a computer, but within a few minutes he became so enamored with the story that he forgot he was watching it on a computer monitor: "How does it look on a computer screen, at about 2 by 2½ inches, framed by a gorgeous, colorful, though over-lit, Art Deco proscenium? The answer is surprisingly good. Ever at odds with the absurdities of the material universe, Keaton and his cool, deadpan humor come across just fine in miniature." At the same time, it's hard to imagine anything but a silent short film, running roughly 22 minutes, working in this format. The classic two-reelers are relatively free of intertitles; they have a strong, clear visual style, and their appeal and meaning, as Miss [Lillian] Gish said, really is universal.

In the end, "we're inventing the medium as we work with it, and the reality is that movies online are still small, jerky, and blurry. But even though the screen is small, the audience we are reaching is huge. Already, over a half of a million people have watched one of our movies in the AFI OnLine Cinema as Hollywood classics become rediscovered by new generations, and our graduate student's work is seen by an international audience." If only AFI could deliver popcorn through the computer, we'd be set — click here for extra butter!

CHAPTER 11
IMMERSIVE ONLINE IMAGING

When you look at a photograph, do you ever wonder what was behind the photographer or just outside the image frame? Wouldn't it be fascinating if, when viewers came to your Web site, they could interact with a photograph? For example, moving through a scene, walking around an object such as a car or a sculpture, or visiting a museum, strolling freely from room to room. If your creative curiosity is piqued by any of these possibilities, then *Immersive Imaging* will intrigue, excite, and literally open new horizons for you and your images on the Web.

David Falstrup, President of eVox Productions, has been working with Immersive Imaging, or VR photography, since May of 1995. In the beginning, Immersive Imaging was called *QuickTime Virtual Reality* (QTVR). But times change, and since virtual reality connotes goggles and wired gloves, which Immersive Imaging does not require, the new term was created to reflect the concept that viewers can pan and zoom to "immerse" themselves in the photograph. Professionals in the field also use the terms *VR photography* and *QuickTime VR* to mean the same thing: interactive photographic images based upon Apple's QuickTime virtual-reality technology. Although the technology and format was developed by Apple Computer, both Macintosh and PC users can see and create cross-platform VR photographs.

Putting semantics aside, viewers that come to *www.evox.com* (11.1) can look around the newest Volkswagen Beetle (11.2 – 11.4), see the first interactive television commercial for Intel (11.5 – 11.7), or visit Monument Valley (11.8) and Lake Powell (11.9).

Immersive Imaging is about photography, and anyone with a 35mm camera, a tripod, and stitching software can start experimenting with it.

DAVID FALSTRUP

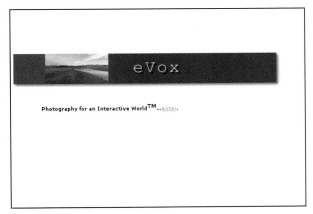

11.1

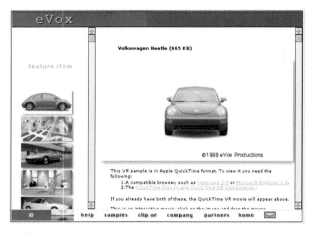

11.2

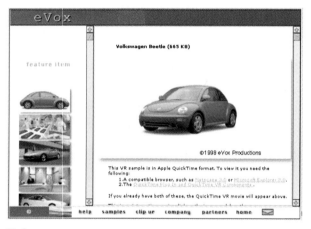

11.3

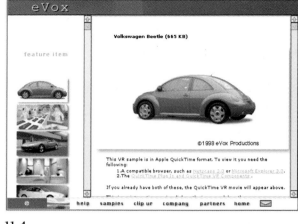

11.4

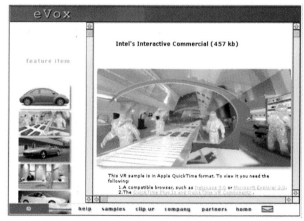

11.5

Pentium II is a registered trademark of the Intel Corporation.

ARTIST:
David Falstrup

ORGANIZATION:
eVox Productions
20432 South Santa Fe Ave., # J
Long Beach, CA 90810
310/605-1400 phone
310/605-1429 fax
New York City Studio
45 West 36th Street, 5th Floor
New York, NY 10018
212/547-8204 phone
212/268-1960 fax
www.evox.com
david@evox.com

SYSTEM, MAC:
Apple Power PC G3
4GB storage/200MB RAM

SYSTEM, PC:
Dell 266 Pentium,
4GB storage/128MB RAM

CONNECTIVITY, ISP:
T-1 and ISDN
Server: Dell 266 Pentium
4GB storage/128MB RAM

PERIPHERALS:
Nikon Fugix E2 and PhaseOne digital
cameras

As David explains, "The viewer can decide where they look in the scene, and this interaction with the image gives the viewer 'ownership' over their experience. Most importantly, Immersive Imaging is about photography, and anyone with a 35mm camera, a tripod, and stitching software can start experimenting with it. The best thing about doing VR photography now is that the software has become much easier to use. We used to have to write code to stitch images together with Macintosh Programmer's Workbench (MPW). Now we can drag the photographs into a folder and the software stitches them together for us."

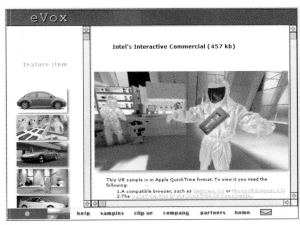

11.7   *Pentium II is a registered trademark of the Intel Corporation.*

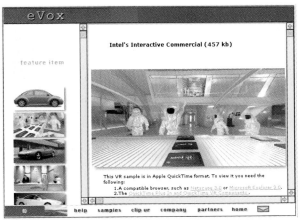

11.6   *Pentium II is a registered trademark of the Intel Corporation.*

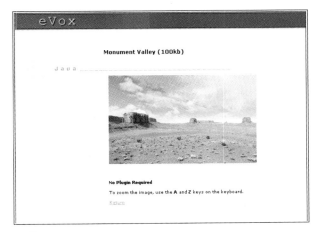

11.8

PRIMARY APPLICATIONS:
Apple QTVR Authoring Studio 1.0, Live Picture Real VR Studio, IPIX Builder, Adobe Photoshop 4.0 and After Effects, Macromedia Dreamweaver, DeBabelizer 1.6, Netscape and Internet Explorer versions 2, 3, and 4

WORK HISTORY:
1981 — Engineering Science degree from the University of Exeter, England; came to the U.S. and headed west. Became an aerospace engineer.
1983 – 84 — First start-up venture converting aerospace technology into products for formula one racing.

1985 – 87 — Management positions in R & D, as well as engineering.
1987 – 89 — Turnaround consulting projects in U.S. and Europe, including analysis of Chrysler's strategic plan for Lee Iaccoca.
1989 – 94 — General management, strategic planning, and consulting; focused on start-up and turnaround operations.
1989 — Masters of Management degree from Northwestern University's J.L. Kellogg Graduate School of Management and Certificate in Advanced International Business Management from the Copenhagen School of Business.

1994 — Introduced to multimedia. Recognized the need for a focused service company.
1995 — Attended the first Apple Developer University for QTVR. Founded eVox Productions in Long Beach, CA, a VR photography studio focusing on automotive and other high-end clients.
1998 — Opened second studio in New York, expanding into fashion work.
1999 — Will open first European QTVR studio.

FAVORITE THRILL:
Sailing on San Fransico Bay in a 40-knot wind.

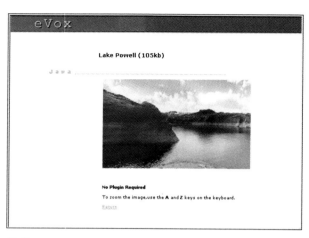

11.9

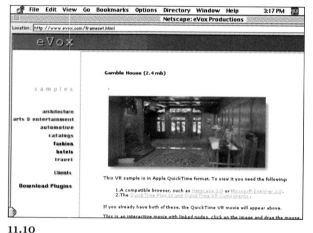

11.10

IMMERSIVE IMAGING FLAVORS

"There are different types of Immersive Imaging. The first one is the *interactive panorama*, in which the viewpoint is from the center out and the viewer can explore a 360-degree environment, such as the Gamble House Museum in Pasadena, California (11.10). The second type of Immersive Imaging is the *interactive object movie*, in which the viewer sees an object and can examine it from different points of view, as seen in the work that we have done for Warner Toys (11.11–11.13). In a nutshell, Immersive Imaging starts by photographing a scene, object, or person in a full 360 degrees, either processing and scanning the film or acquiring the digital camera files, and then stitching the images together with software by Apple or Live Picture. Once the image is on the Web, viewers can choose where they look — up or down, left or right, they can go in for a closer look or 'step back' to enjoy the scenery — all with the click and drag of the mouse. We also partner with IPIX to create BubbleView images (photographs mapped inside a sphere), Black Diamond to create surround videos, and Live Picture, who have developed Real VR. On our Web site, we have a VR photography comparison chart and links to many VR technology providers (11.14)."

11.11

11.12

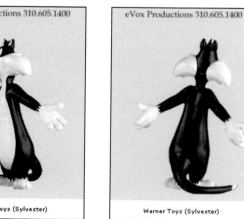

11.13

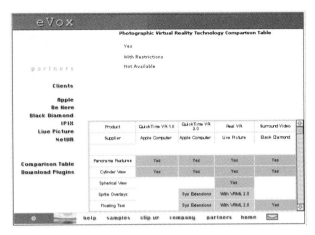

11.14

Product	QuickTime VR 1.0	QuickTime VR 2.0	Real VR	Surround Video
Supplier	Apple Computer	Apple Computer	Live Picture	Black Diamond
Panorama Features	Yes	Yes	Yes	Yes
Cylinder View	Yes	Yes	Yes	Yes
Spherical View			Yes	
Sprite Overlays		Sys Extensions	With VRML 2.0	
Floating Text		Sys Extensions	With VRML 2.0	Yes

INTERACTIVE PANORAMAS

Interactive panoramas are ideal for both interior and exterior shots, such as tours of museums or interesting architectural sites, movie sets, and natural landscapes. "For the Park Hyatt Hotel in Tokyo, we created an extensive interactive tour (11.15). The viewer can 'walk' through the lobby, go up to the rooms (11.16), see the breathtaking view from the presidential suite (11.17), or check out the banquet (11.18), wedding, and spa facilities that the hotel offers. When the viewer comes to the Web site (*www.parkhyatttokyo.com*), they can either download the entire tour, which is a huge 24MB, or go on a freeform online tour to visit the areas that they are specifically interested in. In the full 24MB version, the viewer can move from one area to the next by clicking on the hot spots that we've added. For example, when the viewer is in the presidential suite, they can start in the living room (11.19), move into the dining room (11.20), the study (11.21), or even see the opulent marble baths."

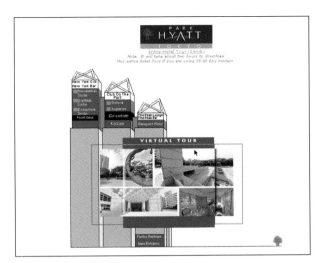

11.15

11.16

11.17

11.18

11.20

11.19

11.21

"The interactive panoramas begin with the camera in the center of the environment being photographed. The photographer 'is shooting from the inside out.' Depending on how wide your lens is, take 12 – 16 overlapping pictures to complete the 360-degree circle of view which will later be stitched together with the QTVR Authoring Studio 1.0 or Live Picture's Photo Vista or Reality Studio to create a single 360-degree image." The most important factors to take into consideration when shooting for professional interactive panoramas are as follows:

■ Work with a panoramic tripod head that can be moved in exact increments.

■ Rotate the camera on the *nodal point* of the lens. The nodal point of the lens is the specific point where light rays intersect on the image plane and the image flips. Aligning the camera on the nodal point will minimize the appearance that the elements in the picture are sliding when the viewer pans.

■ Work with a wide-angle, flat-field rectilinear lens — such as a Nikkor 15mm or Sigma 14mm.

■ Allow for 25 – 40 percent overlap between images, enabling the stitching software to create seamless images (11.22).

11.22

■ Keep exposure consistent. Set the exposure manually so that the auto exposure of the camera doesn't change the f-stop, which influences the images' depth of field and impact the software's ability to stitch the images back together in postproduction. If the light range varies a lot, bracket the exposures. Take a set of images for the light parts of the image and a set for the dark parts of the image. After the shoot, you can merge the files in Photoshop to create one set of images that are well-exposed for both the highlights and shadows. "When we photographed the hotel dining room, the sky in the windows was much brighter than the furniture in the room, so we shot the scene twice, exposing once for the room interior and once for the sky, and merged the shots in Photoshop (11.23)."

■ When using film, work with color negative film because it has greater exposure latitude in regard to lighting and exposure.

■ Shooting in a portrait orientation gives the image visual height.

■ Photographing the correct number of frames simplifies the stitching process. The following tables list the most common lens formats for 35mm cameras (11-1) and consumer digital cameras (11-2) and how many images to take.

11.23

You can learn about Immersive Imaging with much simpler tools, including consumer digital cameras such as the Apple QuickTake 200 or Kodak DC 210, a standard tripod that you've marked in equal increments, and Live Picture's Photo Vista software.

TABLE 11-1   DETERMINING THE NUMBER OF PHOTOGRAPHS FOR 35MM CAMERA LENSES

LENS FOCAL LENGTH	PORTRAIT	LANDSCAPE
14mm	8	6
15mm	8	6
16mm	8	6
16mm Fisheye	8	4
18mm	8	8
20mm	10	8
24mm	12	8
28mm	14	8
35mm	16	12
50mm	24	16

Table 11-2   DETERMINING THE NUMBER OF PHOTOGRAPHS FOR CONSUMER
DIGITAL CAMERAS

CAMERA	PORTRAIT	LANDSCAPE
Apple QuickTake 200	18	12
Canon PowerShot 600N	12	8
Epson PhotoPC 500	18	14
Fuji DC 300	16	10
Kodak DC-50	18	12
Kodak DC-120	18	12
Kodak DC-210	14	8
Olympus D-200L or D-300L	16	12
Polaroid PCD-2000	18	12

Note: Use widest zoom lens setting possible.

Into the Driver's Seat

A straightforward interactive panoramic image is interesting, but eVox pushes the technology further by combining studio shots, natural landscapes or computer-generated 3D environments, and sound to create one-of-a-kind viewing experiences. eVox has worked with over 45 international automobile manufacturers including Toyota, Volkswagen, Ford, Ferrari, Mazda, KIA, and many others. The production begins with the photographer shooting the 360-degree image of the inside of the car. The car is shot in the studio with a green-screen background to simplify and increase the accuracy of the masking process. After the film is processed and scanned onto Kodak Photo CD, the individual images are acquired into Photoshop, where they are retouched, enhanced, and the windows are masked. Then the car image is layered on top of the landscape image and, by using the Offset filter set to wrap around, eVox can see how the landscape fits into the scene. Once position and relationship are set, the layered file is flattened, saved as a PICT file, and brought into QTVR Authoring Studio where the two edges are stitched together. This creates the illusion that a car which was shot and lit in a professional studio is really outdoors on a seaside cliff or in a remote desert (11.24). As viewers move around the interior of the car, they see the landscape changing just as if they were in a car outdoors. In VR panoramas that are combined with object movies, the viewer can open the glove compartment, fold down the seats, honk the horn, and even start the engine — everything but drive away with the Aston Martin pictured here (11.25)!

11.24

11.25

Going Deeper

By adding sound and interactivity to immersive images, the viewer is invited to explore and experience the car, scene, or product more intimately. With the addition of nodes or hot spots, the viewer can move from one point of view to another within the panoramic scene. "Museums and artists use interactive panoramas to document exhibitions, allowing the viewer to pan around the exhibit. And when the viewer sees a painting that they are interested in, they can click on the hot spot to see a high-resolution version, read about the artist, or be linked to another Web site. We use hot spots to give the viewer more information. For example, in a tour we did of the Hard Rock Cafe (11.26), you can walk into the entry way (11.27), look around in 360 degrees, and then click on a hot spot that takes you further into the restaurant (11.28–11.29). Interactive panoramas with hot spots can really add up in file size, so we use them mostly on CDs and interactive kiosks and less on the Web.

"One more thing that we like to do with the panoramic images is to make large photographic quality prints with them. We've created panoramas that are up to 100MB large, which allow us to make prints up to eight feet wide with the Durst Lambda 130 direct digital printer at Infinite Photo and Imaging in Arlington, Virginia (*www.infinitephoto.com*). The prints are really quite spectacular (11.30–11.31)."

11.26

11.27

11.28

11.29

INTERACTIVE OBJECT MOVIES

The second type of Immersive Imaging is the interactive object movie, in which the object is in the center of the image and the viewer can move around it, looking at it from different vantage points. The object can be as small as a single rose or as large as a Toyota van. "For the smaller objects, we use a Virtual Object Rig in which the object is clamped in midair and the camera is rotated around it, taking a picture every 10 to 20 degrees. The decision to use 10- or 20-degree increments depends on how smooth you want the rotation of the final movie to be. For larger objects such as cars, we place the object onto a 30-foot turntable similar to a lazy susan. The camera is stationary and we actually rotate the object in ten degree increments."

Object movies range from simple *spins*, in which the object is photographed from one point of view, to *multi-row object movies*, in which the object is photographed from various perspectives while it is spun. "It all depends on how many points of view you want to give the viewer. For some products, such as the Heineken bottle (11.32), a simple spin is all that is needed (11.33). Often, the client wants the viewer to be able to look at the product from any point of view.

11.30

11.31

11.32

11.33

We'll shoot the object in a grid pattern (11.34 and 11.35) and stitch the set of images together with the Apple QTVR Authoring Studio software. The final result is a file in which the viewer uses the mouse to move the object and look at any side of it — in this case the Nike sneaker (11.36 – 11.39)."

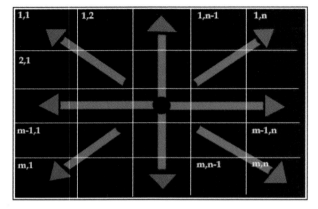

11.34

11.37

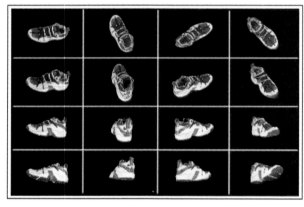

11.35

11.38

11.36

11.39

After acquiring the individual images, creating the required masks, and saving the images as PICT files with Photoshop, the files are imported into Adobe After Effects, where the object images are composited with the desired background or environment. Using the Apple Media Developer Kit, eVox adds interactivity and the ability to spin, zoom, and pan the object with the Navigable Movie Player and then exports the file as a QuickTime movie.

More Than Objects

"Immersive Imaging isn't limited to static objects or empty spaces. We use it to do fashion work and training videos. The fashion work that we are doing for Eddie Bauer and Jhane Barnes, allows viewers to browse the clothing selection and see how the clothing looks on a 'real' model versus just seeing the clothing from one side (11.40 – 11.43).

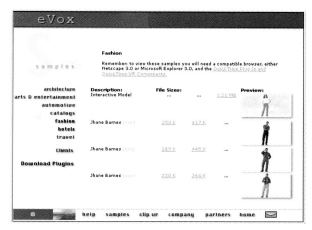

11.40

11.41

11.42   **11.43**

"In the self-defense training video the viewer can scrub back and forth watching the moves of the teachers from many points of view. Shooting moving jujitsu fighters in 360 degrees was accomplished by having the teachers go through their moves a number of times on the turntable that we moved in 10-degree increments. After the instructors had done the jujitsu move a few times, we had all the frames needed to create a 360-degree view of how to flip an assailant. The advantage to using interactive object movies is that the viewer can study each move from different angles and at the pace that they choose (11.44 - 11.49).

11.44   **11.45**

11.46   **11.47**   **11.48**   **11.49**

"When you're shooting outside in environments where there are people, it is always better to shoot an extra set of images. That way, if someone walks into the image, you have the ability to replace frames as needed. What usually happens is that a person will be on the edge of one frame and they will have moved out of the scene by the time you shoot the next shot. This causes 'ghosting' where you see part of a person. In the European street scene, you can see the 'ghost' in the first image (11.50), which we removed to create the second clean image (11.51).

"Among the most interesting work we do, is when we combine interactive panoramic and object movies. In an interactive VR photograph, the viewer would be walking through a museum and see a sculpture that interests them. They would be able to zoom in on the sculpture and look at it from all different sides. The interactivity and dimensionality of these views is fascinating. Right now the bandwidth really isn't there to allow for these large files, but in the future, virtual Web shoppers will be able to walk down the aisles of a virtual store, take a product off the shelf, and turn it around to get a closer look!"

11.50

11.51

11.52

11.53

11.54

THE IMMERSIVE PHOTO STUDIO

Walking into the photo studio of eVox Productions is just like walking into any other high-end photo studio: huge banks of soft lights, a photographer directing the assistant, the client's coffee and snack table are all there. The picture is complete. It is only upon a closer look that you notice that the bright yellow Ferrari is on a room-sized turntable and that the assistant is moving the car in 10-degree increments with the photographer shooting one exposure at each turn with a Nikon E2 digital camera.

Either film or digital capture can be used to photograph images for Immersive Imaging production. In the studio, eVox uses a Nikon E2 digital camera. On location, they prefer to shoot film due to its greater dynamic range in difficult outdoor lighting situations. eVox also works with a Seitz RoundShot, which is a medium-format 120mm strip camera that rotates a full 360 degrees. As the exposure is being made the camera spins and simultaneously the film is transported across the slit that functions as the curtain in traditional 35mm cameras. One advantage to using the RoundShot is that exposures can be made as quickly as one second, allowing you to freeze motion. Another advantage is that the image is on one piece of film which simplifies scanning and stitching (11.52). The processed film is then scanned onto Kodak Photo CD and input into the QTVR Authoring Studio for distortion correction, stitching, adding hot spots, and final image processing. As you can see by the warped ceiling, the original image is distorted by camera optics.

This is the nature of taking a three-dimensional reality and flattening it onto a two-dimensional surface (11.53). The QTVR software resolves this distortion automatically (11.54), analyzing the image as if it was to be laid out on a grid (11.55).

AFTER THE SHOOT

Working in Immersive Imaging requires a combination of good photography, solid lighting skills, and the knowledge to work with digital postproduction tools. When shooting film, eVox has the film processed and scanned onto Kodak Photo CD, after which the files are acquired and brought into Photoshop for cropping, color correction, and retouching (11.56). "We color correct one image with an image adjustment layer (11.57) and then drag that adjustment layer onto all the other images, guaranteeing that all the images have undergone the same color correction." As you can see, the top row has had the image-adjustment layer applied, and the bottom two rows still need correction (11.58). "At this point, we don't do finely detailed image retouching since the stitching process may or may not actually cover up the problem areas."

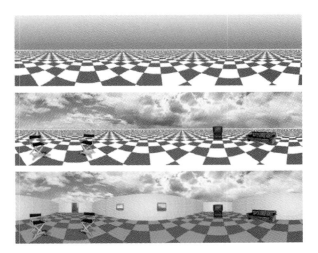

11.55

11.56

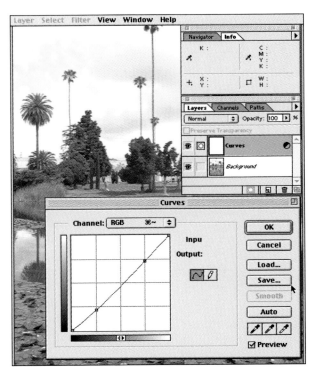

11.57

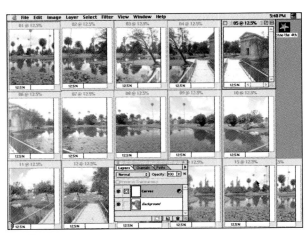

11.58

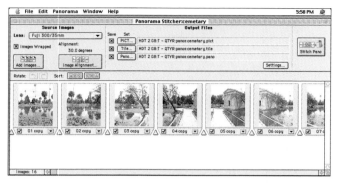

11.59

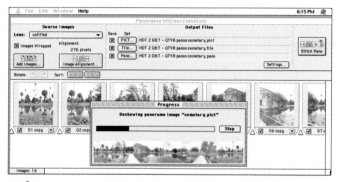

11.60

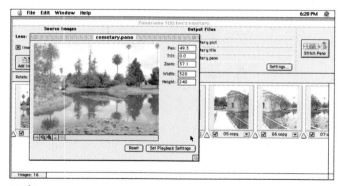

11.61

The next step is to save the files in PICT format and launch the Apple QTVR Authoring Studio.

In the QTVR Authoring Studio, select Panorama Maker, which creates one long PICT file, or Panorama Stitcher, which creates a long PICT file and a QTVR movie. Then import the PICT files (11.59). The software deskews (11.60), stitches, compresses, and previews the immersive image (11.61).

Here are the most important settings to consider when creating VR photography with Apple QTVR Authoring Studio:

- **Compression:** Presently, eVox uses Cinepak Compression set to High. When Apple QuickTime 3.0 is more widely distributed, eVox will test Sorenson compression, especially for larger, multiframed interactive movies.
- **Colors:** "We always use millions of colors to maintain photographic quality."
- **Blending:** eVox uses Gaussian blending which applies a Gaussian Blur filter. This preserves the contrast of the original image, balances image transitions, and minimizes the smearing that may occur when using narrow or normal blending settings.

Once the Panorama Maker or Panorama Stitcher is done, you can bring the long PICT file into Photoshop to retouch frame edges and image blemishes, or to fine-tune exposure. In the working example, the PICT file was brought into Photoshop to clean up the bridge (11.62 and 11.63) and improve the sky (11.64). Then the PICT file was again brought into Apple QTVR Authoring Studio and was stitched together. Remember to use one of the three filename extensions that Netscape Navigator recognizes (.mov, .moov, and .qt) when naming the final panorama or object movie.

11.62

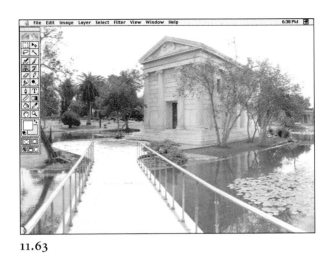

11.63

11.64

"In our work for the Gamble House (11.65), we used Photoshop to improve the ceiling and window density (11.66) before stitching the image together."

11.65

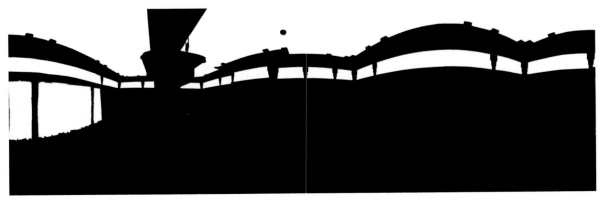

11.66

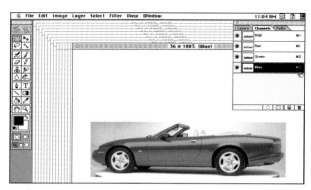

11.67

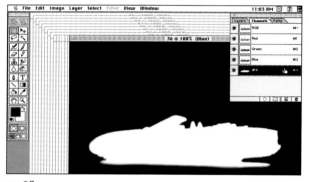

11.68

Interactive object movies often require that each individual frame is first brought into Photoshop to crop (11.67) and separate the object from the studio environment or object rig by cutting a mask (11.68) for each frame.

VR PHOTOGRAPHY ON THE WEB

As with other graphics on the Web, final image size is the most important determining factor to consider when preparing immersive images for Web viewing. A number of places, along the VR photography workflow, influence final file size: whether you use film and Photo CD or consumer digital cameras as the initial input; at what resolution the individual Photo CD files are acquired; using Photoshop's image size to downsize the files before stitching the panorama or object movie; opening the long PICT file that the Apple QTVR Authoring Studio makes and sizing it down in Photoshop; or using higher compression rates than the recommended Cinepak with high settings. "The final file size depends upon the final use for the image, and we work to balance the image-quality-versus-bandwidth issues. The problem with using very low resolution images is that the viewer can't zoom in to see the image details." In the images seen here, the better quality is from a 1.7MB VR movie (11.69), and the low-quality image is from a 132K movie (11.70). "On the eVox Web site, we give the viewer the choice to look at low-, medium-, or high-resolution VR photos.

"Working with film and Kodak Photo CD scans gives us the option to build a number of different resolution files from one photo shoot," as seen in Table 11-3.

11.69

11.70

Table 11-3   PHOTO CD RESOLUTION CHOICES

RESOLUTION	FILE SIZE	STITCHED FILE	MOVIE SIZE
384 × 256 Low-res	288K	1.1MB	260K
768 × 512 Medium-res	1.1MB	5.4MB	490K
1,536 × 1,024 High-res	4.5MB	19MB	1.8MB
3,072 × 2,048 Super Hi-res	18MB	70MB	5.3MB

EMBEDDING VR PHOTOGRAPHY WITH HTML

Adding immersive images to a Web site is straightforward. The simplest and crudest method is to use the `<A>` tag, which will open the movie into an empty gray window. To display the movie in context, use the `<EMBED>` tag as follows: `<EMBED SRC=yourqtvr.mov HEIGHT=320 WIDTH=240>`. Replace the name `yourQTVR.mov` with the name of your movie, and the values for width and height attributes with your movie window dimensions.

The QuickTime plug-in displays QTVR movies with the controller off by default. In order to show it, add the `CONTROLLER` parameter to your `<EMBED>` tag like so: `<EMBED SRC=yourqtvr.mov HEIGHT=320 WIDTH=240 CONTROLLER=TRUE>`. If you use values for `WIDTH` and `HEIGHT` other than those of the movie, the plug-in will scale the movie. If the controller is showing, it can appear cropped. To avoid this, use the `SCALE` parameter with the value "ToFit".

Several parameters control the appearance of the QTVR movie when it is displayed for the first time, including `PAN`, `TILT`, and `FOV`.

- **PAN:** The default setting for when a VR photograph opens centered on the left side of the original image. If you would like to specify a specific starting point use the `PAN` tag `PAN=xxx`, where `xxx` is the number of pixels you want the opening image moved to the left.
- **TILT:** The default setting for when a VR photograph opens centered on the middle (of left side) of the original image. You can have the viewer looking up or down by using the `TILT` tag `TILT=xxx`, where the `xxx` is any number between -42.5 and 42.5 — the negative numbers look down and the positive numbers look up.
- **FOV:** The field of view attribute is where you can define how zoomed in or out the initial opening scene is: `FOV=xxx`, where `xxx` is 5.0 (zoomed in all the way) to 85.0 (zoomed all the way out).

Since QuickTime movie files tend to be large, they are not cached by default. In a case where caching is desired, you can set `CACHE=TRUE`. Additional information regarding playback options can be found at the Apple Web site dedicated to Immersive Imaging (*www.apple.com/quicktime/authors/webmas.html#tags*).

It is polite to let the viewer know that they are about to look at a VR photograph, since time and plug-ins are required to view them. Most Macintosh computers and Netscape Navigator 3.0 have the required QuickTime system extensions loaded, and Windows users can download the extensions from the Apple site (*www.apple.com/quicktime/qtvr/index.html*). "We let the viewers know that they are about to enter a page that has VR photography and how to interact, pan, and zoom in the image (11.71). In fact, we let them know twice (11.72) and also provide the links to download the appropriate plug-ins (11.73). Downloading a VR photograph takes some time, and we give the viewer three resolution choices depending upon their connection speed and quality needs (11.74). When the viewer accesses the VR photograph, at first they see a grid, and as the grid fills in, they can pan and zoom before the download is complete (11.75 and 11.76). Once the image is in the browser cache, the viewer can spin, zoom, and look at the VR photograph (in this case, the Swedish Parliament) as often as they like (11.77 and 11.78).

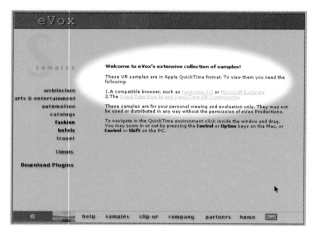

11.71

Working in QTVR requires a combination of photography and lighting skills with digital postproduction finesse. David emphasizes that creating high-quality immersive images is 50 percent photographic and 50 percent digital. When the eVox production team works together, the sum is always better than the parts. If you want to give the viewer more of the picture, incorporating immersive images into your Web site will definitely put a new spin on your photography and the impact of your Web site.

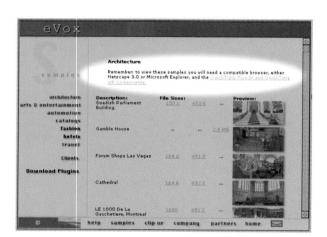

11.72

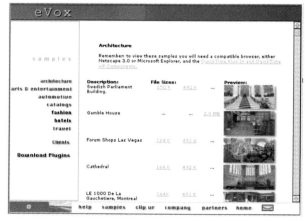

11.74

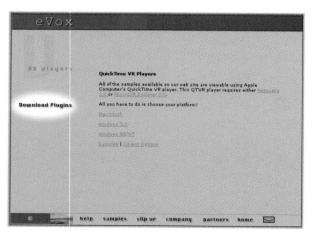

11.73

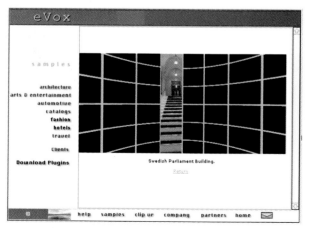

11.75

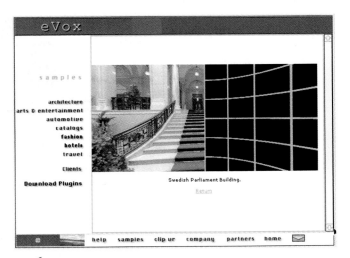

11.76

11.77

11.78

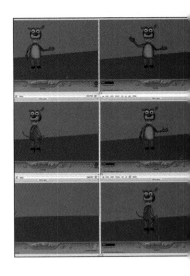

CHAPTER 12
BUILDING 3D WORLDS WITH VRML

If you have ever taken a drawing class or tried your hand at sketching, you know that one of the most telling characteristics of a realistic drawing is the illusion of three-dimensional (3D) space on a two-dimensional (2D) surface. The skills involved in creating a three-dimensional illusion include defining the viewer's point of view, working with scale and size relationships, lighting and shading, and, for many frustrated art students, a lot of highly-developed erasing skills.

Three-dimensional computer graphics started in military and research centers. They were used to visualize variations on yet-to-be-built equipment and scenarios. For example, defining and studying how a fighter plane lands on the deck of a virtual aircraft carrier helps fighter pilots practice landing multimillion-dollar planes. As computers became more powerful and as software operators gave way to artists, the use of 3D evolved from strictly military and scientific applications to defining and advancing the entertainment industry and the fine arts. Who isn't intrigued by Pixar's full-length motion picture *Toy Story*? And who hasn't wondered, "Where do the Budweiser frogs and lizards really live?" (What do you mean they're not real!)

Until recently, talented 3D animators worked with high-end software and computer power that would make our desktop machines hide their mice in shame. Because of the complexity of rendering surfaces, absolute and relative motion, reflections, texture, and bump maps, getting a dinosaur to chase a Jeep at film resolution requires an incredible amount of computer power. The computer-generated scenes in the Hollywood blockbusters *Jurassic Park* and *Titanic* required 20–40MB of computer-generated

For me, the challenge is to start with a cube and by intersecting and extruding it, create shapes that can become imaginative life forms, far-fetched space ships, or accurate scientific illustrations.

TODD GRIFFITH

229

information per frame at a rate of 24 frames per second, averaging 720MB per second!

ENTER VRML

With these mind-boggling and desktop-computer-choking figures, how can a Web designer incorporate 3D objects and environments into Web design? *Virtual Reality Markup Language* (VRML) is the 3D description language for the Web. Similar to the way HTML describes a Web page, VRML is a markup language that describes 3D objects and spaces that allow plug-in-enabled Web browsers to interpret and display true 3D environments and objects. What makes VRML so fascinating is interactivity. The viewer can move freely from room to room, studying an object from any side, and hearing directional sound (as you get closer to the sound it gets louder and as you move away the sound fades).

Another similarity to HTML is that designing with VRML gives you instant feedback. The preview is as quick as dragging the WRL file onto an empty Web browser page. Yet another similarity to HTML is actually a drawback. Just like HTML, VRML code is interpreted, and the visible results of the code may vary from one browser program to another. Developed by Silicon Graphics, Inc. (SGI), two types of VRML exist on the Web: the original VRML 1.0, which supports only 3D objects, and VRML 2.0, which supports environments, objects, animation, user input, and directional sound. Both versions of VRML render on the fly, adding texture, shading, and movement as the viewer changes perspective.

Just as with other Web graphics, rendering on the fly depends on the skill of the artist to minimize file size by minimizing polygon count and texture size, as well as the viewer's connection speed, computer processor speed, and graphics board. If you are surfing the Web with a dial-up connection and come across a VRML world with lots of animation, the first thing that you might do is make a cup of coffee while the VRML file is downloaded. Designing VRML that is visually compelling and small in file size challenges Web-savvy designers to work with finesse and compromises, just as if you were working with HTML and standard GIF and JPEG graphics. Depending on the skill of the designer and the complexity of the VRML piece, the files can range from 50K to a few megabytes.

On a Macintosh, you can experience VRML space with Netscape Navigator 4.0 loaded with a VRML browser. On the PC, you can see VRML with Netscape Navigator 3.0 and 4.0 and Internet Explorer 3.0 and 4.0 loaded with VRML browsers. These interpreter programs, or *plug-ins*, are the VRML browsers, which serve the same purpose as the plug-ins required to see a Shockwave or FlashPix file. They form the frame around the VRML world that gives the viewer the controls to pan, zoom, and rotate. The two most prevalent plug-in browsers are Cosmo (*www.cosmo.sgi.com*) and Worldview (*www.intervista.com*).

ARTIST:
Todd Griffith

ORGANIZATION:
Nichimen Graphics Inc.
12555 West Jefferson Blvd.
Los Angeles, CA 90066
togee@ix.netcom.com

SYSTEM, PC:
Gateway GPG-266
8GB storage/128MB RAM

CONNECTIVITY:
T-1

SERVER ENVIRONMENT:
Sun System

PERIPHERALS:
Accelerated Permedia 3DBoard, Viewsonic 17-inch monitor, Epson Stylus Color 400 printer

PRIMARY APPLICATIONS:
Nichimen Graphics Nendo and Nworld, Adobe Photoshop 4.0, MetaCreations Painter 4.0, Cosmo Worlds 1.0

WORK HISTORY:
<u>1977</u> — Saw *Star Wars*. "It sounds corny, but ever since that, I've wanted to do this kind of work."

Todd Griffith, artist and software designer, has been working with 3D computer graphics since 1992 and with VRML since it's inception. "3D is very similar to painting. The artist starts with a blank canvas and everything you see in the piece comes from within the artist. I love creating fantastic 3D characters, spaces, and experiences, but one of the biggest drawbacks to being a 'traditional' 3D artist is the hours of rendering time for even the shortest animation. This can really cripple your creativity. Additionally, if you want to work in real time doing performance animation, virtual sets, or gigantic *Toy Story*-like scenes, you need extremely expensive and powerful equipment. There is, of course, no way to share any of this creativity over the Web either. It is just impractical in its size. Since VRML is a description language that uses ASCII text, and is small enough to download over the Web, I can apply my 3D skills and knowledge while working on a mail order PC. An additional benefit is that, just like HTML, if I want to see what a file looks like, I just drag the WRL file onto an empty Web browser window and it pops up. Sure beats rendering overnight and coming back the next morning only to see that the computer has crashed or that I forgot to include a certain texture map."

VRML standards are still being developed. As the manufacturers, browsers, and VRML Consortium (*www.vrml.org*) devise and agree on the standards, the three components that are driving VRML forward are affordable software, 3D boards, and viewers wanting

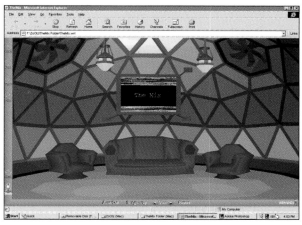

12.1

more from their Web experience. "The cost of good 3D modeling and painting software is coming down. Functionality that cost thousands of dollars only a few years ago now costs only a few hundred dollars. With the price of 3D graphics boards hitting rock bottom, more and more consumer computers are being sold with 3D boards as standard configuration. Finally, people are tired of just looking at flat Web graphics that they can't do anything with.

"For example, I comped up a virtual set for a show called *The Mix* which was going to address environment and technology issues. The virtual set (12.1) is actually a geodesic dome turned inside out or inverted (12.2). It is a great shape to work with because it is fun

---

1980 — Completed first Super 8 movie with cousin Scott. Action figures, rubber bands, and a blanket. . . high-tech production value.

1992 — B.F.A. degree in film from University of New Hampshire, Keene Campus.

1993 — Intern at the Kodak Center for Creative Imaging in Camden, Maine, specializing in 3D and special effects. Manager of the SGI Lab.

1994 — 3D Artist for Graham Nash's virtual-reality show entitled "Life Sighs."

1995 — Lead 3D artist and virtual puppeteer for DEVO's "Jackpot," a sleazy virtual nightclub with performance animation of wacky characters designed by Georganne Deane.

1996 – 98 — Artist and Software designer, Nichimen Graphics in Los Angeles.

1996 – 98 — Independent VRML artist.

FAVORITE COLOR:

That bright reddish-orange you get when you stick a flashlight in your mouth.

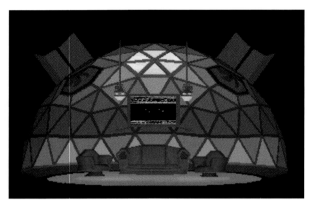

12.2

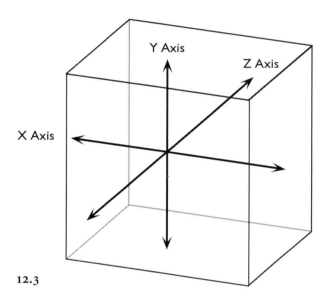

12.3

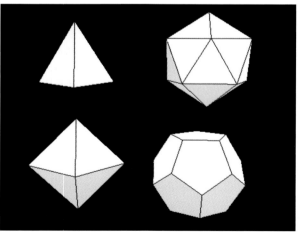

12.4

to look at and loads quickly, and I was planning on changing the wall panels to match the theme of each week's show. Most of the scene's lighting is done with color by vertex, and the cloud texture and video screen textures are only 26K.

"VRML is more than being able to fly through fantastic spaces. Artists are developing autonomous agents, or *avatars*, that have artificial intelligence characteristics. Imagine having a pet in your computer that you take care of and that can learn behavior. Children's hospitals are looking into having a VRML pet friend for children that need to learn how to take care of an illness or to help cope with chemotherapy. These 3D pets don't replace human caregivers, but they do provide a companion that can help the child learn about his illness or be a little friend just when he needs one the most."

3D AND VRML 101

All 3D is based on X (width), Y (height), and Z (depth) coordinates that define shape, position, and viewpoint (12.3). Wherever the XYZ coordinates intersect is where the object is or where your viewpoint is. "Working in 3D combines sculpture, filmmaking, painting, lighting, animation, and digital-imaging skills. In 3D, everything is made-up of points, edges, and faces, which combined, define a surface. Most real-time 3D is accomplished through the combination and refinement of simple geometric shapes. The basic shapes that 3D artists work with are cube, sphere, cone, cylinder, tetrahedron (pyramid), and the following variations of the pyramid (12.4): — *octahedron* (double pyramid), *dodecahedron* (ten-sided double pyramid), and *icosahedron* (twenty-sided double pyramid). For me, the challenge is to start with a cube and by intersecting and extruding it, create shapes that can become imaginative life forms, far-fetched space ships, or accurate scientific illustrations."

The two main types of 3D modeling are *polygonal* and *spline*. "In a nutshell, polygonal modeling is based on straight lines. Spline is curved modeling which uses many more points to describe an edge, increasing the resulting file size dramatically. A primary skill of a VRML artist is to use polygonal modeling to describe a shape concisely and with the smallest number of lines of code. Just like any Web designer, a VRML artist needs to balance image detail and quality with download speed. If I can describe an object in ten lines of code versus 50, I've just cut down on the download time. Keeping the graphic simple is a real challenge. Right now, my gator page is 291K and, as with everything on the Web, 291K is a lot of information and download time. So I'm working on simplifying the graphic without losing the interactivity.

"There are a number of entry-level 3D packages designed specifically for the Web, such as ParaGraph's Virtual Home Space Builder, and Virtus 3-D Website Builder. Plus, there are dozens of sites where you can download models, textures, and sounds. The 3D Café site (*www.3dcafe.com*) is great for all of your 3D needs. It has sounds, textures, models, articles, and reviews. The VRML Repository at *www.sdsc.edu/vrml/* is filled with object libraries, sample scripts, books, and utilities, and it addresses more advanced subjects such as Java applications, parsers, and rendering libraries. The VRML Site (*www.vrmlsite.com*) is a great resource for tutorials, sample worlds, articles, industry news, and related topics.

"Working with established 3D programs such as MetaCreations Bryce 3D and Infini-D, Strata StudioPro, Kinetix 3D Studio Max, Electric Image, and LightWave, you can create original 3D materials and VRML. Creating the VRML code is as simple as saving out a WRL file that the VRML enabled browsers recognize and display. Nichimen's Nendo, the consumer-level program that I am developing, is an intuitive modeling and paint package with pull-down menus for shapes, color, lighting, and camera placement. Using a package that caters to real-time modeling cuts down on complexity and the amount of code, which in turn cuts download and display time."

VRML WORKFLOW

The basic steps in the VRML workflow are sketching, storyboarding, modeling, texturing, defining viewpoints, and incorporating the more sophisticated facets of VRML: animation, interactivity, sound, and linking. "I always start by sketching my ideas out on paper (12.5). Sketching the idea helps me to see relationships, plan lighting, and visualize the work

12.5

process. Some artists do their 'sketching' with plaster sculptures that are later scanned with a 3D scanner. After sketching and storyboarding, I go to the computer, start with a basic cube (12.6), and by subdividing, extruding, and beveling I build the wire frame for the subject (12.7 – 12.10). The wire frame is actually a collection of surface polygons that describe the object. I can interactively move around the object by moving the camera, just as if I were walking around a sculpture with a hammer and chisel."

ADDING COLOR

"Once the wire frame is done, the rendering process begins, in which I apply color, shading, lighting, and texture to the bodies, edges, and faces. There are environmental effects in VRML, like fog, but these are

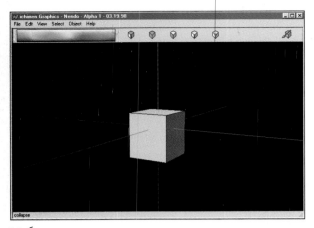

12.6

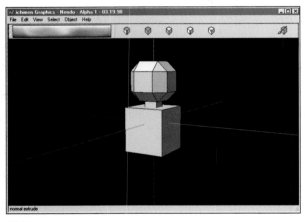

12.7

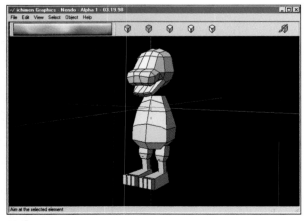

12.8

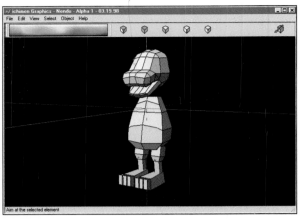

12.9

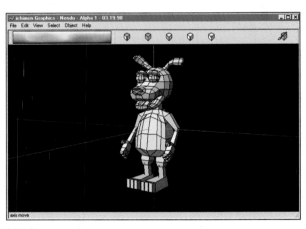

12.10

expensive and don't always run on low-end machines. Adding color to points, edges, and faces is called 'color per vertex' or 'face color.' This allows a computer that cannot handle large textures to display colorful scenes. Adding vertex color allows me to define point, edge, and surface colors that blend evenly between any of these elements.

"Buddy (12.11) began as a flat, white character, but with color per vertex he comes to life, and with no textures at all! First I selected the faces (or surfaces) that make up the eye and made them black (12.11). Then I selected the faces that make up the head to turn them brown (12.12). I continued by coloring all

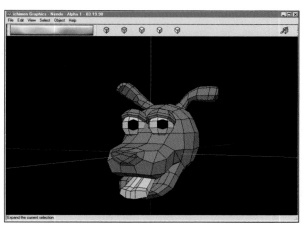

12.11

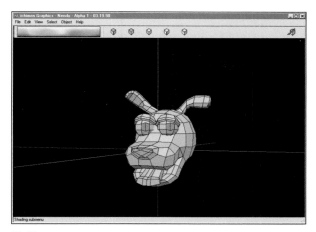

12.12

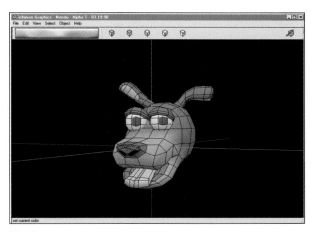

12.13

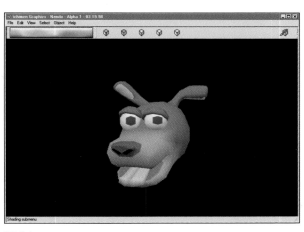

12.14

the different faces of the ears, nose, and tongue, and voila — Buddy looks like a friendly dog rather than a collection of polygons (12.13, 12.14)!

"VRML has a custom sky node that allows you to use color gradients on spheres, but the quality can actually be too good and too high-resolution, which balloons up the file size very quickly. In the online children's book *Stanley Flies Home*, I created a low-resolution sphere and added a color-per-vertex gradient blend (12.15). Working with color in VRML is exactly like working with color in standard Web design. You need to be sure that adding color is what the scene needs, because it can make file sizes huge really fast."

USING TEXTURE MAPS

"In addition to colors, a 3D artist uses *texture maps* created in Photoshop or Painter to add to the surface's visual feel. Texture maps interact with the lighting and viewpoint to give the scene realism and break up that slick computer look. In *Stanley Flies Home*, the clouds are a texture map (12.16) that add a bit of realism to the sky behind. In VRML, you need to use texture maps judiciously since they add to file size and rendering speed. Just as a Web or multimedia artist will create a 'project super palette' for the colors used, I create a super palette of textures that the browser loads once and accesses to display the VRML file more quickly (12.17)."

12.15

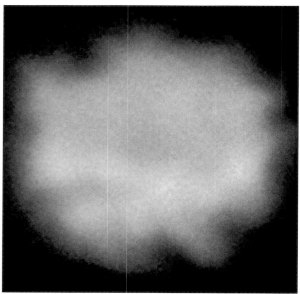

12.16

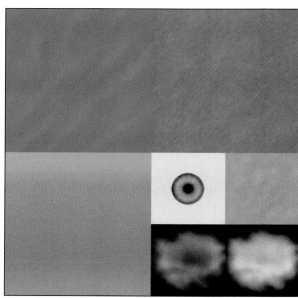

12.17

USING VIEWPOINTS

"Finally, every VRML world has *viewpoints* which the designer can use to give the viewer points of entry into the VRML world or to help the viewer find the best perspective. The viewer is the eye of the camera. Position a camera anywhere that you want to give the viewer a starting point. Setting up your viewpoints helps orient the viewer. In the children's book that I am currently working on, I've set up four cameras: gator cam (12.18), gator far (12.19), gator up (12.20), and grrrr (12.21), which is you being eaten. I may have to edit this when it gets published so that the kids don't get too scared!"

VRML FINESSE

"In VRML 2.0 you can add animation, interactivity, sound, and links. This is where VRML gets really interesting. VRML animation falls into two categories: *automatic* and *triggerable*. Automatic animation, the simpler of the two, is keyframe or time-based, meaning events are automatically generated with the passage of time. Triggerable animation is controlled by touch *Sensors*. As your mouse moves over a touch Sensor, it launches an action, triggers a keyframe animation, and then controls how often to cycle or delay, when to stop—basically everything that defines how an object will behave."

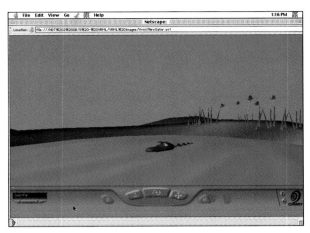

12.19

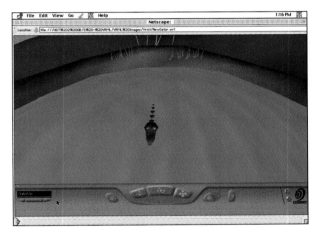

12.20

12.18

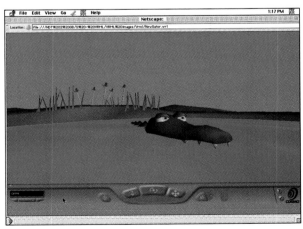

12.21

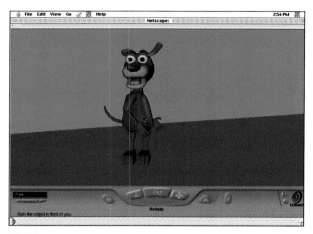

12.22

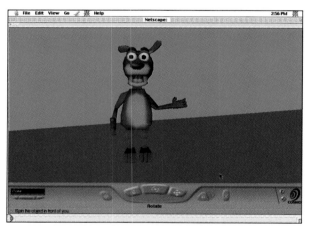

12.23

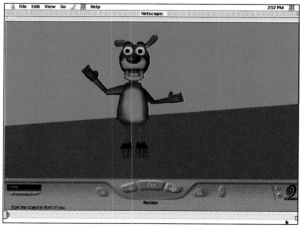

12.24

"I wanted to make Buddy a character that does more than play back an animation file, so I made him interactive by assigning Sensors to his extremities. His torso is a CylindricalSensor, which allows the user to rotate it around on the Y axis. Similarly, his legs, arms, and paws are all set up to rotate using a SphericalSensor (12.22). With a little finessing, I was able to make him a completely positionable character. This way, visitors to Buddy's backyard can manipulate and pose him, making the world a little more fun to be in (12.23, 12.24). A true interactive pet, and better yet, no mess to clean up. (See the *Web Design Studio Secrets* CD-ROM for examples of the code used to make Buddy interactive.)

"I can define how an object will react to the viewer (for example, the position of the viewer's mouse) through the use of proximity and touch Sensors. To make Buddy's character more believable, I made his tail wag as the camera got closer. This autonomous behavior was created by linking the animation of the tail wagging to a ProximitySensor. Buddy's tail wag was set up so that if the user approached Buddy, either by trucking the camera or by changing to a closer viewpoint, he would begin to wag his tail (12.25 and 12.26). Additionally, I added touch Sensors to Buddy's tongue. If you touch it, he'll begin to pant, and if you touch his nose he'll woof. A ProximitySensor can trigger any number of things including animations, sounds, collisions, and even links to other worlds.

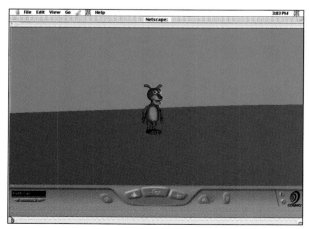

12.25

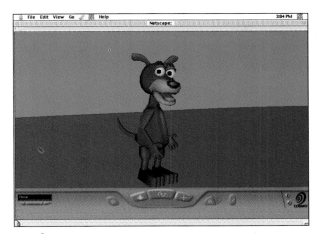

12.26

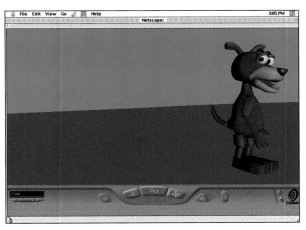

12.27

"Another cool feature about Buddy is that he is always looking straight at you, no matter where you are in the scene. As you pan to the left, Buddy's eyes move to the right (12.27) and as you pan or move to the right he looks to the left (12.28). This makes Buddy look as if he is really watching you all the time. His eyes are actually a child of a special VR trick called a *billboard*. In expensive military simulators, 2D images of trees were placed on 2D squares. These textured chips would rotate to face the camera at all times, creating the illusion that a virtual tank operator is driving through a forest of trees that have width and volume. What appears to be a 3D tree is really a texture map of a high resolution tree image with an alpha channel sitting on a flat surface that is always positioned to your point of view."

12.28

Buddy's eyes are children of Billboards, so he looks at you from any angle! Here is some of the code for the right eyeball:

```
DEF RtEyeBill Transform {
            children    Billboard {
                children      DEF rteye Transform {
                children      DEF Nichimen Group {
                children      [
                DEF NgcCoord_65 Coordinate {
                    point [ -1.37755 2.3149 2.8321,
                            -1.19943 2.3149 2.69738,
                            -1.16875 2.3149 2.47616,
                            -1.30347 2.3149 2.29804,
                            -1.52469 2.3149 2.26736,
                            -1.70281 2.3149 2.40209,
                            -1.73348 2.3149 2.62331,
                            -1.59876 2.3149 2.80142,
                            -1.25012 2.03656 3.32118,
                            -0.763492 2.03656 2.9531,
                            ...
```

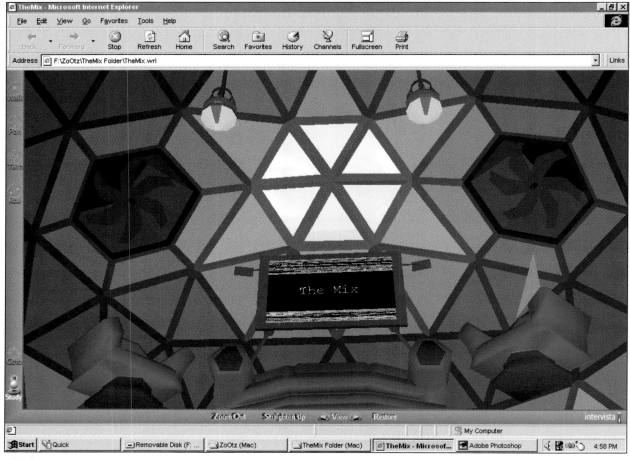

12.29

"I can also add CollisionSensors that help me to guide the viewers or to keep them away from areas that I don't want them to see. On the set for *The Mix*, I was planning on adding CollisionDetection, which would make it impossible for the viewer to look behind the scenes or, in this case, under the chairs of the set (12.29)."

Sound adds another dimension to a story, creating a richer experience for the viewer. "The best thing about VRML sound is that it is directional. As I move closer, it gets louder. Or if I move behind an object, the sound reflects that change, too. Sound is brought in as a standard WAV file so whatever you can record can become sound source material. Finally, I can add links to other URLs, but more importantly to other VRML documents, which is just like adding a link within a Web site to another page in that site. That way, as I walk through

a museum, only the page of the room I am in at that moment is loaded. As I walk towards the next room, I have triggered a link that tells the linked page, or next room, to load. Sometimes this can be quite comical, as walls and rooms pop up when you pass them. In the future, VRML will probably be able to link to QTVR (immersive images) and FlashPix files, so you'll be able to combine 3D with high-resolution photography."

ACCEPTING LIMITS

"The temptation to use all of the possibilities in VRML is strong, such as using a lot of color per vertex, texture maps, links, and animation. What you're doing is compiling line after line of ASCII text (12.30) and ballooning up the file. The rule of thumb

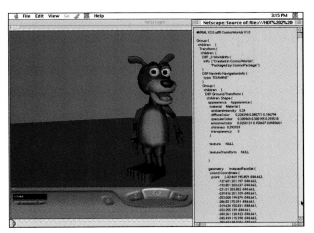

12.30

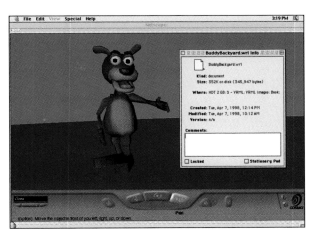

12.31

is 'if you can't see it, it shouldn't be in the file'. For example, if an object is very far away, there is no reason to model it with thousands of polygons when a simpler form will give the same visual information. Think about linking the background information so when a viewer moves towards it, the link will load the VRML file. And as the viewer gets closer, they will see the finely detailed version. Buddy is 353K large, which is a little larger than I'd ideally want him to be (12.31). One way to get around the bandwidth problems of the Internet is to create VRML worlds that are just a series of URLs that link small VRML files to one another. As the viewer gets close to the link, ProximitySensors will trigger the link to load.

"Admittedly, as soon as you start adding interactivity and animation, you are treading into more complex territory. When you see code such as `eventin` and `timeout` and route this to that, you begin to realize that VRML can get complicated very quickly. Coding VRML is similar to walking into a professional sound studio and seeing the audio mixer. I know I would be out of my league and slowly back out of the door to go home and hit the record button on the tape recorder. Writing clean code that triggers and controls animations is similar to fine-tuning a recording with a professional audio mixer. It requires skill and experience. Two of the originators of VRML, Gavin Bell and Rick Carey, have written the definitive resource about programming and triggering of VRML events: *The Annotated VRML 2.0 Reference Manual*. It has a permanent place next to my PC."

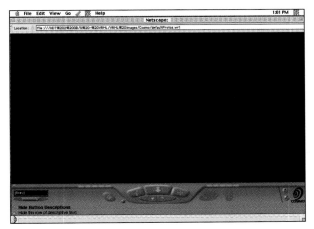

12.32

NAVIGATION CONTROLS

An additional limitation of VRML is that the viewer needs to take some time to practice with the mouse controls and movements. When you enter a 3D world, Cosmo Player (the browser in these illustrations) is automatically launched within your browser window (12.32). At the bottom of your window you'll see the Cosmo Player navigation controls, called the *dashboards* (12.33), that you can use to move around the world with the Movement Dashboard or to examine objects with the Examine Dashboard. Each contains buttons that you use to enter commands, to move around the world, or to affect objects within the world.

12.33

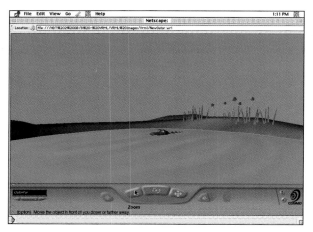

12.34

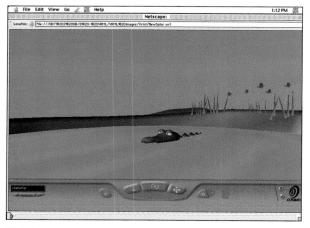

12.35

The Dashboard

The dashboard you see when you enter a world (12.33) is determined by the author, and some worlds don't have a dashboard at all. You can hide the dashboard, or minimize it, by clicking the small triangle at the upper left of the dashboard. To select a control on either dashboard, click a button. Selected buttons display bright green icons and remain selected until you click another button. Unselected buttons display gray-green icons, and buttons that are not available for use are flat and dark gray.

To navigate with the mouse, click a button on the dashboard and then position the pointer in the window containing the world, and drag. The shape of the pointer in the world is similar to the icon on the button. To navigate using the keyboard, press Option/Alt+Ctrl to select a navigation mode without clicking a button on the dashboard, or use the arrow keys to navigate with the currently selected tool.

Most importantly, when using any of the dashboard controls, the following rules apply:

- The farther you drag, the faster you move, turn, pan, or spin.
- Holding down the Shift key as you drag increases your speed.
- You can click and drag any of the three main navigation buttons to perform the same function as if you had pressed the button. When you release the button, the highlight returns to where it was before you dragged. This is useful for quickly performing another navigation function without permanently changing the current one. It is also useful if you get into a place that is difficult to navigate because there are many active objects in the world.

"With Cosmo Viewer, I can zoom (12.34 and 12.35) and pan (12.36 and 12.37) around the gator pond very quickly."

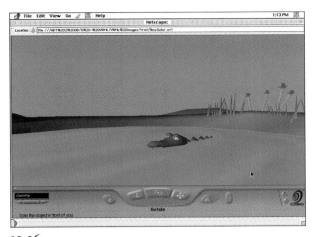

12.36

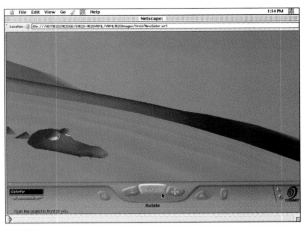

12.37

The Worldview Viewer offers different controls that are clear and are spelled out on the left and bottom of the viewer's frame. They also remind the viewer much less of the spaceship metaphor (12.38).

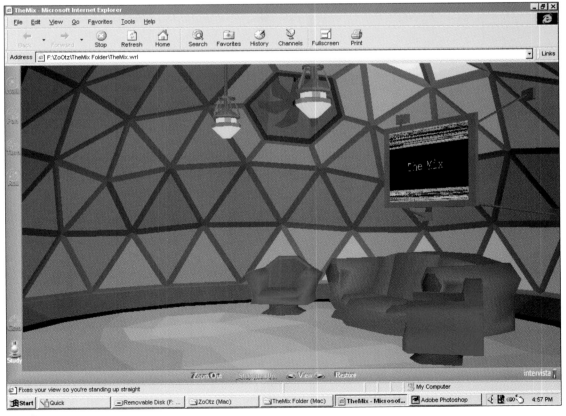

12.38

12.39

12.40

12.41

Navigating with Viewpoints

Viewpoints are author-defined locations that let you travel to different parts of a world. You can choose locations from the Viewpoint menu or by clicking the Next Viewpoint or Previous Viewpoint buttons. If a world does not contain viewpoints, the word Entry is displayed in the Viewpoint list to represent the place where you entered the world. To select a viewpoint, click the Viewpoint List button and then drop down to the desired viewpoint in the pop-up list. "In the children's story *Stanley and Motley Fly Home*, I've set up three cameras—TwoShot (12.39), StanleyView (12.40), and MotleyView (12.41)—that let the viewer get closer to the characters with one click of the mouse rather than having to navigate to them."

Controlling Float and Gravity

Depending on the author's design, you can either fly, walk, or fly and walk through a world. If you can both fly and walk in a world, use the Float (12.42) or Gravity buttons (12.43) to respectively rise up into the air, or to return to the surface of the world. When Gravity is selected, you cannot move off the ground. When you walk along an uneven surface with Gravity selected, you follow the ups and downs of the surface. When Float is selected, you can move off the ground and fly.

EMBEDDING VRML IN A WEB PAGE

There are two ways to have both 2D text and graphics and a 3D VRML world on the same page: embedding the world in a frame and embedding it directly into a Web page. In the first case, use the `<FRAME>` tag inside the `<FRAMESET>` container tag: `<FRAME SRC="yourfile.wrl" NAME="vrmlframe">`. To embed a VRML file, use the `<EMBED>` tag: `<EMBED SRC="my.wrl" WIDTH=500 HEIGHT=280>`.

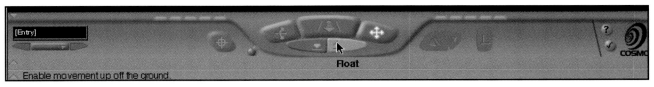

12.42

12.43

THE FUTURE OF VRML

3D and VRML are still being developed as Microsoft, Apple, Sun, SGI, the ISO (International Standards Organization), and 3D browser companies work through developing standards in a world that is constantly changing. The best aspect of VRML is that you don't need to be a programmer to get started with it. There are a growing number of applications, such as V-Realm Builder (*www.ligos.com*), Cosmo HomeSpace Designer (*cosmosoftware.com*), and Virtus 3D Website Builder (*www.virtus.com*), directed toward Web designers that are easy to use and less intimidating than coding VRML by hand in a text editor. 3D is a wonderful medium that until now has had little air time on the Web. New advances in the incorporation of 3D and 2D graphics will create a compelling way to communicate and more fantastic ways to display graphics over the Web.

Adding some 3D to your Web site has been proven to capture viewers' attention, and it just may be the one thing that keeps them there a little bit longer. Immersive 3D worlds can compel people in ways that 2D has been unable to do in the past. If artists and developers can find ways to integrate the best of both worlds, we will be undoubtedly approaching a new age in online entertainment and commerce.

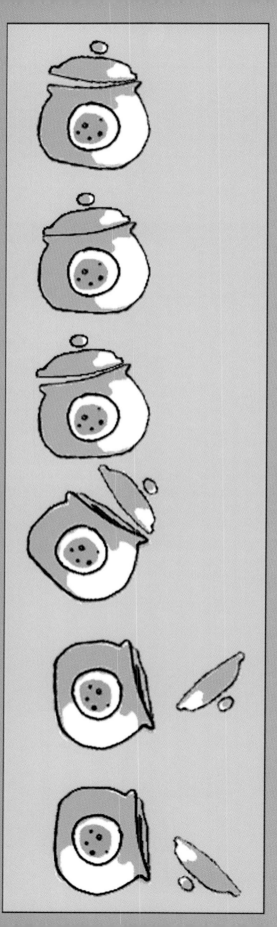

CookieRecipe.com
All cookies. All the time...

Welcome Cookie Bakers! to the CookieRecipe.com Channel. We are proud to present the **Top 10 Most Popular Recipes** for this week on CookieRecipe.com.

(Click on a cookie below to see a recipe)

Last Week's Top 10 Most Popular Recipes at CookieRecipe.com

Old Fashioned Oatmeal Cookies

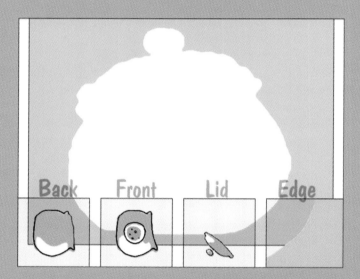

Back   Front   Lid   Edge

CookieRecipe.com
All cookies. All the time...

Old Fashioned Oatmeal Cookies

Submitted by: B. Stoltson

These are the best oatmeal cookies I have ever eaten.

Last Week's Top 10 Most Popular Recipes at CookieRecipe.com

CHAPTER 13
CHANNELING YOUR CONTENT

Whether you know it or not, you're already intimately familiar with "push" technology. When the phone rings, you answer it. When the newspaper hits your porch, you open it up and browse its contents. When you sit down at a restaurant, the waitress hands you a menu and recites the chef's specials. When you want entertainment, you turn on the TV and select from the 50 or so programs that happen to be available. It's not like you're a wind-up toy — you have plenty of options — but they're a relatively few specific options being channeled in your direction.

By contrast, we generally think of the Internet as a "pull" experience. Armed with a Web browser, you become the seeker, the shopper, the student of the world. The sites you visit are as passive as books in a library. They lie in wait like Easter eggs — sometimes hidden, sometimes in plain view, but never jumping into your basket.

On first blush, pull may strike you as more attractive than push. If you're the take-charge type, you want to be the one in control, the one who goes out and gets, particularly where your computer is involved. But think about it for a moment. In your everyday noncomputer life, you spend most of your work day pulling and most of your free time on the receiving end of a push. Pulling takes a lot of effort, but receiving a push is easy.

Now look at it from the perspective of a content provider and push looks even more attractive. A site that can project its information stands a better chance of getting noticed than one that just sits there. A book on a shelf attracts the serious seeker — just as

What you want is constant, random traffic, not a sudden surge followed by a big lull.

DAN SHEPHERD

this book attracted you — but a network beacon gets the mass market. If raw numbers are what you're after, then it's time to start pushing.

PUSHING CONTENT INTO THE HOME

According to confirmed channeler Dan Shepherd, push technology is all about capturing the hearts and minds of the broadest possible cross-section of consumers. "There are two kinds of Web surfers out there — corporate users and home users. The corporate users do most of the actual surfing. They can just hop from one site to another from their office LANs. They're extremely active because their barrier to entry where bandwidth is concerned is really small."

"The problem is that these office surfers represent a narrow demographic of highly paid geeks. The bigger demographic is the vast majority of Web users who are sitting at their home computers dialing up with modems. But by the time they go through the whole dial-up process, they're already tired, so they end up surfing a lot less."

The irony is that the less-active surfers are the ones who will control the future of the Web. "It's generally assumed that if the Web is to succeed as a marketing medium, there has to be advertising. And for companies to advertise, there has to be a more mainstream consumer base. So everyone's very anxious to make it easier for dial-up users to visit their sites. Once you can sit at home and surf with ease, that's when the *really* big bucks will start streaming in."

WHEN SHOVE COMES TO PUSH

If the user can't get to the content, then by golly, the content has to go to the user. In a world where the consumer is king, it's not a question of whether to push, but which push solution will win out.

"The best push technology is the simple e-mail list. Lists like TidBITS (13.1) are becoming more popular because they're easy to subscribe to and you get updates when you check your e-mail. A list is like a newsgroup that gets delivered to your screen automatically. Sometimes it's just a weekly update, sometimes it's daily and you get e-mails all day long, and sometimes you can just get one daily digest of all the stuff that went out that day. It's safe, nonintrusive, convenient — everything that push technology should be."

Unfortunately, e-mail lists are more like industry newsletters than TV shows. While highly informative, they can be equally dry. And without graphics and other design elements, it's difficult to prioritize information on the page. What's needed in the long run is a method to transmit fully fleshed-out page designs.

"One way to push Web pages is to use a proprietary back-end server, like BackWeb (13.2). But then your subscriber has to use a proprietary front-end application as well. The popular PointCast Network (13.3) works along the same lines. Since it doesn't work through the Web browser, you have to install and run a separate application. Not only do these services work better for corporate users, they require too much effort and planning on the part of dial-up folks. Most people would prefer to stay inside their browsers

ARTIST:
Dan Shepherd

ORGANIZATION:
Emergent Media
1804 7th Avenue, Suite 908
Seattle, WA 98101
206/292-3990
www.emergentmedia.com
dans@emergentmedia.com

SYSTEM, MAC:
Power Mac 7500/100
System 7.6
2GB storage/32MB RAM

SYSTEM, PC:
Bear Pentium 166
Windows 95
2GB storage/32MB RAM

CONNECTIVITY, ISP:
Full T1, IXA

SERVER ENVIRONMENT:
Mixed: Macintosh, Windows NT, and UNIX

PERIPHERALS:
Sony 17-inch monitor, Wacom ArtPad, Epson 960 scanner, Kodak DC120 digital camera

when working on the Web. If push can be part of what Joe User is already doing, he'll adapt to it a lot faster."

WHEN IS A PUSH REALLY A PULL?

This brings us to the last type of push technology, which Shepherd calls "timed pull." Here, the browser application seeks out the Web sites you've subscribed to and downloads updated pages to your machine. "Technically, only the server can push. Because the browser is located on the receiving end of a Web page, all it can do is pull. So when you put the Web browser in charge of the push, you're really telling it to pull data at a specified time."

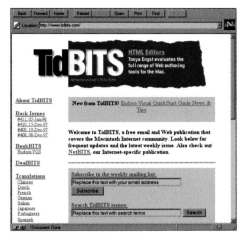

13.1

BROWSER AGAINST BROWSER

Currently, the two browser-based push tools are Netcaster from Netscape and Internet Explorer 4 from Microsoft. According to Shepherd, this is one case where Microsoft provides the superior solution.

"The Netcaster model is basically subscription based, which means that the user has ultimate control. For example, the user is entirely in charge of the timing. But most folks don't pay attention to the time options and end up falling back on the defaults. From a developer's standpoint, this is a big problem. If the default for Netcaster happens to be 12 a.m. on Tuesday, then every week at midnight 100,000 browsers suddenly descend on your site and try to download information. Your server and your bandwidth just can't handle it."

13.2

PRIMARY APPLICATIONS:
Microsoft InterDev Studio, Adobe Photoshop, ULead Web Suite plug-ins, and Macromedia FreeHand

WORK HISTORY:
1991 — Independent solid waste specialist, National Recycling Coalition.
1994 — Saw Mosaic for first time and cofounded Web One Productions, his first venture into the Web.
1995 — Founded Emergent Media, an early Web site development firm.

1997 — Beta-tested Microsoft Internet Explorer 4, decided to focus on push technology and dynamic HTML.

FAVORITE COOKIE RECIPE:
Chewy Peanut Butter Chocolate Chip Cookies
(*www.cookierecipe.com/az/ChwyPBChc. asp*)

13.3

"What you want is constant, random traffic, not a sudden surge followed by a big lull." Internet Explorer lets the Web site developer manage subscription traffic by way of something called a *Channel Definition Format (CDF) file*. "The user still has the ultimate control of deciding whether to subscribe, but the developer can provide scheduling parameters and other default settings. For example, you might permit the user to update at a random time between three and four in the morning. You have to author a CDF file, but it's really not that difficult. It's just a one-page text file that looks similar to HTML, but has a few extra tags in it. From a content producer's standpoint, that's a very good thing."

FROM TIMED PULL TO DIAL-UP YANK

Timed pulling applies mostly to office workers with direct Internet access. Few home and small-business users maintain a constant connection to the Internet, making automated downloads awkward at best. "You might freak if your modem started dialing out in the middle of the night and downloading strange files. It's an invasion of privacy." When pushing to the dial-up crowd, the timed pull turns into something more closely resembling a manual yank.

"Internet Explorer is smart enough to say, okay, your Internet connection is dial-up—not through the LAN—so by default you'll download information

manually. Then it's up to you to choose Favorites ➢ Update All Subscriptions when you want to see the latest stuff." Obviously, you can't control when dial-up folks decide to manually update. It's possible thousands of people could update all at once, just as they might all visit your site at once. But because they're human beings, they tend to behave more randomly without your supervision.

"If the average dial-up user goes online a couple of times a week and they subscribe to a lot of sites, those two dial-ups will involve an awful lot of downloading. Strictly speaking, that's not really push technology, is it?"

TWENTY-FIRST-CENTURY CHANNEL SURFING

If this isn't pushing, what is it? "Microsoft calls it *channeling*, like a TV channel. All ideas about content at Microsoft right now are based on the TV paradigm. The Channels icon even looks like a little satellite dish (13.4)."

And what exactly is a channel? "Again, Netscape and Microsoft see it differently. With the Netcaster model, the user simply subscribes to a site that's already out there. With IE4, you subscribe to a unique collection of pages. The channel is essentially a downloadable site defined by the CDF file." As we'll see, this relatively minor distinction makes all the difference for the end user.

13.4

LATE-BREAKING NEWS

One role for a channel is to broadcast late-breaking news and documentation. "Recently I did some work for the hardware vendor NEC. They wanted to publish technical support documentation directly aimed at new users on their Web site. The problem is accessibility. Once you get to the home page, you have to navigate through the Web site to find your particular niche. How many clicks is it going to take you to get the information you're looking for? The answer is a lot. Marketing usually wins the battle over support for home page real estate, so chances are good that new users are going to get lost."

THE EVERLASTING MANUAL

"So let's say support is a priority, but your client doesn't want it on the home page. The solution is to create a separate tech support channel. You publish a URL in the printed documentation, then you put a button on that page that lets the user subscribe to the channel (13.6).

"When someone clicks on the button, Internet Explorer downloads a CDF file to the user's machine. The CDF file tells IE4 which pages make up the channel. Perhaps the channel comprises three pages of very pertinent, time-sensitive information. The browser downloads those pages to your machine so you can view them anytime you like offline. Then the CDF file references five other pages located in different areas of the Web site. These don't get downloaded; you have to go online to see them. Suddenly the user has an eight-page reference system—a three-page offline quick reference with a five-page online encyclopedia. After that, the user can update the quick reference any time he or she wants just by going online and choosing the Update All Subscriptions command."

DEFAULT CHANNELS INCLUDED

Just out of curiosity, is there any option for hardware and software vendors to automatically install a channel onto a user's system, so the developer doesn't have to print a URL in the documentation? "Sure, that's a possibility. For example, when you install IE4 for Windows with the Active Desktop turned on, you get a default set of channels for MSNBC, Disney, and

others. Then the next time you go to one of those sites, it'll let you know whether or not there's new content."

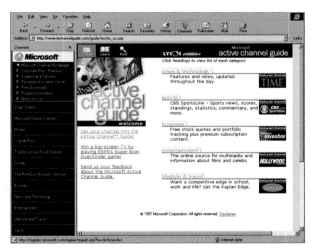

13.5

13.6

"Microsoft is also encouraging developers to use the CDF format to create timed environments that check to see if the user has the latest version of a piece of software. Piracy could go bye-bye if your version of Photoshop has a channel installed and Adobe finds out that you have someone else's registered copy."

Naturally, this potential Big Brother scenario is mitigated by the fact that the user holds the trump card. The owner of a computer can, at any time, delete a channel and avoid contact with any vendor he or she chooses.

DAN'S FANTASTIC COOKIE MACHINE

But not every channel has to provide button-down occupational content like technical support. Consider the whimsical CookieRecipe.com (13.7), a site owned and operated by Shepherd's Emergent Media. The site plays host to a library of more than 1,000 cookie recipes, most submitted by the site's fans. (These are traditional baking cookies, by the way, not electronic cookie scripts. Or as Shepherd calls them, "Actual eat-'em-up, yum-yum cookies.")

Recipes are organized alphabetically, by category (13.8), and according to popularity. The site even includes baking tips and an international cooking glossary. And you can search for a recipe by word or ingredient. At last check, "chocolate chip" turned up 136 matches.

"There's also the Top Ten, and that changes every week. The server tracks the recipes that get the most

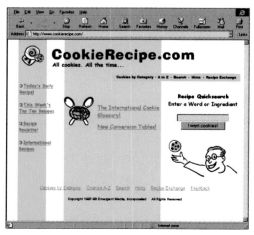

13.7

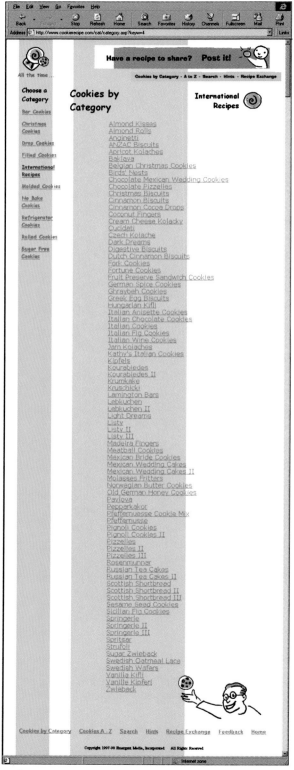

13.8

hits, the ones that were actually clicked and viewed the most often. Every week that gets updated and we start brand new again.

"The channel for the cookie sight carries this weekly Top Ten list (13.9). The idea is that even though you aren't there every day—maybe you don't even know what kind of cookie you want—the channel gives you the ability to browse through the latest and greatest recipes really quickly. Each time you update the subscription, the recipes download to your hard drive so you can view them offline."

The next time you click the CookieRecipe.com channel in IE4's Channels list, a message appears asking you to be patient as the channel loads (13.10). Then comes the actual channel, which features an animated series of cookie icons—numbered according to popularity—trailing out from an overturned jar. The icons pass across the base of a large white cookie jar silhouette (13.11). If you hover your cursor over a cookie, you see the name of the corresponding recipe for the week. Click the cookie icon and the full recipe appears above it. "If any of the recipes make you hungry for more, just click on the CookieRecipe.com logo at the top of the screen to go to the on-line Web site."

EXACTLY HOW DOES THIS COOKIE CRUMBLE?

"The amazing thing is that every element in the channel—the wait screen, the animated cookies, the recipes, everything—is the result of one Dynamic HTML file. There's also a CDF file, as I mentioned earlier, but in this case it's really just a scheduler. The guts of the channel come from the HTML file."

Shepherd's channel makes extensive use of Dynamic HTML and customized functions. You need a logical mind to fully understand what he's up to, and a bit of coding experience certainly doesn't hurt. In the following sections, I make every effort to keep the explanations as straightforward as possible. And as always, the channel file is included on the CD-ROM at the back of the book so you can examine its source code. But remember, what's most important is that you understand the options available to you. If the tags seem like so much Greek to you, you can always hire a professional coder.

13.9

13.10

13.11

MORE CACHE, LESS WAIT

At the end of his HTML file, Shepherd lists the URLs for all the multimedia files that he'll be using (13.15). "Some of these files get loaded elsewhere in the script. But I still go ahead and include this complete list just to make sure I didn't miss anything that I might want to use. I instruct the browser to load the files under the guise of a style called `precache`, which I defined earlier (green inset). This style includes the line `visibility:hidden` so the images go unseen until I turn them on in my script." Everything gets copied to cache during the Wait message so that it's ready to go when called by `start`.

```
<HTML>
<HEAD>

<TITLE>CookieRecipe.com Weekly Channel</TITLE>
</HEAD>
<BODY ONLOAD ="start()" bgcolor="ffcc00" >
<STYLE>
body    {   font:16pt Impact;
            font-weight:normal;
            font-style:normal;
            color:336699;
            text-decoration:none;
            margin-left:
            }
```

13.12

```
<SCRIPT LANGUAGE="Javascript">
<!--
function start()
{

    LOADPAGE.style.visibility = "visible"

    Seq.item("AS").At(3.000,"begin()")
    Seq.item("AS").At(4.000,"fadein(logo)")
    Seq.item("AS").At(5.000,"showanim()")
    Seq.item("AS").At(10.000,"showaction()")
    Seq.item("AS").Play()

}
```

13.13

SETTING UP A SEQUENCE OF EVENTS

Lots of Web pages contain multimedia elements, but Shepherd's simple cookie channel is a carefully crafted sequence of timed events. "Using Dynamic HTML within the context of a channel, I can load the entire file — including all GIFs — without showing them. Using the `<VISIBLE>` tag, you can set these things to be seen or not seen by Internet Explorer."

Like any HTML document, this one starts off with the standard `<HTML>`, `<HEAD>`, `<TITLE>`, and `<BODY>` tags. Shepherd's `<BODY>` tag includes the code `ONLOAD = "start ( )"` (13.12). The `ONLOAD` command is a piece of JavaScript code that tells the browser to do something right when the page starts to load. In this case, IE4 is instructed to perform the function `start`.

Shepherd uses the `start` function to lay out the order of events (13.13). "The first thing `start` does is display the Wait message, which gives the browser time to load all the images into cache. That way, when you ask IE4 to show a particular image, you don't have to wait for it to download. It's already in cache, ready to go." After giving the browser sufficient opportunity to collect its data, `start` orchestrates a succession of operations that comes to a climax mere seconds after you first load the channel.

SEPARATING THE WAIT MESSAGE

The very first thing the `start` function does is set something called `LOADPAGE` to `visible`. Shepherd defines `LOADPAGE` later in the HTML document using a `<DIV>` tag (13.14). "`<DIV>` stands for a *divisional area*. It's a tag you can use with Dynamic HTML to separate a set of elements into its own space." In this case, `<DIV>` separates "Please wait: Cookie Channel

```
<DIV ID=LOADPAGE
    STYLE ="
        position:absolute;
        top:200px;
        text-align:center;
        font: 22pt comic sans ms;
        color:white;
        ">
        Please wait: Cookie Channel loading
</DIV>
```

13.14

```
<!-- Precached images -->
<IMG CLASS="precached" SRC="images/jarlid.gif" WIDTH=59 HEIGHT=57 BORDER=0>
<IMG CLASS="precached" SRC="images/cookie_1_50x47.gif" WIDTH=50 HEIGHT=47 >
<IMG CLASS="precached" SRC="images/cookie_2_50x47.gif" WIDTH=50 HEIGHT=47 BORDER=0 >
<IMG CLASS="precached" SRC="images/cookie_3_50x47.gif" WIDTH=50 HEIGHT=47 BORDER=0 >
<IMG CLASS="precached" SRC="images/cookie_4_50x47.gif" WIDTH=50 HEIGHT=47 BORDER=0 >
<IMG CLASS="precached" SRC="images/cookie_5_50x47.gif" WIDTH=50 HEIGHT=47 BORDER=0 >
<IMG CLASS="precached" SRC="images/cookie_6_50x47.gif" WIDTH=50 HEIGHT=47 BORDER=0 >
<IMG CLASS="precached" SRC="images/cookie_7_50x47.gif" WIDTH=50 HEIGHT=47 BORDER=0 >
<IMG CLASS="precached" SRC="images/cookie_8_50x47.gif" WIDTH=50 HEIGHT=47 BORDER=0 >
<IMG CLASS="precached" SRC="images/jar_corner.gif" WIDTH=157 HEIGHT=131 BORDER=0 >
<IMG CLASS="precached" SRC="images/jartilt_fr.gif" WIDTH=81 HEIGHT=106 BORDER=0 >
<IMG CLASS="precached" SRC="images/jartilt_bk.gif" WIDTH=81 HEIGHT=106 BORDER=0 >
<IMG CLASS="precached" SRC="images/cookie_84x600_banner.gif" WIDTH=600 HEIGHT=84 BORDER=0 >
<IMG CLASS="precached" SRC="images/jarbig.gif" WIDTH=600 HEIGHT=420 BORDER=0 >
<IMG CLASS="precached" SRC="images/jarshake_an.gif"  WIDTH="184" HEIGHT="121" BORDER=0>
<!-- End precached images -->
<!-- Precached Audio -->

<EMBED AUTOSTART="FALSE" LOOP="FALSE" ID="jarAudio"
  SRC="audio/jar11.wav" CLASS="precached">
<!-- End Precached Audio -->

</BODY>
</HTML>
```

```
<STYLE>
.precached {
  position:absolute;
  top:0px;
  left:0px;
  visibility:hidden;
  z-index: -100; }
</STYLE>
```

13.15

Loading" onto its own page, aligned center and spaced 200 pixels from the top of the screen. It also formats the text as white 22-point Comic Sans.

"The <DIV> tag lets me set up an object that I can move around into different places. I can define an area of any size and segregate it from the rest of my page within a single HTML file. That way, the stuff inside the <DIV> tag acts like its own little HTML page."

SEQUENCING WITH ACTIVEX

So when LOADPAGE turns to visible, the Wait message appears onscreen. No sweat. But while we look at "Please wait," what's happening in the background? "Next in the start function, you see a list of object tags that begin with Seq (13.15), short for *sequence*. These refer to objects that I've defined using

ActiveX." ActiveX is the name given to a collection of controls included with Internet Explorer. You can call up one of these controls by entering a numerical class ID (CLSID) address. The addresses are long — not the kind of thing you want to be entering over and over — so Shepherd assigns the name Seq to the one he wants to use (13.16). He also sets the default visibility attribute for Seq to hidden, ensuring that the elements in the sequence are invisible until he specifies otherwise.

"Seq calls an ActiveX control that plays functions at specific intervals. Each of those numbers listed in the start function (13.13) spell out an amount of time in seconds. At the specified number of seconds, IE4 plays a script (13.17). Everything happens according to a very definite schedule."

```
<!-- Sequencer Object -->
<OBJECT ID="Seq"
 CLASSID="CLSID:B0A6BAE2-AAF0-11d0
                 -A152-00A0C908DB96"
 STYLE="width:0; height:0;
        visibility:hidden;
        position:absolute;
        top:0px; left:0px">
</OBJECT>
```

13.16

```
function begin() {
    LOADPAGE.style.visibility = "hidden"
    theback.style.visibility = "visible"
    corner.style.visibility = "visible"
    }

function fadein(obj) {
    obj.filters.item(0).apply()
    obj.style.visibility = "visible"
    obj.filters.item(0).play()
    }

function showanim() {
    play_sound(jarAudio)
    shake.style.visibility = "visible"
    }

function showaction() {
    shake.style.visibility = "hidden"
    intro.style.visibility = "visible"
    cookieslide.style.visibility = "visible"
    footer_conveyor_start()
    }
```

13.17

13.18

■ Three seconds after the Wait screen comes up, IE4 plays the `begin` function, which hides the Wait page. "I chose three seconds because that's about how much time it takes to load all the images into the cache."

■ At the fourth second, IE4 performs the `fadein` function, which fades the CookieRecipe.com logo onscreen. "The `fadein` script uses one of IE4's transition filters. The filter fades the text onscreen in a dither pattern."

■ At five seconds, we come to `showanim`, which plays the sound of a wobbling cookie jar lid while playing a GIF animation file (13.18).

■ After ten seconds, the sound and animation have completed. The `showaction` function kicks in, displaying a "Welcome Cookie Bakers!" message and then initiating a procession of cookies that flow out from the overturned jar.

The cookie procession is triggered by a little function called `cookieslide`, which turns out to be the most extensive function of them all. Not surprisingly, this portion of the HTML file consumes a few hundred lines of code, but like so much of life, it becomes easier to understand when you look at it one cookie at a time.

THE CONTINUOUS COOKIE PROCESSION

Once the cookie channel finishes loading—that is, once the `start` function completes—a succession of ten cookies cycles slowly across the screen. In the next two figures, "I've colored the cookies to make a couple of points:

■ As I mentioned earlier, you can hover the cursor over a cookie to see the corresponding recipe name (13.19) or click the cookie icon to see the full recipe (13.20). The figures show me bothering the green cookie.

■ But also notice how the cookies interact with their environment. The cookies appear to exit the overturned jar (purple cookie, 13.20) and pass behind the lid (red cookie, 13.19). Then they flow across the screen and disappear into the right-hand edge of the large white silhouette (blue cookie, 13.19)."

13.19

13.20

Shepherd achieves this effect by overlaying a series of graphic elements (13.21). The front side of the cookie jar is separate from the back side and lid. Shepherd also created an extra edge behind which cookies can disappear along the right side of the screen. The key to putting these images together — with the cookies — is absolute positioning and stacking order, both permitted by Dynamic HTML.

PRECISE POSITIONING

As with the Wait message, Shepherd uses the `<DIV>` tag to stake out his territory (13.22). "I set out a `cookieslide` space that's 505 pixels wide and 120 pixels tall. That space sits 80 pixels in from the left side of the window and 265 pixels down from the top. This area contains the jar graphics, the lid, the edge, and the cookies. And thanks to Dynamic HTML, this space is absolute. The images can overlap each other, just like they do in Photoshop."

Shepherd was likewise deliberate about positioning the individual graphics inside the `cookieslide` space. But rather than using the `<Z-INDEX>` tag to stipulate layering order — one Dynamic HTML option — he let the order of his code do the work for him (13.23). Images that are tagged first appear in back; later images appear in front. So right after the opening `<DIV>` tag, Shepherd coded the back side of the jar (`jartilt_bk.gif`) so it would appear in back of the other images. Later he tagged the edge (`jar_corner.gif`), the front side (`jartilt_fr.gif`), and the lid (`jarlid.gif`), so that they would appear in front. Notice how the back and front sides of the jar are positioned identically — 30 pixels from the top and 0 from the left — ensuring that they register exactly.

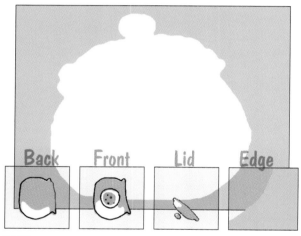

13.21

```
<DIV ID="cookieslide"
    STYLE="position:absolute;
        left:80px; top:265px;
        width:505px; height:120px;
        background-color:;
        background-image:URL();
        overflow:hidden;
        clip:rect(0, 505, 135, 0);
        visibility:hidden">
```

13.22

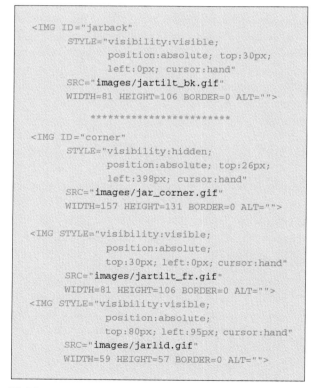

```
<IMG ID="jarback"
    STYLE="visibility:visible;
        position:absolute; top:30px;
        left:0px; cursor:hand"
    SRC="images/jartilt_bk.gif"
    WIDTH=81 HEIGHT=106 BORDER=0 ALT="">

    *************************
<IMG ID="corner"
    STYLE="visibility:hidden;
        position:absolute; top:26px;
        left:398px; cursor:hand"
    SRC="images/jar_corner.gif"
    WIDTH=157 HEIGHT=131 BORDER=0 ALT="">

<IMG STYLE="visibility:visible;
        position:absolute;
        top:30px; left:0px; cursor:hand"
    SRC="images/jartilt_fr.gif"
    WIDTH=81 HEIGHT=106 BORDER=0 ALT="">
<IMG STYLE="visibility:visible;
        position:absolute;
        top:80px; left:95px; cursor:hand"
    SRC="images/jarlid.gif"
    WIDTH=59 HEIGHT=57 BORDER=0 ALT="">
```

13.23

COOKIE MARQUEE

In between the back side of the jar and the other images (as indicated by the green asterisks in 13.23), Shepherd coded the march of the cookies. That way, the cookies appear in front of the back side of the cookie jar but in back of the other graphics.

To put the cookies into perpetual motion, Shepherd employed the `<MARQUEE>` tag (13.24). "`<MARQUEE>` has been around since Internet Explorer 3, but it was about as lame as Netscape's `<FLASH>` tag — people just used it to make text run across the screen. Nowadays, you have more controls than you used to. You can size the marquee, put images inside it, and scroll them in a specific direction — left, right, what have you.

"Next, I list all the cookies, in the order that they scroll across the screen (13.25) — `cookie_1`, `cookie_2`, and so on." (Because each cookie is coded more or less the same, only the first two appear in the figure.) For the present, the cookies are static GIF files, but in the future, Shepherd may have them rotate as they scroll along. How would he do that? "Oh, I'll use animated GIFs, definitely. I could write a really convoluted IE4-specific rotate script, but it'd take up a lot more CPU power than just loading an animated GIF.

"You can see a little tag called `cursor` — this permits me to set what the cursor looks like when you're moused over a particular item. After this comes the in-line JavaScript tag `ONMOUSEOVER`. When you move your cursor over the cookie, this tag calls the `showit` function, which simply makes the name of the cookie recipe visible." Similarly, `ONMOUSEOUT`

calls a function that hides the recipe name when you move the cursor off the cookie, and `ONCLICK` shows the recipe when you click the cookie icon.

Shepherd spaced the cookie graphics apart using nonbreaking spaces, indicated by ` `. "I suppose I could have used a blank spacer GIF, but then that's one more thing I'd have to download. You may notice that I vary the number of spaces pretty wildly to give the cookies a more random feel. It's just touch and feel — I code a few spaces and then hit Reload inside Internet Explorer to see how it looks. Made on a computer, but crafted by hand.

"After I code all the cookies, I close the `<MARQUEE>` tag. And then finally, after I tag the corner and jar images (13.23), I close out the `<DIV>` tag so it's all part of my `cookieslide` function."

```
<IMG STYLE="visibility:visible;
         position:relative;
         top:20px; left:0px; cursor:hand"
     SRC="images/cookie_1_50x47.gif"
     WIDTH=50 HEIGHT=47 BORDER=0
     ALT="Click Me!"
     ONMOUSEOVER="showit(title1)"
     ONMOUSEOUT="hideit(title1)"
     ONCLICK="display_item(recipe1)">1
       
       

<IMG STYLE="visibility:visible;
         position:relative;
         top:25px; left:0px; cursor:hand"
     SRC="images/cookie_2_50x47.gif"
     WIDTH=50 HEIGHT=47 BORDER=0
     ALT="Click Me!"
     ONMOUSEOVER="showit(title2)"
     ONMOUSEOUT="hideit(title2)"
     ONCLICK="display_item(recipe2)">2
       
       
       
```

13.25

```
<MARQUEE ID="conveyorMarquee"
     STYLE="position:absolute;
         background-image:URL();
         top:40px;
         height:60px; width:505px;"

     BEHAVIOR="scroll"
     DIRECTION="right"
     SCROLLAMOUNT=0
     SCROLLDELAY=150
     TRUESPEED="FALSE">
```

13.24

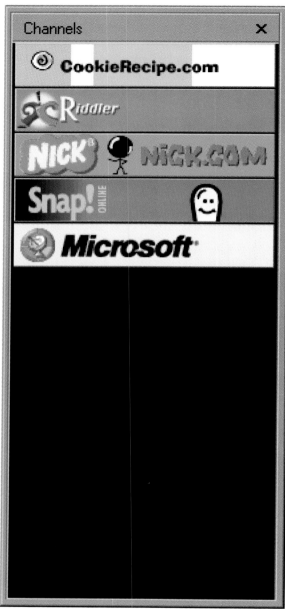

13.26

13.27

13.28

THE THREE CHANNEL LOGOS

"Now that I've scripted the HTML page, there's one more set of graphics I need to create before I write the CDF file. Internet Explorer lets you assign three icons — or *logos* — to a channel. All the logos are optional; you don't have to include them. But they're a good idea if you want to set your channel apart from the others."

Each of the logos must be a specific size in order to fit into the right place. I describe each logo below according to its CDF tag:

- `image-wide`: The largest logo appears in the Channels list inside the Internet Explorer application window (13.26). It measures 192 pixels wide by 32 pixels tall.
- `image`: The next smaller logo is applicable to Windows users only. It appears in the Channel Bar when the user has Microsoft's Active Desktop function turned on (13.27). The `image` logo measures 80 pixels wide by 32 pixels tall.
- `icon`: Lastly, you need a tiny 16 × 16-pixel icon for the Favorites ➢ Channels submenu (13.28) inside Internet Explorer.

"A subscriber can load your channel just by clicking on the logo. The sheer convenience of this feature makes it more likely that users will visit your site."

UNITING THE CHANNEL ELEMENTS

"After you get all your pages and logos in order, you need to write a CDF file to pull all the parts of the channel together. It sounds hard, but by comparison to the HTML file, CDF scripting is really a piece of cake." Indeed, the entire CDF script fits on a single screen (13.29). "CDF is a subset of XML — the *Extensible Markup Language.* And XML is a subset of SGML, which is where HTML comes from. So if you can write HTML, you shouldn't have any problem with CDF.

"You start off the file by telling the browser that this is an XML file — `<?XML VERSION="1.0" ENCODING="UTF-8"?>`. This is a standard line; you don't ever have to change it. The next line is the `<CHANNEL>` tag. It includes a standard `HREF` that tells the browser the URL for the channel. So you open up the `<CHANNEL>` tag, give it an `HREF` and `<TITLE>`, and put everything else inside that `<CHANNEL>` tag, just as you do with `<HTML>`."

```
<?XML VERSION="1.0" ENCODING="UTF-8"?>
<CHANNEL HREF="http://emergentmedia.com/cookiechan/" LEVEL="1">
<TITLE>CookieRecipe.com  Channel</TITLE>
<ABSTRACT>CookieRecipe.com  - Top 10 Recipe List | This
    channel gives you the weekly update of the most popular
    recipes on CookieRecipe.com. </ABSTRACT>
<LOGO HREF="images/chanbar_wide.gif" STYLE="image-wide" />
<LOGO HREF="images/chanbar.gif" STYLE="image" />
<LOGO HREF="images/chanicon.gif" STYLE="icon" />
<Item HREF="http://emergentmedia.com/cookiechan/" Precache="YES" >
    <TITLE>CookieRecipe Channel Screen Saver</TITLE>
    <ABSTRACT>CookieRecipe.com  - Top 10 Recipe List | This
        channel gives you the weekly update of the most popular
        recipes on CookieRecipe.com. </ABSTRACT>
    <USAGE VALUE="ScreenSaver" />
</Item>

<SCHEDULE STARTDATE="1997.11.17" ENDDATE="1997.11.24">
    <INTERVALTIME DAY="7" />
    <EARLIESTTIME HOUR="12" />
    <LATESTTIME HOUR="18" />
</SCHEDULE>

</CHANNEL>
```

13.29

POP-UP DESCRIPTION

"The <ABSTRACT> tag lets you create a text description of your channel. If the user hovers the cursor over your logo in one of the Channels lists, the abstract pops up (13.30). The idea is to write something that's fairly compelling so when someone mouses over your button, they'll think, 'Oh yeah, that's what that channel's for.' The abstract is also handy to have around if for some reason IE4 doesn't load the logo graphic, which can definitely happen."

TAGGING THE LOGOS

"Next comes the three <LOGO> tags, one for each of the icons you've created. If you look at the code (13.29), you'll see that unlike <TITLE> and <ABSTRACT>, <LOGO> does not require a closing tag. It's open ended. You need to enter HREF and the path to the icon graphic. But the STYLE tag is what sets <LOGO> apart. STYLE tells how the icons are going to be used— image-wide (13.26), image (13.27), or icon (13.28). These styles aren't made up by me; they're part of XML.

"At the end of the <LOGO> tag is a slash close. If you don't put the closer slash in, the tag won't get read."

SWITCHING CHANNELS IN YOUR SLEEP

"The <Item> tag spells out additional pages and other elements in the channel. But in the case of the CookieRecipe.com channel, there's just one <Item>, a Windows screen saver. The tag points to the same cookiechan HTML file used for the channel, the only difference being that I set the <USAGE VALUE> tag to ScreenSaver. When you go to subscribe to the channel on a Windows machine, this tag tells IE4 to give you the option of using the channel as a screen saver (13.31).

"The channel will also appear as an option in the user's Screen Saver Properties dialog box (13.32). Either way, if you accept this option, the CookieRecipe.com channel will play any time your screen goes to sleep." It's yet another way to make your content more apparent to the user.

"Because I set the Precache tag to YES (13.29), the screen saver will pull the channel locally from your hard drive." What happens if you clear the cache or the cache fills up and displaces the channel file? "Then the screen saver option will probably just disappear. You have to rely on users to update the subscription if they like your content. You can't expect to just pollute their systems indefinitely— and that's a good thing."

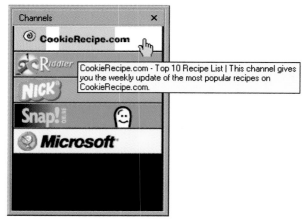

13.30

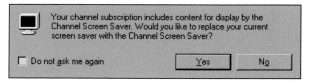

13.31

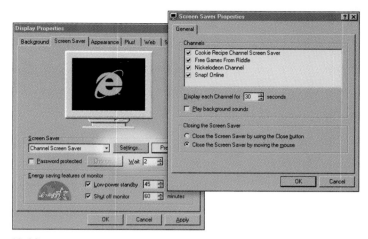

13.32

SCHEDULING PARAMETERS

"As I mentioned at the outset, one of the main purposes of the CDF file is to act as a scheduler for automatic updates, so your subscribers' computers don't hit your site and download content all at once. That's what the <SCHEDULE> tag is all about.

"In my CDF file (13.29), the <SCHEDULE> tag shows a STARTDATE of November 17 followed by an END-DATE a week later. There's also an INTERVALTIME tag that tells IE4 how often to update the channel, plus a couple of HOUR tags in military time. So here's how IE4 reads my SCHEDULE script: Between November 17 and 24, update the channel once a week at some random time between noon and 6 p.m."

What happens after November 24? "In theory, I'll change out the channel content and the CDF file every week, so the ENDDATE info will always get updated. Of course, you don't have to work this way. If you didn't want to update the CDF very often but still planned on updating the content, you could set the ENDDATE to sometime way in the future."

TWO TREATS IN ONE

After all this intense code, the question that crosses my mind is why? Why is a scripting expert like Shepherd hosting a cookie site? "Because we love cookies! Everyone loves them! A couple of us here like to bake, so it seemed a natural fit."

That's it? "Hey gang, let's make a cookie site"? Seems like a lot of work just to satisfy your personal sweet tooth. "If you really want to know, it's based on a market survey we did looking into the kind of reference sites that people might be interested in. This particular niche looked promising, and sure enough, it has taken off. We're serving up 65,000 impressions a day. Also, the demographics of the site are 92 percent female. It's an advertising niche that's not currently exploited."

It's good to know you really can follow your dreams and still ensure a tidy profit. "Absolutely," Shepherd agrees. "We have PieRecipe.com and CakeRecipe.com in the works right now."

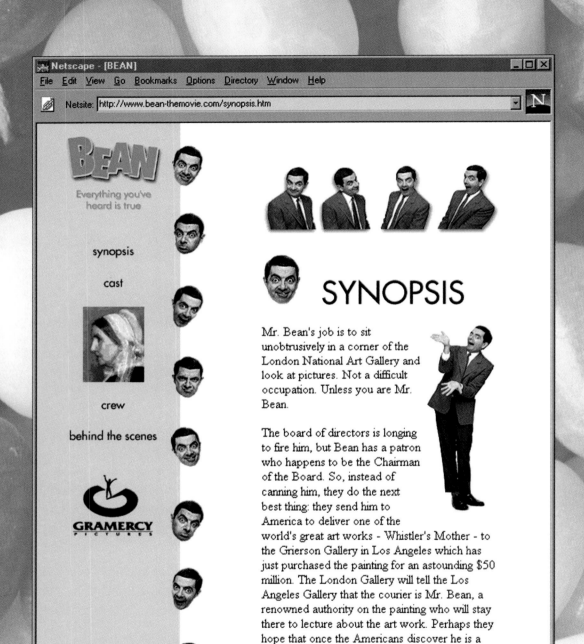

CHAPTER 14
ANNOUNCING YOUR WEB SITE

You might question what Eric Ward is doing in this book. He's not a graphic artist. He's not a designer. Perhaps most telling, he's the only person featured in this book who doesn't list Photoshop among the tools he uses on a daily basis. "I wouldn't recognize Photoshop if you set it right in front of me. I'm a little embarrassed to admit this, but I know nothing about graphics. Nothing. When I was first putting together my site, I paid college students to create my graphics." The good news is, Ward chose good people to help him. "The college kid who I hired back in 1993 is now the creative director at CyberGold."

And yet Ward maintains that what he does is an art. Ward's business? Web site promotion. We're not talking about a guy who blasts a company's URL willy-nilly to a billion different search engines and says to his client, "There you go, consider yourself a player." Ward methodically matches each client's site with the people and places most likely to be interested in it. And he's been at it longer than anyone in the business.

"When I went back to college in '92, I saw the Internet for the first time. It was completely the domain of academia. There weren't any graphical browsers yet. But when Mosaic became available and suddenly the Internet had graphics, I knew it was all going to change. I hate to say this, but I could tell right away that business and commerce were going to take over the Web in a big way. I didn't know how long it would take or when it would happen, but I knew it was just a matter of time."

Like any business entity, an online presence doesn't serve any purpose if nobody knows it's there. So having cut his teeth in traditional marketing, Ward

You need to take a holistic approach. Look at your Web site as a whole, based on its quality and content, and find the outlets that need to know about it.

ERIC WARD

quickly saw that the forthcoming professional Web sites were going to need his services. "Five years ago, I went to an ISP that had just opened up in Knoxville, Tennessee. At this time, they probably had four or five corporate companies that had built some kind of Web presence. I told them I wanted to start a business promoting Web sites. All I really wanted to know was whether they thought my plan was feasible or not. But instead they said, 'Hell, if you can do that, we'll hire you to announce all our clients. We're having to do that now and it's a pain in the neck.' That's when I knew it was going to work. If the first ISP I talked to responded this enthusiastically, I had no doubt that my services were going to be needed."

So the question remains: What is a non-designer doing in a book about Web design? The answer is very simple. Ward knows how to unlock the door between you and your intended audience. After spending hours upon hours and weeks upon weeks establishing a Web presence, most of us don't have a clue about how we should go about announcing ourselves to the world. And let's face it, there's no point in launching your personal vision onto the million-lane information superhighway only to pile up and stall a few feet from the entrance ramp.

Eric Ward knows how to keep the traffic moving. And after all is said and done, this may be the most important art of them all.

<META> TAGS AND SEARCH ENGINES

Not surprisingly, Ward doesn't condone the build-it-and-they-will-come philosophy. "I'm sorry, but the simple fact that you have a Web site isn't news. Everybody has a Web site. If you came to me and told me your company *didn't* have a site, now that would be remarkable."

Okay, so you can't hang up a sign and hope that the world decides to stop by for a visit. But what do you do? Should you put a ton of <META> tags in your pages (14.1) so that the almighty search-engine "spiders" snag you and put you in their databases (14.2)? "A lot of people think <META> tags were invented for the benefit of AltaVista and Infoseek. But when <META> tags first came into use, there weren't any search engines. <META> names and keywords are just ways of identifying your documents, so you can keep track of what all the different pages inside your site are doing. Then along came the automated search engines, and the <META> tags became a convenient way for the engines to categorize sites.

"As a publicity tool, <META> tags are most useful if your site includes a lot of artistically designed pages that are nothing more than a series of graphics. If there's no text on a page, it becomes literally invisible to the search engine. All you've got is a bunch of <IMG SRC=X>, which tells the search engine absolutely nothing about what your page has to offer. In this case, <META> tags become crucial. In the absence of any text in your HTML document, the

ARTIST:
Eric Ward

ORGANIZATION:
The WardGroup
Knoxville, Tennessee
423/637-2438
www.netpost.com
netpost@netpost.com

SYSTEM:
Dell Dimension 486/300MHz
Windows 95
8GB storage/64MB RAM

CONNECTIVITY:
56 Kbps modem

PERIPHERALS:
Dell 17-inch monitor

PRIMARY APPLICATIONS:
Netscape Communicator, Microsoft Access, EWAN (Telnet client), and Microsoft Office

WORK HISTORY:
1986 — Published Knoxville-based franchise of *Travel Host* magazine, which gets distributed in hotels.

1991 — After employer went bankrupt, took night courses at University of Tennessee.

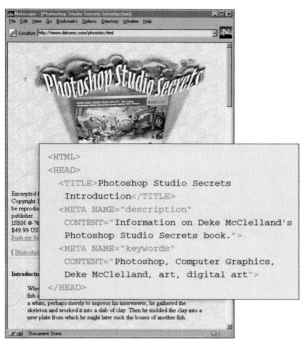

14.1

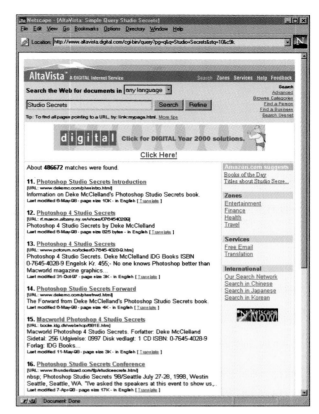

14.2

`<META>` description and keyword tags are all AltaVista and others have to go off of."

Two of Ward's clients, coolshopping.com and Gramercy Pictures, are cases in point. The home pages for *www.coolshopping.com* (14.3) and *www. bean-the-movie.com* (14.4) both feature lone GIF images against solid-colored backgrounds. A look at the source code

1992 — Turned on computer for first time and discovered potential of Internet through the eyes of a marketing person.

1993 — The WardGroup was born when local ISP began forwarding all its clients who needed promotion.

1994 — Asked Yahoo to create a new category for site-promotion businesses, now grown to include hundreds of companies.

1997 — Named in *Websight* magazine's list of the 100 most influential people on the Internet.

FAVORITE TOM HANKS MOVIE:
Joe Versus the Volcano ("I relate to the beginning where he's stuck in this depressing job.")

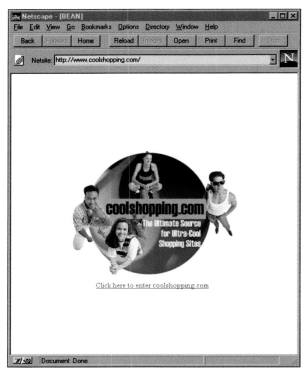

14.3

14.4

for the coolshopping.com page shows an extensive list of <META> descriptions and keywords that are likely to help a search engine digest the site. The description text appears verbatim in the AltaVista hit (14.5). Like the movie it promotes, the *Bean* site source code is a little more peculiar (14.6). Although the <META> description is undeniably funny, it's less successful in conveying a sense of what the sight is about. As a result, it takes some effort to locate this site through AltaVista.

In fact, in every search we performed on the movie *Bean*, the first 40 or 50 hits were exclusively third-party reviews of the movie. Ward guesses that Gramercy wasn't very concerned with the search engines. "These movie sites generally come out a week or two before the movie premiers. Since the search engines take two to six weeks to list a site, they really don't drive much of the movie-going traffic."

But the movie will still be out in six weeks. Shouldn't the designers have worked harder to massage the <META> tags so the site would get the first spot on a search? "Well, yes and no. I think these movie sites tend to be too focused on the cinema experience. They should be thinking longer term. How can they use the site to roll out the movie on Pay Per View? What happens when it comes out on video? I don't think the studios are exploiting the sites to their full advantage.

```
<HTML>
<HEAD>
    <TITLE>coolshopping.com</TITLE>
    <META NAME="description"
    CONTENT="The ultimate source for ultra-cool
    shopping sites, including cool shopping
    site of the day, coolblue heat soap opera,
    chat, personals, online cards.
    Handpicked by the coolteam.">
    <META NAME="keywords"
    CONTENT="shopping,cool,shop,mall,submit,
    award,advertise,gifts,fashion,jewelery,
    software,cds,art,books,toys,banner,flowers,
    videos,travel,clothes,clothing,hardware,
    contests,sports,crafts,pets,accessories,
    children,kids,food,coffee,cigar
    collectibles,gourmet,gallery">
</HEAD>
```

14.5

coolshopping.com
[URL: wwww.coolshopping.com/]
The ultimate source for ultra-cool shopping sites, including cool shopping site of the day, coolblue heat soap opera, chat, personals, online cards.
Last modified 3-Mar-98 - page size 4K - in English

"But let's say that they actually did shoot for number one. Maybe the *Bean* `<META>` tags—strange as they are—were exactly what the search engines wanted. Maybe they had the first spot for a week or so and then they dropped to number 207 after that. Then maybe they massaged the code some more and got up to number three, only to be knocked down again a few days later. How long are you supposed to keep doing this? My feeling is, it's not a game you can win, so why even try?

"The fact is, you can spend thousands of hours trying to be number one with AltaVista. A lot of people do. But there's no point. First of all, search engines are fickle, so there's no telling what they want. But also, you have no secrets, because everyone out there has access to your HTML code. If you somehow manage to figure out the right keywords to come up high on a search, another person can go to your site and look at your source code and steal it. So if you decide you're going to tweak your code to come up high on a search, keep in mind that you're going to have to do it eight hours a day, 365 days a year, and everything you do can be stolen by your competitors because there's no way to stop them unless you spend a fortune in time and money building bait-and-switch pages. It becomes your own version of Dante's *Inferno*—a hell with many levels of madness. It's insane.

"`<META>` tags are a good tool, but they're just one of many. And hard as you might try, you can't leverage a search engine when 10,000 other sites are doing the same thing. I like to tell people, instead of massaging your HTML code, you're better off massaging the Webmaster at Infoseek. It's a joke, but it's true. The manual ways are better."

SUBMITTING TO THE DIRECTORIES

In addition to making your site accessible to automated search engines, Ward advocates that you make manual submissions to Web directories. Just so we're all on the same page, what's the difference? "Search engines all rely on spiders to automatically crawl around and investigate Web pages. The spiders generate an enormous index. When you enter a few words

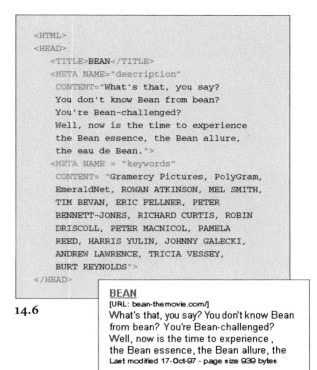

14.6

and hit Enter, the search engine looks through its index and comes back with a few hundred or thousand results. There are no humans involved."

"Directories rely on human beings. Unlike the search engines, they don't try to index every single site on the planet. They just go for the best sites. But directories also tend to be a better vehicle for promoting your site. Yahoo in particular is an immensely popular site. Its categories are predefined and well organized. So instead of sifting through hundreds or thousands of matches, as you do with a search engine, users can get to the sites they're looking for in a matter of a few clicks.

"The problem with Yahoo is that something like one third of the people who apply to be listed never get in. And it can take months to get a listing. But it's well worth the effort. If you make submissions to all the directories, you're bound to get on a few of them. And it doesn't hurt if you have a killer site. When it comes to directories, quality counts."

AVOIDING THE APPEARANCE OF SPAM

There are lots of clever tricks for getting the attention of search engines. But Ward generally advises against them. Most of the tricks have been used to death by spammers, giving them a bad name with the search engines.

"There's a lot of <META> tag abuse going on. People add <META> tags that have nothing to do with what their sites are really about. Like a soft drink manufacturer might list the names of its competitors in its description field. Then when you search for Pepsi, you also get hits for Coke. That's not a real-life example, of course, but it's indicative of the kind of thing that happens all the time.

"There are so many different techniques for spamming, it's awful. For example, let's say you use a white background for your Web page. Some sites will then include a bunch of text on the page and color it white. The white text blends into the white background so the user can't see it. But the search engine can see the text just fine."

See, now to us, that sounds like a hot tip, especially for artists with very little text on their pages. "Well, in theory, there's nothing wrong with including invisible text so long as it's an honest description of your page. But there are search engines that will disqualify a page for it. The search engine figures invisible text means you're trying to pull a fast one so, bang, you're eliminated."

The search engine doesn't know if you're playing fair. It just knows that this trick is used by spammers, so you're guilty by association. "These are machines. They don't know clever from crooked. So the safest thing is to steer clear of the tricks."

TIPTOE THROUGH THE YAHOO

Yahoo does a good job of documenting how you should go about making a submission. But speaking from experience, the more right-brained among us sometimes have problems following even the simplest of left-brained instructions. So we thought it might be helpful to watch over Ward's shoulder as he makes a directory submission for a real client, coolshopping.com (14.7).

"The client came to me with the idea of launching a site that was designed to be a directory of nothing but really high-end shopping-related Web sites. There are a billion people out there who will sell you stuff over the Web, but who's doing some really unique or unusual things? The idea behind coolshopping.com was to be a port of entry to the best shopping sites out there."

Before making your submissions, Ward recommends that you put together a brief text-only document that lists your name, URL, e-mail address, and other specifics, along with a few brief descriptions of your site. "It's good to include separate 15-, 25-, 50-, and 70-word site summaries. That way, they can just lift the summary that matches the length requested

14.7

by the directory. By preparing in advance, you don't have to type the same information over and over every time you make a submission.

"Next I go to Yahoo (*www.yahoo.com*). It's not like Yahoo's the only directory out there, but it's a darn fine starting point. Then I type *shopping directories* into the Search field and hit Enter. I'm just doing some research here — I don't know if I'll find anything or not. I get a total of five category matches along with a bunch of internal Yahoo site matches (14.8). I want the categories because I need to announce a site that's not part of Yahoo. So now I'm scanning the list for a good category. I like the sound of the first one, *Business and Economy: Companies: Shopping Centers: Shopping: Directories*. I'm thinking this category might make sense.

"So I click on the category name. Yahoo takes me to the category, where I see a whole list of shopping directories, and sure enough, midway down is *cool-shopping.com* (14.9). But let's say I'm submitting the site for the first time. I've found this category and I'm thinking this is the one for me. At the very bottom of the page is a link that says 'Suggest a Site.' And there begins the process."

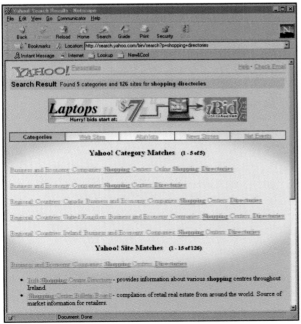

14.8   *(Text and artwork copyright © 1998 by Yahoo!, Inc. All rights reserved.)*

WHERE TO FIND THE SEARCHERS

We can't begin to list every search engine and directory out there. But here are a few of the most popular and influential. According to Ward, you should make an effort to submit your site to every one of them.

SEARCH ENGINES

AltaVista	*www.altavista.digital.com*
Infoseek	*www.infoseek.com*
Lycos	*www.lycos.com*
WebCrawler	*webcrawler.com*
Excite	*www.excite.com*
HotBot	*www.hotbot.com*
OpenText	*index.opentext.net*
PlanetSearch	*www.planetsearch.com*
NorthernLight	*www.northernlight.com*
AOL NetFind	*www.aol.com/netfind*

DIRECTORIES

Yahoo	*www.yahoo.com*
MiningCo	*www.miningco.com*
Magellan	*www.mckinley.com*
LookSmart	*www.looksmart.com*

All of these sites permit you to make manual submissions. The search engines then automatically gather the information from your site. The directories are manually juried and therefore take some time to turn around results.

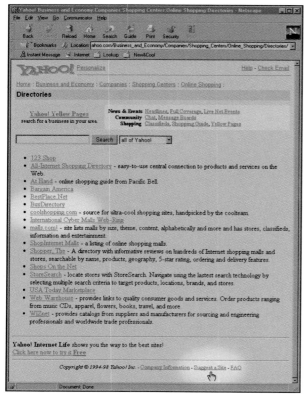

14.9   *(Text and artwork copyright © 1998 by Yahoo!, Inc. All rights reserved.)*

"From here, I'm asked for a bunch of different pieces of information. I open that text-only document that I created earlier. Then I just sit there and copy and paste from it. If you're organized up front, it takes maybe five minutes to go through the whole process."

It may be a few weeks or months before your site shows up on Yahoo. And even then, it may not show up in the category you suggested. "That's the funny thing about Yahoo — just because you say you want to submit your site somewhere doesn't mean that's where it's going to end up. There are human reviewers here and they make the decisions."

SEARCH ENGINE SUBMISSION

What about the automated search engines? Do they permit manual submissions? "Oh, yeah, you can and you should. Search engines rely on spiders, but it's still a good idea to show the spiders where to go. If you go to AltaVista (*www.altavista.digital.com*), you'll

see a link at the bottom that says 'Add a Page.' Just go ahead and click on it.

"Now you see how easy submissions can be. Yahoo and AltaVista represent opposite ends of the submission difficulty spectrum. Where Yahoo has five or six screens of options, AltaVista just asks for one thing — your URL. That's it. Every few months, AltaVista will go out and fetch your site and index it automatically according to the text in your HTML files. It doesn't need or permit any more input from you."

INDUSTRY-SPECIFIC DIRECTORIES

Yahoo and AltaVista aren't the only games in town. "Yahoo offers a great directory for other directories and search engines that you should definitely look into. But you have to go deep into Yahoo to get to it.

"Starting at the top of the Yahoo hierarchy — right after you enter *www.yahoo.com* — click on the Computers & Internet category. Then click on World Wide Web@, then Searching the Web. Now you've burrowed pretty far into the Yahoo directory system and you've discovered a mother lode of promotion information (14.10). You can see in this list that there are 152 search engines, 226 Web directories, and a bunch of articles comparing search engines. It's everything anybody could ever want for announcing a Web site.

"So if I were new to announcing Web sites, I would come to this page and click on the Web Directories link. Suddenly, I have this amazing list of the kinds of places I want to be submitting to (14.11). Keep in mind, not every one of these fits every kind of site, but you can definitely find a handful that are right up your alley.

"If you scroll through this list of directories, you start to see some familiar ones. But there are a lot of industry-specific directories as well. Like here's one called Achoo, the directory of Internet health-care sites (14.12). If you're a graphic designer and you're building a site for a hospital, an HMO, a private practice, or anyone else in the health-care profession, you need to submit them to Achoo. I used this directory when I was consulting with the American Medical Association (14.13). It was an obvious marriage. Once you know where to look, it's just a matter of common sense."

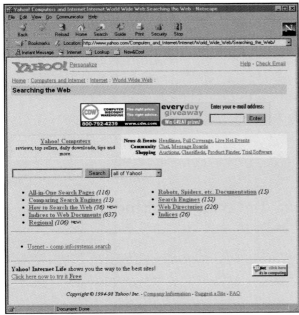

14.10   *(Text and artwork copyright © 1998 by Yahoo!, Inc. All rights reserved.)*

14.12

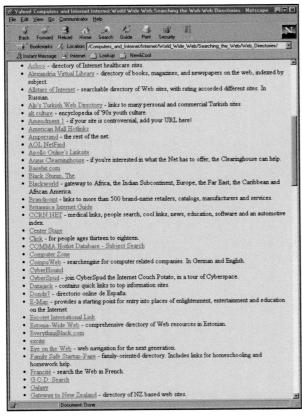

14.11

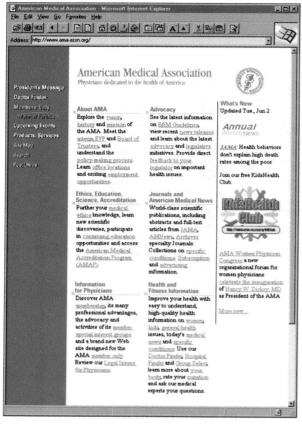

14.13

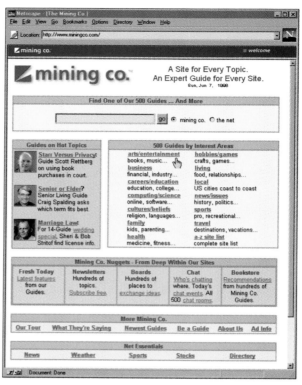

14.14

PUTTING A FACE WITH A NAME

"Often, a directory will present you with a specific person who you should e-mail. Then you know precisely who the arbitrator is. This is often the case with smaller directories, like the Mining Co (*www.miningco.com*, 14.14). Incidentally, I have to say, the Mining Co is a great tool. It's really an awesome site."

"So let's say I want to promote Gramercy's *Bean* site (14.15). I'd go to that area called 500 Guides by Interest Areas and click on the first link, 'Arts/Entertainment.' Now I'm thinking, do they have anything about movies? And I see a headline for 'Movies' with a category called Hollywood Movies/Reviews. So I click there and I'm presented at this point with the Mining Co Guide to Movies.

"Right at the top of the page is a name, Bruce Diamond, and an e-mail address, *hollywoodmovie. guide@miningco.com* (14.16). If I was promoting this site today, I would certainly want to submit *Bean* to

him. See that Net Links section on the right? 1997 Movies Sites, 1998 Movie Sites — there you go. *Bean* came out in '97 so it would definitely need to be submitted there.

"Now if we follow the 1997 Movies Sites link, hopefully we'll find the *Bean* site. Hopefully Bruce decided that *Bean* was a worthy enough Web site to list. That's always an issue. As you move more into the human-reviewed directories, you take your chances. These guys aren't obligated to promote your stuff, and it really doesn't pay to hound them. Just tell them you're here, and let them decide whether to include you.

"Sure enough, there's a link for *Bean* here. But you know what's interesting? He pointed to the UK version of the site. *www.mrbean.co.uk* (14.17). It doesn't matter, of course, I'll take the plug either way. The movie gets promotion, so my client will be happy."

14.15

14.16

14.17

PROMOTING OUTSIDE THE BOX

There's no denying that the tools we've explored so far are indispensable when it comes to promoting a Web site. But Ward insists that real creativity comes into play when you start thinking beyond the two walls of search engines and directories. "This is where the art comes in. You need to take a holistic approach. Look at your Web site as a whole, based on its quality and content, and find the outlets that need to know about it. Only then can you come up with announcement angles that will give your site the competitive edge it deserves.

"There are two basic lessons I've learned in my years promoting Web sites. First, every site has a very specific audience. There are people out there who want to see it. There are services that want to classify it. There are writers, reporters, and editors who want to cover it. Your goal should be to connect your site with all of those things, with all those outlets that make sense and want to know about it. Figure out exactly who you're trying to appeal to, then go out and hunt down the sites that can do you the most good.

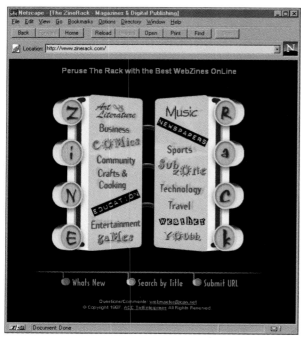

14.18

"Second, a Web site is more than just a URL. A lot of people think too small. They think, 'Okay, I've got this Web site and here's the URL for it. Now I need to submit the URL to all these places.' That's fine, but it's not enough. Think of your URL as a front door to all kinds of different content. Let's say at *www.site-x.com*, not only do I find a Web site that talks about what you do for a living and the services you offer, but I find out that you also publish a monthly Web-zine on the art of Web site design. Well, that zine itself is promotable. It has its own URL. It might be *www.site-x.com/artweb* or whatever you call it. There are directories of Web zines out there like Zine Rack (*www.zinerack.com*, 14.18). Here's a place that doesn't care about Web sites, it just wants to know about Web zines. It divides those up and categorizes them by topic. If you went there now and did a search for graphic design for the Internet, you might find that there are 40 Web zines. In other words, your zine is an added hook to draw people to your site.

"Or let's say you sponsor an e-mail discussion group. It's not Web based, it's just plain old e-mail. Every time one person in the group sends an e-mail,

everyone gets it. So you sponsor a discussion group about Web design tips, and it's just for people to share tips back and forth, nothing else. You're the moderator, so every post that gets sent goes to you first and then you decide if you want to release it to the entire group. There are list-serve programs that let you do exactly that. You have a little button at your Web site for people to sign up for the discussion group, and suddenly you have people signing up left and right.

"Again, that discussion group is separately promotable. In other words, there are directories and guides and editors, writers, and reporters who do nothing but highlight the best e-mail discussion groups. So there's another element of *www.site-x.com* that's promotable.

"Then let's say you're also an expert at Shockwave or some other authoring tool that lets you add cool elements to your Web site. There are about ten Web sites that do nothing but highlight cool Shockwave applications, with a Shockwave App of the Day.

"I could follow this same kind of concept through a dozen different elements of your Web site. You have to think beyond your URL and develop elements that are separately promotable. If you don't have any elements like this, you may want to consider adding them. The idea is to have as many separately promotable elements as possible."

SPEAKING TO THE ZINES

We asked Ward to walk us through a few specific examples of sites he's promoted that demonstrate the holistic approach at work. The first that came to mind was a specialized section of The Weather Channel's site christened Breaking Weather (*www.weather.com/breaking_weather*, 14.19).

"The Weather Channel has had a Web site up for a long time. But they came to me and said, 'We're building a major new section within our Web site dedicated to breaking weather. And we're going to launch this section of the site right at the beginning of the hurricane season.' In other words, they timed the launch of a topical site with a real-world event, which gave me that much more reason to think I could get it covered."

SEARCHING FOR DOMINANCE

According to Ward, one of the best ways to set up your site as the foremost authority in an area is to implement a search engine. "I know, a lot of people think it's counterintuitive. I once had this client, a boating manufacturer. I told them, 'You know, there's no search engine for the boating industry. But by God, there will be — it's just a matter of when. Why don't you guys use Swish or one of these other free tools to put together a search engine now while there are only 30 or 40 boating Web sites out there? You'll grow with it and eventually you'll be known as *the* source. You'll also have a vehicle for attracting banner ads.'"

"Well, they said, 'Oh. that's nuts! Why would we want to do that? You can't sell any boats that way. A search engine would just help people leave our site!'"

"No pun intended, but they missed the boat. These elements I'm mentioning, they become an extension of your Web presence. It's more than, 'Hey, come to my Web site and buy my product.' Instead it's 'Come use the search engine that I sponsor to help find what you're looking for.' Suddenly you have regular traffic, repeat customers, people who think of your company's name before any of the others. You control that market."

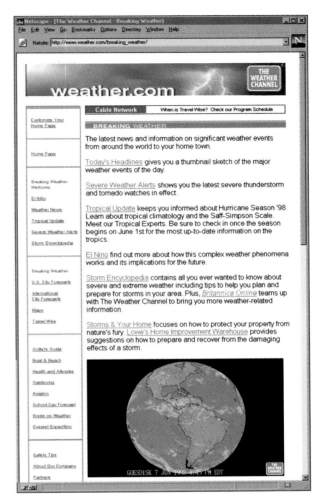

14.19

"Now, because this is an additional element of an existing Web site, the search engine and directory submissions have most likely already been done. I'm fairly certain that *www.weather.com* is already widely indexed. But there are sites out there that are interested in events as opposed to entire sites. For example, Netsurfer Digest (*www.netsurf.com/nsd*) is a Web-zine that comes out every two weeks and it highlights Web launches and happenings. They're looking for sites that make news. Because Breaking Weather is timed to a specific weather pattern, Netsurfer Digest is a perfect place to make an announcement."

TIMING IS EVERYTHING

Ward suggests that timing can be a crucial factor in how your Web site is received. "The Breaking Weather page brings up an important point: Just because your Web site is done doesn't mean you should be eager to get the thing out the door. You might consider, when's the best time to launch? What else is happening that might bring a little added excitement to my site? If you can find an event that gives your site greater relevance, you'll be rewarded for it."

So how does Ward go about submitting a partial site to a Web zine? "Near the bottom of the Netsurfer Digest index page is a link that says "Contact Information." Clicking on that link takes you to a page of editorial contacts. Midway down, you see where it says "Submit Networthy Items" (14.20). Click on that e-mail link and away you go."

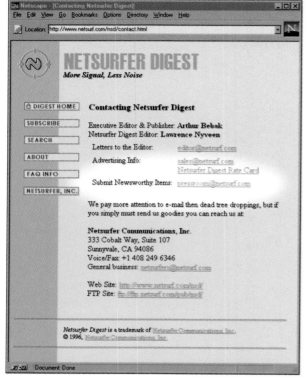

14.20

So what does Ward include in his e-mail? A press release? "Well, I'll go ahead and distribute my client's press releases, yes. But press releases don't always get read. So I try to make my notes as personal as possible. I might say, 'Hey, the Weather Channel is launching a new portion of its site this week timed with the beginning of hurricane season. The company-issued press release is below. Feel free to read it, but here are some things that I think are particularly cool about this launch.' Then I'd list a few items. Certainly, you can automate e-mail to send out a million press releases in one chunk. But it's a waste. That kind of mail gets thrown away. It misses the human element—and I have to say, even over the Internet, the human element is extremely important.

"Obviously, Netsurfer Digest is just one example of the literally hundreds and hundreds of Web zines that exist. But it demonstrates a point: the Breaking Weather page isn't a brand new Web site, it's an extension of an existing site. But it's still a newsworthy Web launch, in my opinion, and there are people out there who will take it seriously and give it the attention it deserves."

GIVING PEOPLE A REASON TO STOP BY

Often, Ward's client is the one who comes up with the idea that makes it all work. "One of my favorite clients was Norbest (*www.norbest.com*, 14.21). Norbest is a turkey manufacturing co-op. They have all these turkey farmers market their turkeys under the name of Norbest. So you would think they'd be really boring. It's like, my God, how do you promote a turkey Web page?

"Well, they launched a section of their site filled with Thanksgiving recipes and tips (14.22), all based on a diner motif. It was extremely clever. An editor friend at *USA Today* highlighted the site in the print edition. In many print publications, there's something about the Web each month. I tend to stay away from those because the odds of coverage are so small. But here a turkey site makes it into *USA Today*. This site attracted a lot of attention."

14.21

14.22

BRINGING NEW ATTENTION TO AN OLD SITE

"Another favorite of mine is the Acme Pet site (*www.acmepet.com*, 14.23). This is a community site for pet lovers of all kinds. If you have a pet, you can go there and find out why Fifi has fleas or whatever. I really love this site. The sites I enjoy most are the ones that have nothing to do with the Web or technology. They're about a real topic, something that people care about. It demonstrates that the Web has a purpose other than to promote itself.

"When Acme Pet came to me, the site was already in every search engine and directory they could find. But they were looking for some new way to promote the site. So I asked them, 'Do you have any events or special promotions coming up?' And they said, 'Well, we got a Halloween party where we're asking people to submit pictures of their dogs dressed up in

Halloween costumes (14.24).' And I said, 'Damn that is so brilliant! If you were here, I'd kiss you. This is so insane that I can get you coverage. My editors will eat it up when I tell them that I have an online Halloween picture party for puppies.'

"I asked the site's creators to build a special page as an entryway into the contest. And they put a banner on their home page so that people would see that the contest was going on. And then I sent out a news release about a week before Halloween to all my appropriate online media contacts.

"But also, here's an event about pets. I know that there are online mailing lists for pet lovers. There are Usenet newsgroups for pet lovers. And each of those represent a place I could go to let people know about this costume contest.

14.23

"I was not trying to promote the Acme Pet Web site itself. But I knew by promoting the Halloween picture contest, I would do just that. The spillover would be that I would tell a lot of people about a site they hadn't seen yet."

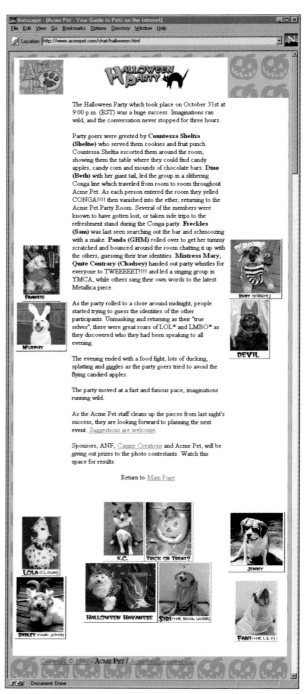

14.24

DO IT RIGHT, DO IT YOURSELF

Earlier in this chapter, Ward mentions automating press releases through mass e-mailings. Can't you likewise automate search engine and directory submissions and save yourself a lot of headache? "Yes you can, but it won't save you any headaches. It would take me a heck of a lot of pages to explain all the pluses and minuses with automatic submission software. But it's basically like this: an auto-submitter tries to replicate the submission forms for Yahoo and all other search engines and directories. It tries to pass this information *en masse* to hundreds of forms at once. The program never actually goes to the Yahoo form, it uses its own version of the form and tries to make it fit.

"The first potential problem is that the auto-submit form may not exactly match the Yahoo form. It could be missing fields. The categories may not fit or they may not be offered at all. And the descriptions may be the wrong length. Second, some search engines and directories just flat-out don't like auto-submitters. If you're auto-submitting, then you're not seeing Yahoo's banner ads. I understand there are times when Infoseek refuses to take auto-submissions.

"The point is, if you use an auto-submission program, some sites will list your page, others will turn it down. And you'll never know why. Was it because you didn't give them what they needed, or was it because you used the auto-submission program? Instead of saving time, you've wasted it.

"If for whatever reason, you simply don't have enough time, then the best auto-submission program is SubmitIt (*www.submitit.com*). But I really urge you to do it yourself. You spend six months of your life putting together a Web site, right? So why would you believe you can announce it to the world in 30 seconds? Yeah, there are some things you can automate, and they might work okay, but announcing your Web site is just too important. If you're just willing to roll up your sleeves and spend some time at the keyboard, you can do a much better job than any machine."

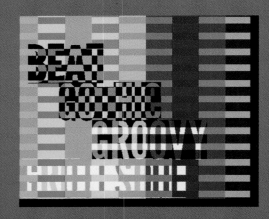

APPENDIX
ABOUT THE CD-ROM

The CD-ROM at the back of this book gives us the opportunity to do something we can't always do inside the book — show as opposed to tell. Oh, sure, we can wax poetic about Neil Robertson's whimsical JavaScript rollovers or David Falstrup's creative use of QuickTime VR, but until you see a few examples for yourself, your socks will fail to be knocked off.

If you're having problems accessing the files and programs included on the CD-ROM, here's the skinny: Start by inserting the CD-ROM into your CD-ROM drive. On the Mac, the CD-ROM appears as a WebDesignSS icon on your desktop. Under Windows, you probably need to double-click the My Computer icon on your desktop to find the WebDesignSS icon. In either case, the WebDesignSS icon features a cropped view of a globe trapped in an elaborate cable maze (A.1).

Double-click the icon to open the CD-ROM. Depending on your platform, you will see one of two independent partitions, one for the Mac (A.2) and the other for the PC (A.3). If you own Virtual PC on the Mac, you can check out the PC half of the CD-ROM from inside Windows 95. While the Mac and PC partitions are similar, each contains a few extras that are exclusive to the respective platform.

The main item on the *Web Design Studio Secrets* CD-ROM is the Chapter Support Files folder. This folder contains support elements for every chapter in this book. For the most part, the chapter elements are self-explanatory, and many are referenced in the chapters themselves. If a folder contains a sound file — in the AIFF format on the Mac or WAV on the PC —

A.1

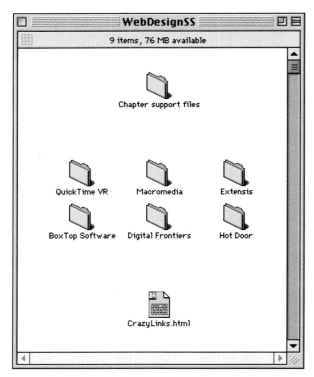

A.2

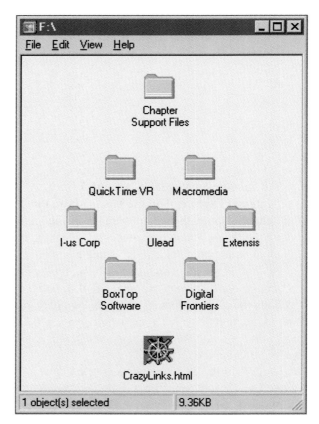

A.3

double-click the file to listen to the artist explain a topic in his or her own words. Beyond that, here are a few words of wisdom about the specific folders:

■ **Chap04 Worthington**: Among other things, this folder contains three Shockwave files (with .DCR extensions). To open these files, you need to install Shockwave in your browser. If your browser isn't already Shockwave enabled, run the Shockwave installer from the Macromedia folder. Then create a new window in your browser and drag a DCR file into it. One is interactive, reacting to your mouse movements, the other two play without your help. Interesting stuff.

■ **Chap08 Goto:** If you're using a Mac, you can check out the Voyager demo, which was designed to sell Paramount on launching and promoting the UPN television network. The demo was never intended to appear on a book

CD-ROM, so it isn't optimized for each and every machine, but it provides excellent insights into the production process. On the Mac and PC, you have access to the Phamis interactive kiosk (included with permission from IDX Systems Corporation). Double-click the Phamis icon to run the program. Granted, neither of these are Web sites, but this is a CD-ROM and a CD-ROM deserves great multimedia.

■ **Chap09 Oehl:** This folder contains animated GIF files. Open them in Netscape Navigator or Internet Explorer to watch them run. No other special software is required.

■ **Chap11 Falstrup:** To look at these marvelous VR files, your machine must be equipped with QuickTime VR. If it isn't, run the installer included in the QuickTime VR folder.

- **Chap12 Griffith:** The Buddy & Code folder contains three Word documents explaining how to script VRML code for an animated dog named Buddy. The folder also contains a WRL file. To run this file in your browser, you need a VRML player such as CosmoPlayer or Worldview . See Chapter 12 for more information.
- **Chap13 Shepherd:** The contents of this folder work only on a PC equipped with Internet Explorer 4 or later. (You can also open the files under Virtual PC equipped with Internet Explorer 4 on the Mac.) To run the channel, open the default.htm file inside Internet Explorer and watch it go.

In addition to the Chapter Support Files folder, the CD-ROM contains free and demonstration software from a variety of top Web graphics vendors, including Apple, Macromedia (Portions Copyright © Macromedia. 1996-1998 All Rights Reserved.), Extensis, BoxTop Software, and Digital Frontiers. Hot Door has included a special Photoshop plug-in for Macintosh users, and ULead and I/us Corp. have included plug-ins and utilities for Windows folks. A typical demo runs for 30 days before expiring and inviting you to buy the fully functioning program, but some last for shorter periods. (One in particular, Hot Door Harmony, expires after only three days. Erk!)

Finally, you'll find a file called CrazyLinks.html. Open this file in your favorite Web browser — or your not-so-favorite browser if you're feeling masochistic — to gain access to a plethora of Web sites that provide additional instruction, advice, and resources beyond the confines of this finite book (A.4). These links are so great, we must be crazy to offer them. At least, that's what we say in our infomercials.

A.4

CD-ROM TECHNICAL SUPPORT

If you have any problems getting the CD-ROM to work with your computer, it's very likely that some of your settings files or drivers are not working properly. For assistance, call IDG Books' technical support hotline at 1-800-762-2974, option 2. This is also the number to call if your CD-ROM is damaged.

INDEX

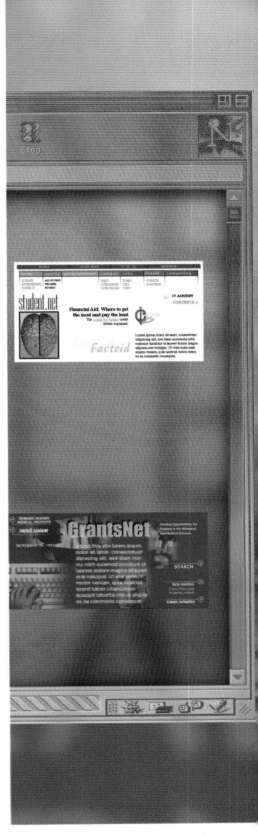

"...er thrills"

...a on archival paper
...ox 6' x 5'

H

(continued)

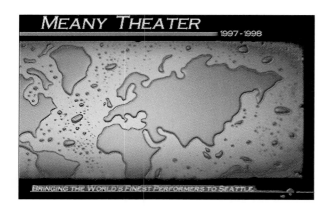

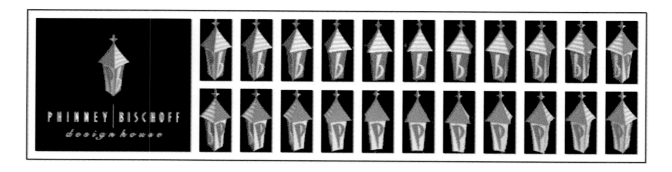

Netscape push technology, 249–250. *See also* Web browser support
NetShow, 192, 199
Netsurfer Digest Web site, 277
Never Enough Coffee creations, 92–93. *See also* HTML
news broadcast channels, 251
Nichimen Graphics Inc., 230–231. *See also* VRML
<NOBR> tags, 103
nodal points, 210
nodes, 213
Norbest Web site, 278
NorthernLight Web site, 271
numbered lists, 104
NW Federal Credit Union Web site, 158–159

O

object movies, 208, 214–217
objects, aligning, 127–129
octahedrons, 232
Oehl, Yann, 172–173, 284. *See also* GIF animations
Offset filter (Photoshop), 67–68
<OL>, </OL> tags, 102
online presence. *See* promoting Web sites
ONLOAD JavaScript command, 254
OpenText Web site, 271
OpenType, 79–80
ordered lists, 104
outside environments, 219
overlapping images, 56

P

<P> tags, 78, 102
page layout. *See* design issues; site management; tables as layout tools
page length, 12–13
page weight, 9
page width, 11
PageSpinner Web site, 122
paintings, displaying on Web, 60–61
PAN attribute, <EMBED> tags, 225
panoramas, interactive, 208–213
paragraphs, 102
Park Hyatt Hotel Web site, 209
patchwork color file, 180
PFR (Portable Font Resource) file, 80
Phamis kiosk, 155, 284
Phinney/Bischoff Design House, 138–139. *See also* JavaScript rollovers
photographs, 175. *See also* Immersive Imaging
Photoshop
    Actions, 18–19, 178
    antialiasing fonts, 75
    Copy Merged, 177
    file sizes, 47
    Goodies folder, 47
    History Palette, 178
    icons, adding to images, 48
    layers, 15–18, 221
    as layout tool, 15–18
    Motion Blur filter, 179
    Offset filter, 67–68
    tiled backgrounds, 67–68
    transparency techniques, 57–58
    Unsharp Mask, 176
    Web Scrub filter, 178
PICT files, 175, 222
pixel dimensions, reading, 58
pixels per inch (ppi), 42
PlanetSearch Web site, 271
planning, 156–159. *See also* design issues
PNG (Portable Network Graphics), 44
PointCast Network, 248–249
polygonal modeling, VRML, 232–233
pop-up channel descriptions, 262
Portable Font Resource (PFR) file, 80

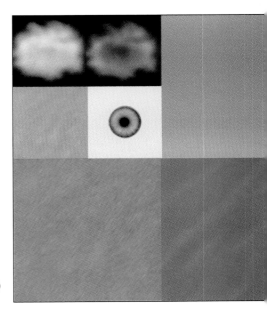

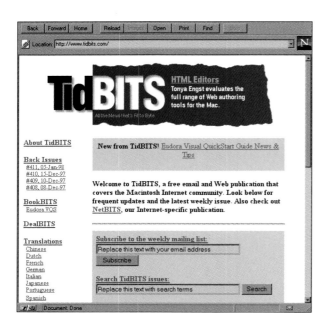

SYNOPSIS

Mr. Bean's job is to sit unobtrusively in a corner of the London National Art Gallery and look at pictures. Not a difficult occupation. Unless you are Mr. Bean.

The board of directors is longing to fire him, but Bean has a patron who happens to be the Chairman of the Board. So, instead of canning him, they do the next best thing: they send him to America to deliver one of the world's great art works - Whistler's Mother - to the Grierson Gallery in Los Angeles which has just purchased the painting for an astounding $50 million. The London Gallery will tell the Los Angeles Gallery that the courier is Mr. Bean, a renowned authority on the painting who will stay there to lecture about the art work. Perhaps they hope that once the Americans discover he is a fraud, they will kill him. Even if only in self-defense.

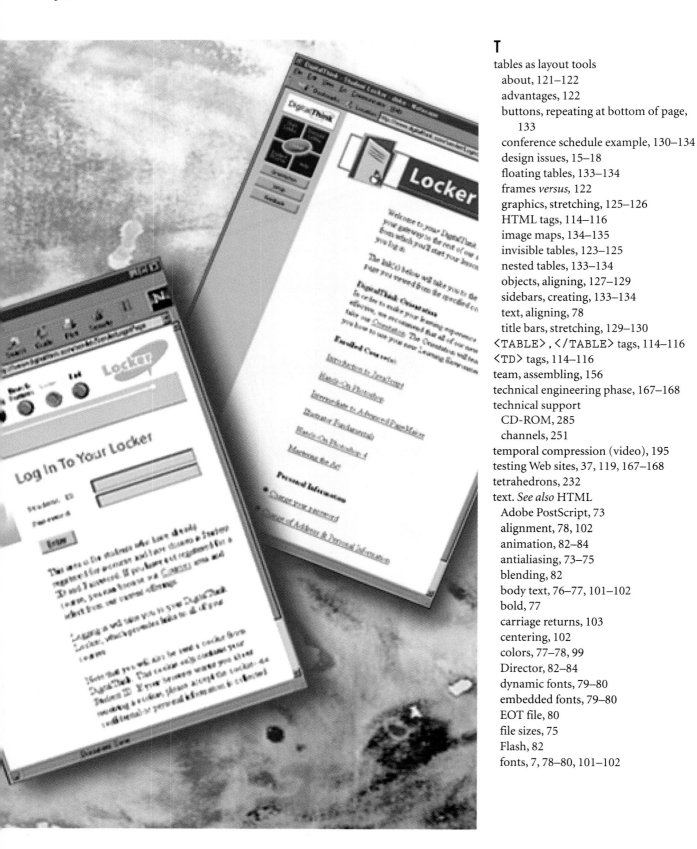

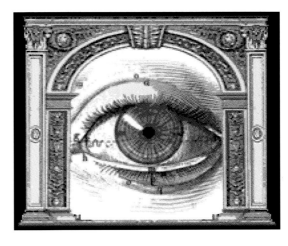

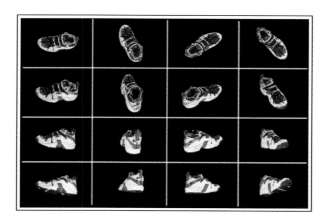

ABOUT THE AUTHORS

Deke McClelland is a contributing editor to *Macworld* and *Publish* magazines. He has authored more than 40 books on desktop publishing and the Macintosh computer, and his work has been translated into more than 20 languages. Deke also hosts *Digital Gurus*, a syndicated TV show about personal computing, from his home base in Colorado. He started his career as artistic director at the first service bureau in the United States.

Deke won a Society of Technical Communication Award in 1994, an American Society for Business Press Editors Award in 1995, and the Ben Franklin Award for Best Computer Book in 1989. He also won the prestigious Computer Press Association Award in 1990, 1992, 1994, and 1995.

Deke is author of the following books published by IDG Books Worldwide, Inc.: *CorelDRAW 8 For Dummies, FreeHand 8 Bible, Macworld Photoshop 5 Bible, Photoshop 5 For Windows 95 Bible, Photoshop 5 For Dummies,* and *Photoshop Studio Secrets.*

Katrin Eismann is an internationally respected lecturer and teacher on the subject of imaging and the impact of emerging technologies upon the professional photographer. She is the conference chair for the Thunder Lizard Productions Photoshop Conferences. Her company, PRAXIS Digital Solutions, teaches and lectures throughout Europe, North America, and the Asian-Pacific region.

Katrin's creative work is based on investigating concepts and working with the appropriate technologies to create intriguing images. Her images have appeared in the books *Photoshop WOW!, Photoshop 4 Studio Secrets, Essentials of Digital Photography, Make Your Scanner a Great Production Tool,* and *Essentials of Computing* and in *Macworld, PhotoDistrictNews, American Photo, Photonics, Computer Artist, Image World, International Photography, IdN,* and *Mac Art & Design* magazines.

COLOPHON

This book was produced electronically in Foster City, California. Microsoft Word Version 7.0 was used for word processing; design and layout were produced using QuarkXPress 4.03 and Adobe Photoshop 4 on Power Macintosh computers. The typeface families used are Minion, Myriad Multiple Master, Prestige Elite, Symbol, Trajan, and Zapf Dingbats.

Acquisitions Editor: Andy Cummings
Development Editors: Amy Thomas, Katharine Dvorak
Technical Editor: Ted Padova
Copy Editor: Timothy Borek
Project Coordinator: Susan Parini
Book Designers: Margery Cantor, Cátálin Dulfu, Kurt Krames
Graphics & Production Specialists: Vincent F. Burns, Elsie Yim
Graphics Technicians: Linda Marousek, Hector Mendoza
Quality Control Specialists: Mick Arellano, Mark Schumann
Proofreader: Laura Bowman
Indexer: Ann Norcross
Cover Art: Glenn Mitsui
Back Cover Art: Chris Gollmer, Neil Robertson, David Falstrup

IDG BOOKS WORLDWIDE, INC.
END-USER LICENSE AGREEMENT

<u>**READ THIS.**</u> You should carefully read these terms and conditions before opening the software packet(s) included with this book ("Book"). This is a license agreement ("Agreement") between you and IDG Books Worldwide, Inc. ("IDGB"). By opening the accompanying software packet(s), you acknowledge that you have read and accept the following terms and conditions. If you do not agree and do not want to be bound by such terms and conditions, promptly return the Book and the unopened software packet(s) to the place you obtained them for a full refund.

1. <u>**License Grant.**</u> IDGB grants to you (either an individual or entity) a nonexclusive license to use one copy of the enclosed software program(s) (collectively, the "Software") solely for your own personal or business purposes on a single computer (whether a standard computer or a workstation component of a multiuser network). The Software is in use on a computer when it is loaded into temporary memory (RAM) or installed into permanent memory (hard disk, CD-ROM, or other storage device). IDGB reserves all rights not expressly granted herein.

2. <u>**Ownership.**</u> IDGB is the owner of all right, title, and interest, including copyright, in and to the compilation of the Software recorded on the disk(s) or CD-ROM ("Software Media"). Copyright to the individual programs recorded on the Software Media is owned by the author or other authorized copyright owner of each program. Ownership of the Software and all proprietary rights relating thereto remain with IDGB and its licensers.

3. <u>**Restrictions On Use and Transfer.**</u>

(a) You may only (i) make one copy of the Software for backup or archival purposes, or (ii) transfer the Software to a single hard disk, provided that you keep the original for backup or archival purposes. You may not (i) rent or lease the Software, (ii) copy or reproduce the Software through a LAN or other network system or through any computer subscriber system or bulletin-board system, or (iii) modify, adapt, or create derivative works based on the Software.

(b) You may not reverse engineer, decompile, or disassemble the Software. You may transfer the Software and user documentation on a permanent basis, provided that the transferee agrees to accept the terms and conditions of this Agreement and you retain no copies. If the Software is an update or has been updated, any transfer must include the most recent update and all prior versions.

4. <u>**Restrictions On Use of Individual Programs.**</u> You must follow the individual requirements and restrictions detailed for each individual program in the appendix, "About the CD-ROM," in this Book. These limitations are also contained in the individual license agreements recorded on the Software Media. These limitations may include a requirement that after using the program for a specified period of time, the user must pay a registration fee or discontinue use. By opening the Software packet(s), you will be agreeing to abide by the licenses and restrictions for these individual programs that are detailed in the appendix, "About the CD-ROM," and on the Software Media. None of the material on this Software Media or listed in this Book may ever be redistributed, in original or modified form, for commercial purposes.

my2cents.idgbooks.com

Register This Book — And Win!

Visit **http://my2cents.idgbooks.com** to register this book and we'll automatically enter you in our fantastic monthly prize giveaway. It's also your opportunity to give us feedback: let us know what you thought of this book and how you would like to see other topics covered.

Discover IDG Books Online!

The IDG Books Online Web site is your online resource for tackling technology — at home and at the office. Frequently updated, the IDG Books Online Web site features exclusive software, insider information, online books, and live events!

10 Productive & Career-Enhancing Things You Can Do at www.idgbooks.com

- Nab source code for your own programming projects.

- Download software.

- Read Web exclusives: special articles and book excerpts by IDG Books Worldwide authors.

- Take advantage of resources to help you advance your career as a Novell or Microsoft professional.

- Buy IDG Books Worldwide titles or find a convenient bookstore that carries them.

- Register your book and win a prize.

- Chat live online with authors.

- Sign up for regular e-mail updates about our latest books.

- Suggest a book you'd like to read or write.

- Give us your 2¢ about our books and about our Web site.

You say you're not on the Web yet? It's easy to get started with IDG Books' *Discover the Internet*, available at local retailers everywhere.

Publish

THE MAGAZINE FOR ELECTRONIC PUBLISHING PROFESSIONALS

FREE 101 Tips Book!

Pixel-Perfect Scans

Managing Color: Get Consistent Results From Start To Finish

The Next Generation of Publishing Software

Affordable Big-Screen Monitors

Top Products of the Year

Choose The Right Paper For Dramatic Effect

Can You Trust Onscreen Proofing?

To receive your FREE ISSUE and FREE *101 TIPS* book, simply detach this postcard return it today. No purchase required.

CUT HERE – MAIL NOW – NO POSTAGE NECESSARY

1 FREE ISSUE AND A FREE BOOK
absolutely free

Yes, I'd like to sample 1 issue of *Publish*. I understand that I'll also receive 101 Best Electronic Publishing Tips FREE just for trying Publish. If I like my sample issue, I'll pay just $29.95 for 11 more issues (for a total of 12 issues). I'll save $29. That's 50%!– off the annual cover price.

If I don't choose to subscribe, I'll return your subscription bill marked "cancel" and owe nothing.

The FREE issue and 101 TIPS book will be mine to keep – free.

**Trial only.
Don't send money.
Just mail this card!**

Name

Title

Company

Address

City   State   Zip

E-mail

H80111

Just an hour a month with *Publish*

gives you the edge in mastering your electronic publishing tools—from design to → print → web screen → or CD-ROM!

With today's explosion of new electronic publishing technologies, you have more options than ever before. To keep up, you need the magazine that pioneered the digital publishing revolution... and still sets the pace for graphics professionals.

It's *PUBLISH*. Month after month, *PUBLISH* improves your skills at every step in the electronic publishing process.

PUBLISH provides the ongoing education you need to save time and money in today's competitive world of electronic publishing. Our experts not only discuss new digital technologies, they show you how to use design and imaging tools to achieve spectacular results.

Defy the limits of Web production. With Macromedia.

Fireworks

Flash 3

Dreamweaver 1.2

Introducing three ways to take the Web further, faster.
Macromedia® announces a major leap in Web production:
a powerful set of design tools, made for the Web, that
dramatically push the boundaries of what you can do.
All, while supporting the standards that make the Web
the world's most perfect open forum for ideas.

Leap graphical barriers with a single tool. With Fireworks.
Creating powerful Web graphics used to require an unholy
shuffling of applications, utilities, filters, and add-ons. Now, it
simply means Macromedia Fireworks®. The first comprehensive
graphics tool designed expressly for the Web. Create JPEG,
GIF, animated GIF, and PNG files and rollovers; preview for
quality and optimize for size-all in one place. Once created,
your graphics remain editable all the time.

Challenge the conventions of interactive design. With Flash.
Flash™ 3 takes the possibilities for riveting Web content even
further. Create compact, yet dramatic vector graphics, text,
sound, animation, and morphing effects that download instantly.
Even at 28.8. Preview at varying modem speeds. Reach a
worldwide audience—with or without plug-ins. Cool was never
so practical.

Draw it all together with pristine code. With Dreamweaver.
It all comes together in Dreamweaver™ 1.2. Compose your site
visually. Use Roundtrip HTML™ to stay in control of your live
source code. Drop in optimized Fireworks graphics. Add Flash
animations. Add JavaScript™ behaviors without coding. And
send it all to the Web, to view in old and new browsers. In a
fraction of the time. For a fraction of the budget.

Download a FREE trial at www.getmacromedia.com/mw
It's your Web. Your rules. Our tools. See Macromedia Fireworks,
Flash 3, and Dreamweaver 1.2 in action. Visit our site to
down-load FREE trial versions of all three, or to order a demo
CD. But whatever you do, jump to it.

macromedia®

CD-ROM INSTALLATION INSTRUCTIONS

USING THE CD-ROM

Insert the CD-ROM into your CD-ROM drive. On the Mac, the CD-ROM appears as a WebDesignSS icon on your desktop. Under Windows, you probably need to double-click the My Computer icon on your desktop to find the WebDesignSS icon. In either case, the WebDesignSS icon features a cropped view of a globe trapped in an elaborate cable maze.

Double-click the icon to open the CD-ROM. Depending on your platform, you will see one of two independent partitions, one for the Mac and the other for the PC. If you own Virtual PC on the Mac, you can check out the PC half of the CD-ROM from inside Windows 95. While the Mac and PC partitions are similar, each contains a few extras that are exclusive to the respective platform.

The main item on the *Web Design Studio Secrets* CD-ROM is the Chapter Support Files folder. This folder contains support elements for chapters in this book:

- **Chap04 Worthington**;
- **Chap08 Goto**;
- **Chap09 Oehl**;
- **Chap11 Falstrup**;
- **Chap12 Griffith**;
- **Chap13 Shepherd**.

In addition to the Chapter Support Files folder, the CD-ROM contains free and demonstration software from a variety of top Web graphics vendors.

Please read the "About the CD-ROM" appendix for instructions on installing and copying files. Also note, to view files with the .psd extension you must have Photoshop installed on your machine.